# THE ELECTION PROCESS

# IN CANADA

# mcgraw-hill series in canadian politics

Paul W. Fox, *General Editor*

# THE ELECTION PROCESS IN CANADA

TERENCE H. QUALTER
*Professor of Political Science,*
*University of Waterloo, Waterloo, Ontario*

*Toronto*
McGraw-Hill Company of Canada Limited
*Montreal*
*New York*
*London*
*Sydney*
*Johannesburg*
*Mexico*
*Panama*
*Dusseldorf*

THE ELECTION PROCESS
IN CANADA

Cover design by Arjen F. de Groot.

Library of Congress Catalog Card Number 75-127187
ISBN 0-07-092664-6
1234567890 MB-70 9876543210

Printed and bound in Canada

# FOREWORD

Despite the fact that Canadians have displayed great interest in elections, especially in recent years, there has been no book available until now to explain all the ins and outs of the requirements and principles of the electoral process at both the federal and provincial levels of government. A zealous citizen could always have consulted, of course, the *Canada Elections Act* or the comparable provincial law but no doubt few citizens ever found their enthusiasms carrying them so far that they wanted to wrestle with the ponderous clauses of a bulky election statute.

The result has been that while most Canadians have participated in the simple act of voting many times — indeed, it is probably the political experience which is most common to Canadian adults — the details of the process in which they have engaged have remained obscure and no doubt somewhat puzzling. Voters, and even prospective candidates, may well have asked themselves some of the following questions. Who can vote? What are the qualifications and disqualifications for voting in a certain jurisdiction? Who can be a candidate? What role does the party play and why do party labels not appear on most ballots? How are the boundaries of constituencies determined, and how and when are they altered? What is "gerrymandering"? Where do we elect only one member from a constituency and where do we elect several? What are corrupt and illegal election practices? What are the roles of the various election officials, and what are the steps in a typical election?

It is questions such as these that Professor Qualter answers in this book. The author explains clearly and simply the many regulations and details that make up election procedures in Canada. One of the great merits of his work is that he examines not only federal practices but the procedures in each of the ten provinces, which are probably even less well known, if that is possible, to most Canadians. At many points he provides a table of data which permits handy comparisons.

The other great merit of Professor Qualter's book is that the author does not confine himself solely to presenting information, as valuable as that is. He is concerned also with the principles involved, and he is not hesitant to criticize them and to suggest improvements.

Both students and voters will find that *The Election Process in Canada* is a very useful book. It provides for the first time a definitive account of an important but hitherto neglected aspect of Canadian government and it also raises for further consideration a number of significant issues. On both scores it suits admirably the purposes for which the McGraw-Hill Series in Canadian Politics was designed.

April 27, 1970,                                                 Paul W. Fox,
University of Toronto                               GENERAL EDITOR

# PREFACE

This book would not have appeared without the assistance of a great many people. A grant from the Canada Council provided the initial financial support. Professor John Meisel, and Queen's University, provided me with a pleasant refuge whilst on sabbatical leave during which the ideas for this study emerged. A special debt of gratitude is due to the Chief Electoral Officers in the provincial capitals and in Ottawa who so generously and promptly responded to requests for copies of statutes, reports, and documents and who gave patient and detailed replies to innumerable letters. Professors Paul Fox and John Wilson gave valuable advice and assistance at various stages in the preparation of the manuscript. Professor Wilson, in particular, was a constant counsel and guide. My research assistants, Mr. Andrue Anstett and Miss Sandra Burt, spent many hours searching for obscure pieces of information and in compiling tables. Miss Marilyn Roycroft assisted in proofreading and preparing the index. Finally, I ought to thank my colleagues who bore with me while I used the writing of this book as an excuse for not doing other things more valuable to them but less interesting to me.

December, 1969,                                         Terence H. Qualter
University of Waterloo

To my students and colleagues

# CONTENTS

Foreword                                                                          v

Preface                                                                         vii

Introduction                                                                     xi

ONE        WHO VOTES?                                                             1
           Control over Franchise; Property Qualifications;
           Citizenship; Age; Sex; Race, Language, and Religion;
           Residence; Voters' Lists; Advance Polls, Absentee
           Ballots, and Proxy Ballots.

TWO        FOR WHOM?                                                            45
           Legal Qualifications of Candidates; Nomination
           Formalities; The Need for a Party Label; Selection by
           Parties; The Socio-Economic Considerations.

THREE      WHERE?                                                              81
           Criteria for Constituencies; The Measurement of
           Maldistribution; The Case for Redistribution; The
           Machinery of Redistribution; Redistribution Procedures
           in the Provinces; Distribution of Federal Seats Among the
           Provinces; Gerrymandering; Single- and Multi-Member
           Constituencies; Conclusion.

FOUR    HOW AND UNDER WHAT CONDITIONS?           129
        The Electoral System; The Election Officials; Bribery,
        Corruption, Intimidation, and other Unsavoury Practices;
        Election Finance; The Official Agent; Taking the Vote;
        Diary of an Election.

        Conclusion                                              170

        Appendix One   Classification of Voters' Lists.         174

        Appendix Two   (A) Provincial Returning Officers:
                           Terms of Office                      177

                       (B) Provincial Returning Officers:
                           Classes of Persons Disqualified
                           From Serving as Returning Officers   178

                       (C) Provincial Returning Officers:
                           Grounds for Removal.                 180

        Appendix Three Manner of Voting in Canada and
                       the Provinces.                           181

        Addendum                                                184

        Index to Tables                                         187

        Abbreviations                                           189

        Index                                                   193

# INTRODUCTION

This book starts from the assumption that the manner in which we elect our representatives — the election process — is a vitally important sub-process within the broader democratic political process, setting the character and style of that broader process and, to a large extent, determining the success of its operation.

It conceives of an election as being a dynamic process operating within a specific political system. The participants, the actors in the process, are the electors, the candidates, and the election officials, who interact within given territorial limits, the constituencies, according to definite electoral procedures, and subject to a set of administrative rules and regulations.

There are thus five principal variables. First of all there are the voters, actual and potential. The voters may affect the process both directly as positive actors who determine the fate of candidates, and indirectly through their perception of the integrity of the process and of their individual influence within it, which perception will tend to modify the character and style of the process. They will also in turn be affected by the statutes, administrative practices, customs, and political-cultural factors which together determine which members of the total population will be voters, and of the non-voters, which will be voluntary and which will be involuntary abstainers.

The candidates compose the second variable. They, too, play both a direct and indirect role. They must actively compete with each other for the support of the voters, but before this they must be chosen as candidates. Their selection is determined in the first instance by the social, cultural, political, and economic considerations which draw certain individuals out from the total population as possible candidates and then by the more or less formal procedures by which the political parties nominate some of these possibles as their official standard-bearers.

The constituencies, the third variable, are the arena within which individual contests take place. The constituencies will have an impact on the process, both in the manner in which it is conducted, and in its outcome, according to such things as the number of candidates to be elected within each constituency, the criteria for determining the composition of constituencies, and the machinery for drawing boundaries and for their periodic revision.

The fourth variable, the electoral system (as distinct from the election system) refers to the particular procedures by which votes are recorded and counted, and translated into legislative seats. More specifically, the electoral system involves consideration of such voting systems as alternative ballots, plurality votes, proportional representation, and so on.

Finally there is the administrative machinery, a term used to cover all the official administrators of the process from the chief electoral officer to the enumerators and poll clerks, as well as the procedures by which such people come to be appointed. The term also embraces the laws, regulations, and customary usages through which the election officials compile lists of eligible voters, make known to the voters the facts of the existence of an election and of the date and places at which they may record their votes, attend to the official nomination of candidates, print ballot papers, establish polling places, supervise the voting, count the ballots, and make official returns of the results. The administrative machinery controls the efficiency of the total process and the accuracy with which it translates the wishes of the voters into official results. It influences not only the objective honesty, fairness, and integrity of the process, but also, what is equally as important, the voters' perception of them.

It is further assumed that while Canada as a whole constitutes a political system within which an election process operates, the several provinces also constitute separate systems, sufficiently alike to be considered under one general heading but sufficiently different to make comparisons meaningful and rewarding.

It is hoped that this study which, as far as can be discovered, is the first to attempt systematic comparisons of Canada and its provinces as individual political systems (using the term in its loosest popular sense) will stimulate further much more intensive and sustained research within provinces and between provinces. Especially it is hoped that others will explore more deeply the relationship between the political-social culture of any one province or region particularly as it differs from other provinces or regions on the one hand and, on the other, any unique elements in any aspect of the total political process.

# ONE
## WHO VOTES?

Although we commonly think of an election as a process by which some people choose other people to be their representatives, it is obvious that even under universal suffrage not all the people can be choosers, or voters. This chapter deals with those factors which determine whether a person will be a voter or non-voter. Although simple categorizations are often misleading one can begin usefully by recognizing three types of non-voters: the statutory, the administrative, and the voluntary. The rest are, of course, the voters.

A statutory non-voter is a member of a class which is denied the right to vote by law. It is a whole class or section of the population which is disfranchised. At various times in history and in different countries, women, Jews, Negroes, Catholics, the landless, and the illiterate have all been statutory non-voters. In Canada today the majority of the statutory non-voters are the under-age, the non-citizens, the non-residents, certain of the insane, those confined in penal institutions and certain election officers.

An administrative non-voter, on the other hand, is a person who, as a member of a class, has the right to vote, but as an individual is unable to exercise that right. Inadequate provisions for those who must be absent from their districts on election day, voting instructions and ballots too complicated for the poorly educated to understand, limited voting hours and too few or inaccessible voting places, violence and intimidation, and corrupt or incompetent election administrators can all be administrative barriers to voting.

A voluntary non-voter is one who chooses not to vote, whether this decision be based on a positive conviction of the undesirability of voting, or as a product of varying degrees of apathy and alienation.

1

Quite obviously these categories are neither exclusive nor watertight. What appears on the surface as a statutory restraint against the whole class of illiterates may become an administrative barrier if in actual practice it is enforced only against Negroes. An individual who claims that he was prevented from voting because the polls were closed too early may be rationalizing a deeply entrenched political apathy so that even if the polls were open until midnight, he would find other excuses for not voting. On the other hand, those who admit to a lack of interest in politics may well have reached their present state of political alienation because of administrative barriers to the exercise of the vote. Long years of denial of the vote may produce a feeling of disinterest in it, even when the denial is retracted.

This study will neither examine the motives of the voluntary non-voters[1] nor attempt to determine which of the legally eligible voters are kept from the polls by administrative hurdles and which refrain from voting by choice. The purpose is rather to examine the nature and the extent of the statutory and administrative barriers to voting in Canada today and to suggest some of the ways in which these barriers have impact on the total political process.

## CONTROL OVER THE FRANCHISE

In any federal system the question of which level of government controls the franchise is always an important one, the answer to which can materially affect the power bases of the various elements in the political process. Within the United States, for example, the divisions of opinion as to the most appropriate basis of representation were deep and irreconcilable. Unable to determine commonly acceptable standards for a federal franchise, the constitution framers had perforce to defer to state provisions. Apart from those sections of the Constitution which prohibit discrimination on the grounds of sex, race, colour, or previous condition of servitude, the United States Constitution does not confer the franchise on anyone. The Senate, the House of Representatives, and the Presidential Electors are all chosen in a manner ultimately under state control.

The existing pattern in Canada is quite different. In respect to provincial elections, each province controls its own franchise and there are no overriding constitutional provisions, such as the 15th or 19th Amendments in the United States, protecting the vote of any class of citizens at the provincial level. A Canadian province could, even now, quite legally deny the vote to women, Negroes, those earning less than $10,000 a year, or to any other category of voters. At the same time, however, the federal franchise is firmly in Ottawa's hands and there are no indications of any pressure to grant the provinces control over it.

But, although the question of the control over the federal franchise is not now a major political issue, the position has not always been so settled and Canada has experienced various forms of provincial control over federal voting rights. It is worth reviewing some of these stages briefly.[2]

The constitution framers intended that the national parliament would have control over the federal franchise, although, as a temporary expedient the franchise would, in the beginning, be that in force in the provinces.[3] The phrase "until the Parliament of Canada otherwise provides" clearly indicated the intention to establish a federal franchise. Various factors in Canada, however, delayed its introduction for eighteen years (from 1867 to 1885). The original Canadian franchise was thus determined by the franchise in the four original provinces. The voting qualifications varied in detail although in every case the basis was property.

The right to control the federal franchise increased the influence of provincial politicians on the federal scene and some began to see the advantages of altering the provincial franchise in a manner which could affect the party balance in Ottawa. Nova Scotia, for example, proposed to disfranchise all federal employees, all of whom held their appointments as patronage gifts of the Conservative party in power in the federal government. Such a move would have deprived the federal Conservatives of many grateful voters within the province and their reaction was to pass federal legislation to prohibit such maneuvering by stipulating that the federal franchise in each province would be the same as the provincial franchise as it existed in 1867 regardless of any subsequent change.[4] This control, however, lasted only until the return of the Liberal government in 1874 when, once again, the provinces regained full control over federal voting rights.

The entry of new provinces in the federation and the changes in the provincial election laws produced a varied and complicated federal franchise, ranging from what was virtually manhood suffrage in British Columbia[5] to a complex property or income qualification in Ontario.[6]

It appears from several accounts of the period that while the main pressure for a centrally controlled federal franchise came from the Conservative party, the dominant motive was less one of principle than of recognition of the dangers in leaving the franchise in the hands of Liberal governments in the provinces, especially in Ontario where the Liberal party was overtly manipulating the franchise to increase Liberal support.

The Conservatives were returned to office in 1878, but it was not until 1885 that they were able to enact the first comprehensive federal franchise law, *The Electoral Franchise Act*, 1885.[7] The attempt to produce a uniform franchise was only partially successful and, as one authority has stated, on balance "the uniform federal franchise of 1885 may be fairly described as more diversified than the varied provincial qualifications it supplanted."[8] The extraordinarily complex franchise provisions of the 1885 *Act*, contained basically in sections 3 to 10, do not at this point concern us, except insofar as that very complexity and diversity was a major source of the dissatisfaction which led to a second return to a provincial franchise.[9]

The Liberal party consistently opposed the principle of Dominion control over the franchise and promised a return to provincial control when re-elected. The opportunity came with the Liberal victory in the elections of 1896, and in 1898 legislation was passed[10] to restore control over the federal franchise to the provinces. It sought to avoid the complication which led to the first abandonment of the provincial franchise by stipulating that: "No person possessed of the qualifications generally required by the provincial law to entitle him to vote at a provincial election, shall be disqualified from voting at a Dominion election merely by reason of any provision of the provincial law disqualifying him from having his name on the list or from voting . . . ."[11] The same section specifically prohibited the disfranchising of federal or provincial civil servants who otherwise possessed the provincial voting qualification. It should be noted that the *Act* of 1898, by adopting a provincial franchise, which in most of the provinces meant manhood suffrage, produced a wider and more uniform franchise than under the former federal provisions.

For a brief period (from 1917 to 1920) control over the franchise was exercised by both the federal and the provincial governments. To the basic provincial franchises which remained the effective foundation of the right to vote the federal government made certain specific amendments, granting the vote to certain persons not otherwise enfranchised and denying it to others who might normally have been expected to have exercised it. These quite extraordinary measures were carried into effect through two statutes in 1917: *The Military Voters Act*[12] and the *War Time Elections Act*.[13] More will be said in a later section about the provisions of these acts.

The final stage came with the passing of the *Dominion Elections Act*, 1920,[14] which set up a uniform federal franchise under Dominion control. Today, with universal adult suffrage in force at the federal level and in all the provinces, provincial control over federal voting rights, if based on the same qualifications as for provincial elections, would neither extend nor limit the federal franchise (except in some very minor details). There is thus nothing to be gained or lost by a departure from the existing procedure. The question of the locus of control over the federal franchise is no longer a live issue in Canadian politics.

## PROPERTY QUALIFICATIONS

The assumption that good government implies universal suffrage is not self-evident and was far from widely accepted in the British North American colonies. It is true that throughout the nineteenth century there were many who stressed the idea that the vote should be extended to as many people as possible. In accordance with the liberal faith in the rationality of man, those urging the widening of the franchise assumed that once all men (and perhaps even all women) received the vote, all privilege and vested interest would disappear, for the voters would listen to the arguments of rival candidates and rationally choose that course of action which would be for the greatest good of all.

The opposition was founded on two basic considerations, deeply interwoven: the determined preservation of self-interest and entrenched privilege, and a sincere belief that extension of the suffrage to the "unfit" would be detrimental to the general good of the society. From the vantage point of the mid-twentieth century one can see that the cynical motive of self-interest was dominant, but it would be grossly misleading to neglect the reality of the more noble aspirations. To many the "ignorance of the multitude" was an insurmountable barrier to any extension of the franchise. There is a natural tendency for the rich to fear and distrust the ambitions of the poor, for the educated and cultured to dislike the boorishness of the working classes, and for the members of one faith or race to suspect the motives of rivals. It is not difficult to express such fears, dislikes, and suspicions in terms of the noblest principles and to believe sincerely in the universal validity of such principles.

Thus, although the actual requirements for the suffrage in most western democracies have been reduced to a relatively few minimal standards, denying the vote to a few broad and more or less readily identifiable classes such as those below a certain age, those in prisons, or lunatic asylums, and so on, almost every extension of the franchise has been opposed by those who anticipated the loss of their special privileges, on the grounds that such extension would lead to disaster by granting the privilege of voting to those unworthy or incapable of exercising it.

One of the oldest forms of franchise qualification, one subject to the most vehement attack and the most determined defence, was that of property, especially property in land. The basic assumption, unchallenged until the mid-nineteenth century, was that a man derived his right to vote from his property and not from anything else, although the property qualification might itself be further restricted by other criteria such as residence, age, sex, or race.

As already mentioned, the Canadian franchise at the time of Confederation was based on the voting qualification in the provinces and so varied from province to province. In each case, however, the base of the qualification was the ownership or occupancy of real estate of varying annual values. Nova Scotia expanded the real property qualification to include personal property, while New Brunswick added, as a third option, an annual-income qualification. By 1885, when the first Dominion franchise was introduced, there were seven provinces, in six of which a property qualification was maintained, even though in most cases, as an alternative, there were provisions for the qualification to be met by income of some kind. In Prince Edward Island the alternatives offered to the basic property qualification were so extensive as to approach universal suffrage. In British Columbia alone, the franchise ignored property qualifications altogether.[15] In the succeeding years the property qualifications were gradually broadened and finally abandoned altogether. The last three provinces to retain a property qualification were Nova Scotia,[16] Quebec,[17] and Prince Edward Island.[18]

One negative variation of the property qualification survived for a longer period. Until 1948, inmates of charitable institutions, other than war veterans, if they were disqualified from voting at provincial elections, were also disqualified from voting at federal elections. When, in 1948, the federal disqualification was repealed by an Amendment to the *Dominion Elections Act*,[19] it affected voters in only three provinces: Ontario, Nova Scotia, and New Brunswick, all of which have since removed the disqualification from the franchise regulations.

## CITIZENSHIP

Within the Commonwealth the question of citizenship has special complications as different countries have attempted to extend voting privileges beyond their immediate citizenship to a broader "British" citizenship, normally with some greater or lesser qualifications. The *Canada Elections Act*, for example, grants the vote to a person of full age of twenty-one who is "a Canadian citizen or other British subject," although it is required of a "British subject other than a Canadian citizen," that he "has been ordinarily resident in Canada for the twelve months immediately preceding polling day."[20]

Again complications arise over the precise definition of "British subject" and over the special privileges to be accorded to the citizens of Ireland. Canadian federal law puts the Irish into a very special category of non-British who are treated as though they were British. The *Citizenship Act* provides that: "Any law of Canada, including this Act, and any regulation made under the authority of any law of Canada shall, unless it otherwise provides, have effect in relation to a citizen of the Republic of Ireland who is not a British subject in like manner as it has effect in relation to a British subject."[21] Thus citizens of the Republic of Ireland, once they have met the twelve months' residence requirement, have the right to vote in federal elections.

A further complication arises in that the Canadian Government has been slow to amend the schedule of Commonwealth countries specified in the

*Citizenship Act* and so South Africans, for example, are still regarded as British subjects for electoral purposes and are entitled to vote, although South Africa left the Commonwealth in 1961.

The same general provisions extending the right to vote to British subjects who are not Canadian citizens apply in all but two of the provinces. Since 1945 Quebec law has required that voters in provincial elections be Canadian citizens, and not just British subjects.[22] Then, in 1954, Prince Edward Island amended its *Election Act* to provide that "wherever the words 'British subject' appear in this Act, the same shall be stricken out and the words 'Canadian citizen' substituted therefore."[23]

Table 1: 1 sets out the several provisions regarding citizenship in the federal and provincial election acts.

### Table 1: 1
### CITIZENSHIP QUALIFICATIONS IN FEDERAL AND PROVINCIAL ELECTION ACTS

| Voting Rights Extended to | Election Act | Section |
|---|---|---|
| A British Subject | Ontario | 17 (1) |
| A Canadian Citizen or other British Subject | Canada | 14 (1) |
| | Alberta | 17 (2) |
| | Saskatchewan | 31 (2) |
| | Manitoba | 17 (1) |
| | New Brunswick | 43 (1) |
| | Nova Scotia | 25 (b) |
| | Newfoundland | 3 (b) |
| A Canadian Citizen | Quebec | 133 |
| | Prince Edward Island | 21 |
| A Person Entitled Within the Province to the Privileges of a Natural-Born Canadian Citizen or British Subject | British Columbia | 3 (1) |

The actual position of citizens of the Republic of Ireland in provincial elections is ambiguous. Those provinces which extend the right to vote to "other British subjects" are governed by the definition of "British" as it appears in the *Canadian Citizenship Act*, but it is not at all certain how far the special provisions for Irish citizens apply in the provinces. It will probably remain a disputable matter until the issue is tested in the courts.

The political impact of voting by British subjects who are not citizens of Canada, and by Irish Republic citizens, is extremely hard to determine. Such people are not separately identified on the electoral registers and, as far as can be gathered, there have been no voting-behaviour surveys with a category for "eligible voters — non-citizens." It seems safe, however, to hazard the guess that in most cases the numbers involved are so small that the total effect is insignificant. Perhaps in some districts the Irish, and in others the large numbers of English immigrants who have never taken the trouble to take out formal Canadian citizenship papers, may play a decisive role. Such circumstances are almost certainly rare and their existence is still highly speculative. Perhaps some survey researcher will take up the hint and explore the characteristics of these non-citizen voters.

## AGE

Invariably there is an age limit on the right to vote. But while there is general agreement that those who are too young to vote responsibly shall not do so there is less agreement on how young is "too young." Recently there has been considerable pressure in many parts of Canada to lower the voting age and it seems highly probable that further changes will be made. The fact that the voting age has already been reduced below twenty-one in several provinces without any obviously disastrous effects will undoubtedly add stimulus to the move towards similar changes in the remaining provinces and at the federal level. Indeed, at the federal level the change is imminent. The lowering of the voting age to eighteen years was a widely publicized item in the Speech from the Throne at the opening of Parliament in October, 1969.

Undoubtedly the principal considerations in the minds of those with power to extend the franchise to younger age groups will be the anticipated voting pattern of the new voters and, perhaps, the additional votes to be

### Table 1: 2
### MINIMUM VOTING AGE IN CANADA AND THE PROVINCES

| Age | Province |
| --- | --- |
| 18 on or before polling day | Saskatchewan |
| | Manitoba [since October 10, 1969] |
| | Quebec |
| | Prince Edward Island |
| 19 on or before polling day | British Columbia |
| | Alberta |
| | Newfoundland |
| 21 on or before polling day | Manitoba [until October 10, 1969] |
| | Ontario |
| | New Brunswick |
| | Nova Scotia |
| | Canada |

gained from the young by being the party which grants them the vote. Table 1: 2 sets out the current position on voting age throughout Canada.

## SEX

The question of votes for woman, while often bitterly and passionately argued, has now been settled. Women have won the right to vote, if perhaps belatedly in some parts of Canada, and they are not likely to surrender this right in the foreseeable future. The history of the struggle for women's franchise in Canada, a struggle which, incidentally, was mostly waged by a small section of the feminine population and as much against widespread feminine apathy as against male hostility, has been admirably dealt with by Catherine Cleverdon and needs no repeating here.[24]

Perhaps one brief quotation will serve to illuminate the character of the male opposition which, after many trials, tribulations, false starts, and disappointed hopes, women finally overcame. The speaker was Jean Joseph Denis, arguing in the House of Commons against granting votes

### Table 1: 3
### PROGRESS IN VOTES FOR WOMEN

| Canada and Province | Date of Royal Assent to Legislation Granting Votes to Women |
| --- | --- |
| Manitoba | January 28, 1916 |
| Alberta | March 6, 1916 |
| Saskatchewan | March 14, 1916 |
| British Columbia | April 5, 1917 |
| Ontario | April 12, 1917 |
| Canada | September 1917, **The Military Voters' Act** and the **Wartime Elections Act** gave the vote to women who had participated in any branch of the Canadian armed forces or who had a close relative serving in the armed forces of Canada or Great Britain. |
| | May 24, 1918 — full female franchise |
| Nova Scotia | April 26, 1918 |
| New Brunswick | April 17, 1919 |
| Prince Edward Island | May 3, 1922 |
| Newfoundland | April 13, 1925 — for women 25 or more years of age. Women's voting rights ceased with the renunciation of self-government in 1934. **The Terms of the Union of Newfoundland With Canada**, 1948 (Term 15) granted women full voting rights at the age of 21. |
| Quebec | April 25, 1940 |

to women: "I say that the Holy Scriptures, theology, ancient philosophy, Christian philosophy, history, anatomy, physiology, political economy, and feminine psychology, all seem to indicate that the place of women in this world is not amid the strife of the political arena, but in her home."[25] Table 1: 3 summarizes the stages in the development of female suffrage in Canada.

## RACE, LANGUAGE, AND RELIGION

As in the case of franchise discrimination on the basis of sex, discrimination on the grounds of race, language, or religion is now of greater concern to students of Canadian political history rather than to those interested in the practice of contemporary Canadian politics. There are, however, still some survivals. Quebec, for example, still maintains the once widespread disqualification of Indians living on reservations.[26]

While, today, Quebec is the only province to retain such a disqualification, it was once far more common and it was as recently as March 1963 that New Brunswick repealed a similar disqualification for reservation Indians. The disfranchisement of such Indians lasted in Ontario until 1954.

Most of the discriminatory measures have been directed at Indians and, especially in the West, at Asians. A British Columbia statute of 1875,[27] for example, declared that, "No Chinaman or Indian shall have his name placed on the Register of Voters for any Electoral District, or be entitled to vote at any election of a Member to serve in the Legislative Assembly of this Province." Until 1945 the right to vote in British Columbia provincial elections was still denied to "every Chinese, Japanese, Hindu, or Indian," although the Japanese who had served in the Canadian forces in the first World War were not so disqualified.[28] The right to vote as a reward for military service was gradually extended to the other groups who suffered from racial discrimination although it was not until a new *Provincial Elections Act* was introduced in 1953, that all references to race were finally dropped in British Columbia. The Canadian *Electoral Franchise Act* of 1885, in the interpretations and definitions in Clause 2, stated that: " 'person' means a male person, including an Indian, and excluding a person of Mongolian or Chinese race."[29] As in the provinces, Indians on reservations experienced special treatment in federal franchise legislation and it was not until 1960 that these discriminatory laws were removed from the statute books.[30]

The position of the Eskimos is even more peculiar than that of the Indians. It does not appear that any mention was made of the voting rights of Eskimos until 1934 when the *Dominion Franchise Act*[31] included among the lists of those not entitled to vote, "every Esquimeau person whether born in Canada or elsewhere." It is assumed that prior to this date

Eskimos were entitled to vote, although it is unclear whether many did, in fact, do so. The special provisions of 1934, which applied to all Eskimos, were repealed on June 30th, 1950, although large numbers of Eskimos were still unable to vote for another reason. At that time and, indeed, until 1962, the Territories of Keewatin and Franklin were not included in any federal electoral district, since the district of the Northwest Territories embraced only the Territory of Mackenzie. Thus no Eskimos, and no Europeans for that matter, living in Keewatin or Franklin could vote in a federal election prior to 1962.[32] Eskimos may now vote under the same conditions as other Canadians.

Apart from Asians, Indians, and Eskimos, other groups have from time to time suffered. The wartime franchise of 1917 denied the vote to all naturalized British subjects born in an enemy country and naturalized after March 31, 1902. Even those similarly naturalized British subjects whose "natural language, otherwise described as 'mother tongue'," was the language of an enemy country, irrespective of the country of birth, lost the right to vote.[33] Earlier, in 1901, the Manitoba legislature took action to minimize the political effectiveness of recent Ukrainian immigrants by limiting the franchise to those who could read English, French, German, Icelandic, or any Scandinavian language.[34]

In British Columbia, for provincial elections, the right to vote is still denied to "every person who does not have an adequate knowledge of either the English or French language."[35] It is assumed that this disqualification is directed primarily against the large numbers of Asians in British Columbia and particularly in Vancouver and the lower mainland. The criterion for the language qualification appears to be that the would-be voter must satisfy the Registrar of Voters that his knowledge of English or French is "adequate."

No other provinces impose a statutory language requirement and the right to vote is not conditional on the language one speaks. However, this is an area where statutory right can be obscured by administrative regulations. In Ontario and all provinces to the west, English is the language for the conduct of elections. For those in Ontario who do not speak English an interpreter may be engaged "to translate the oath as well as any lawful questions necessarily put to the voter and his answers." The deputy returning officer may hire an interpreter, but he is under no obligation to do so, and "if no interpreter is found or presents himself at the polling place, the voter shall not be allowed to vote."[36] Presumably a French-speaking Canadian cannot vote in any provincial election held west of Quebec unless an interpreter is available.

Language can still be a barrier to voting in the eastern provinces, although there is a somewhat stronger obligation on the deputy returning officer to provide an interpreter, and English is not specifically mentioned as the language that is to be understood. Both New Brunswick and Nova Scotia have almost identically worded provisions: "Whenever the deputy returning officer does not understand the language spoken by an elector, he shall if possible appoint an interpreter. . . ."[37]

In Nova Scotia and New Brunswick it is, in effect, the responsibility of the deputy returning officer to understand whatever language the elector speaks. If he does not, he is to try to obtain an interpreter. This is close to the federal regulation on language which, since it makes no reference to any particular language, puts the duty of finding an interpreter on the deputy returning officer, but which adds that if an interpreter cannot be found, the elector cannot vote.[38] Quebec alone decrees that English and French shall be the official languages for the conduct of elections, but in the treatment of electors who speak neither of these languages, it makes provisions basically the same as those applying in Nova Scotia and New Brunswick and at the federal level.[39] The election acts of Prince Edward Island and Newfoundland are silent on the question of language.

At the moment there does not seem to be any information available as to the numbers of non-English-speaking electors in Ontario and points west who are unable to vote because they are unable to find an interpreter although one may speculate that there may be large numbers in such cosmopolitan cities as Toronto, Winnipeg, and Hamilton. Some may not even attempt to vote and would thus be classified as voluntary non-voters.

Religious discrimination in recent times has been confined largely to members of those faiths which forbid one to fight for Queen and country. The last full statement of exclusion on this ground appeared in the *Canada Elections Act* of 1952,[40] where those listed as being ineligible to vote included:

> In any province, every person exempted or entitled to claim exemption or who on production of any certificate might have become or would now be entitled to claim exemption from military service by reason of the Order in Council of December 6, 1898, because the doctrines of his religion made him averse to bearing arms, and who is by the law of that province disqualified from voting at an election of a member to the legislative assembly of that province.

This provision was repealed on July 11, 1955.[41] In 1953, Doukhobors, who had been denied the vote in British Columbia, were enfranchised also. Thus at present no otherwise eligible voter is excluded for reasons of his religious beliefs, even if they include rejection of military service.

## RESIDENCE

As in the case of citizenship the question of residence poses some interesting points of legal definition, although in practice there does not seem to be any evidence that the amateur, part-time election officials entrusted with the enumeration of voters have concerned themselves too much with the technical niceties.

The language of the *Canada Elections Act*,[42] repeated in similar terms in most of the provincial acts, sets the criteria for residence clearly and precisely:

> (3) The place of ordinary residence of a person is, generally, that place which has always been, or which he has adopted as, the place of his habitation or home, whereto, when away therefrom, he intends to return; specifically, when a person usually sleeps in one place and has his meals or is employed in another place, the place of his ordinary residence is where the person sleeps.
> (4) a person can have only one place of ordinary residence and it cannot be lost unless or until another is gained; although, generally, a person's place of ordinary residence is where his family is, if he is living apart from his family, with the intent to remain so apart from it in another place, the place of ordinary residence of such person is such other place; temporary absence from a place of ordinary residence does not cause a loss or change of place of ordinary residence.

For electoral purposes the key provision is the first part of subsection (4) which means, in effect, that every otherwise eligible voter must have one, but only one, place of residence. There are, as we shall see, some few special exceptions to this principle.

For federal purposes residence is a fairly simple matter. Every Canadian citizen, and every British subject other than a Canadian citizen who has had residence in Canada for at least twelve months prior to polling day,[43] has a place of residence, which is the place at which he resided on the date of the issue of the writ. This is the place at which he will vote and should he move between the date of the writ and polling day, his place of residence will remain, with some exceptions, that which it was when the writ was issued. There is no requirement for federal purposes that one should have been at any particular place of residence, or have resided in any particular constituency, for any minimum length of time to qualify as a voter. All the provinces, however, require a minimum residence within the province as one of the qualifications for voting at provincial elections. These residence requirements are set out in Table 1: 4, page 14.

One would expect, of course, that the extent of migration between provinces would be reflected in the smaller numbers of electors on provincial lists as compared with federal. Unfortunately direct comparisons are hard to make. Provincial and federal elections are not normally held at the same time and there is an unmeasured population shift between the two elections. Again, as already noted, the voting age is not the same in all provincial and federal elections. Then too, one must expect a certain amount of error in the compiling of lists. Personal experience indicates, for example, that provincial enumerators, especially those who have previously

Table 1: 4

## RESIDENCE REQUIREMENTS FOR VOTING IN PROVINCIAL ELECTIONS

| Province | Residence requirements (with reference to the relevant section of the provincial acts) |
|---|---|
| British Columbia | 12 months in Canada, and in the province for six months immediately preceding the date of application for registration as a voter. sec. 3 (1) |
| Alberta | 12 months prior to the date of issue of the writ. sec. 17 — 2 (c) |
| Saskatchewan | 6 months prior to the date of issue of the writ. sec. 31 — 2 (b) |
| Manitoba | 12 months prior to the date of issue of the writ. sec. 17 — 2 |
| Ontario | 12 months prior to polling day. sec. 17 — 1 (1) |
| Quebec | One year before the first day fixed for enumeration. sec. 133 (d) |
| New Brunswick | 6 months prior to the date of issue of the writ. sec. 43 — 1 (c) |
| Nova Scotia | 12 months prior to the date of issue of the writ. sec. 25 (c) |
| Prince Edward Island | 12 months prior to the date of issue of the writ. sec. 21 (c) |
| Newfoundland | 12 months prior to the day of the election. sec. 3 (c) |

conducted a federal enumeration, do not always check the length of residence within the province.

It would be useful to know how many people are unable to meet the residence requirements in provincial elections, how many are permitted to vote without fulfilling residence requirements (as a result of careless enumeration) and how these figures vary from province to province and from time to time. However, the answers to these questions have not yet been determined.

In addition to the normal residence regulations there are, in the various election acts, further residence provisions for special categories of voters. In national elections, ministers of religion, priests, "ecclesiastics," school teachers and the dependents of these, who, in the course of their duties, move to another federal constituency between the date of the writ and polling day, may vote in federal elections in their new districts.[44] The Prince Edward Island,[45] Nova Scotia,[46] and New Brunswick Acts[47] make no mention of ministers, but contain similar provisions allowing school teachers and their dependents who are teaching school at a place other than their normal residence to decide for themselves in which districts they will vote. Manitoba differs only in that there is no mention of a teacher's dependents.

Students are almost everywhere given special consideration. In both federal elections and elections in New Brunswick, students who are in residence at a university may register in both the constituency in which the university is situated and in that of their family home or place of normal residence. They may then decide, on election day, to vote in either, but not in both.[48] Quebec has a similar provision which, however, refers not to "student" but to "a child who is absent from his father's or his mother's abode, with his or her consent, to attend a course of study or apprenticeship."[49]

Some of the difficulties which led to the enactment of the federal provision were raised by the Chief Electoral Officer in 1940.[50] Certain ambiguities in the *Dominion Elections Act,* 1938[51] were finally interpreted to mean that a student could vote in the constituency wherein his university was situated only if he had his place of permanent residence there. It was the opinion of the Chief Electoral Officer that this was not the intention of the original drafters of the provision, and he recommended changes making it easier for students to vote while at university. The present regulations allowing dual registration with an option to vote in either constituency were introduced in 1948.[52]

A further complication in the voting position of students arose in the 1965 elections. The writ was issued on September 8th at which time few students were in residence at university and therefore were unable to take advantage of the dual registration system; but when the enumerators began their work in the week commencing September 20th (the 49th day before polling day) most of these students were back at university. The enumerators were instructed not to add the names of such students to their lists, except for those who could demonstrate that they had in fact been in full-time residence at the university on September 8th. As the *Act* now reads, even those who affirmed that they had not been, or would not be, enumerated in their "home" constituencies could not be registered in the university district. The general rule was that as, on September 8th, their only place of residence was their family home, they could vote in that district or not at all. This situation will arise for any election held between about the middle of September and about the middle of November, if the writ is issued before the opening of term and the election is held after students have returned to university. The 1965 election was the only such instance in the eight elections since the present student-voting regulations were introduced in 1948.

Saskatchewan and Prince Edward Island both permit those students whose normal place of residence is within the province, but who are attending university outside the province, to retain their provincial residential status and to vote at provincial elections.[53] Saskatchewan, in addition, grants residence status and voting privileges to those whose normal residence is outside the province, but who are attending university in Saskatchewan.[54] Presumably, therefore, a student from Prince Edward Island attending university in Saskatchewan, would retain residence in P.E.I. and gain it in Saskatchewan and would be eligible to vote in elections in both provinces.

Alberta has unique provisions for students, allowing them, while at a "designated educational institution," to cast absentee ballots for their constituencies of normal residence.[55] This seems to combine the best elements of all systems. It allows the students to vote at the university but ensures that the votes will be counted in their "home" constituencies. This, if nothing else, protects the constituency housing the university from the disturbing influx of several thousand student voters. This is a particularly important provision in Alberta where the voting age is nineteen.

Nova Scotian legislation achieves a somewhat similar effect by giving unmarried students at university a proxy vote for their "home" constituency.[56] In Newfoundland, students, and several other categories of electors, are permitted to decide for themselves whether to be registered in their place of temporary residence or in their normal "home" constituency.[57]

Another group of transients also receives special treatment. In the federal act, a worker who is temporarily employed away from his place of normal residence may register and vote in his place of temporary employment, but not if his temporary work is for the "execution of any federal or provincial public work," nor if his temporary residence is in "any camp temporarily established in connection with any such public work under federal or provincial government control," unless he has been "in continuous residence therein for at least thirty days immediately preceding the issue of such writ."[58] The purpose of such provisions are, of course, to prevent the government making doubtful seats safe by moving in large numbers of temporary public employees, and to the extent that they prevent even the allegation of such manipulations, they are probably to be recommended. Somewhat similar provisions are included in the *Quebec Elections Act*.[59]

There is a lengthy correspondence submitted with the *Report* of the Chief Electoral Officer following the 1949 general elections which discusses the position of workers engaged on Hydro projects in various parts of Canada. The debate centred round the question of whether or not such projects were public works within the meaning of the *Public Works Act* of 1937. Inasmuch as the details are much too complex to summarize here and too lengthy to reproduce in full, it is suggested that the interested reader consult the C.E.O. Report.[60]

The situation in 1965 which led to a considerable number of students not being enumerated affected another section of the community in 1962. In this case in Newfoundland a number of logging camps were opened after the issue of the writs and the majority of the men working in the camps on election day were unable to vote. A defeated candidate for the constituency of Grand Falls-White Bay-Labrador set out the plight of the loggers, as it affected the one constituency in which he was interested, in a letter to the Chief Electoral Officer which was published in the C.E.O.'s *Report* following the June 1962 elections. This particular set of events apparently involved more than simply difficulties with the enumeration and there were allegations of deliberate failure to establish polling divisions in the logging camps and an inadequate supply of ballot papers at those polling stations which were established.

One final class of residents ought to be mentioned; these are the summer cottagers. There is great concern lest the summer vacationers from the big cities upset the traditional power structures in the rural areas so that federal and most provincial legislation makes it quite clear that premises which are "generally occupied only during some or all of the months of May to October, inclusive, and generally remain unoccupied during some or all of the months of November to April"[61] shall not be regarded as the place of residence of those people who do, in fact, occupy other premises during the winter months. A voter must come home from the cottage to vote in a summer election.

Several other smaller disfranchised groups need to be mentioned only briefly and simply to make the account complete. While there may be detailed variation in the wording, all the election acts contain clauses denying the vote to those who are undergoing a prison sentence for the commission of some offence, those who are confined in a hospital for the insane, and those who have, within some specified recent period, been convicted of some corrupt practices under the terms of the election act. The only point that is perhaps worth noting is that the disqualification for a criminal offense applies only while the person is undergoing punishment in a penal institution. Once he has served his time he is free to take up again the responsibilities of citizenship. Many election acts in other countries, notably in some of the state election acts in the United States, render the law much more rigid and conviction for a criminal offense may disfranchise for life. Insofar as the law is intended to have some rehabilitative element, this permanent denial of the rights of citizenship is quite indefensible.

Finally there are groups of people who, by reason of their office, are denied the vote. Again the details vary from province to province, but the principle remains the same. The Chief Electoral Officer, and often his deputy, the returning officer (although the returning officer may sometimes be given a casting vote), sometimes the Election Clerk, and various categories of judges, are generally specified in the lists of those who may not vote. These are fairly normal provisions and perhaps the only category which might cause some dispute is that of judges, and here it is interesting to note that the *First Report* of the Ontario Select Committee on Election Laws contained the proposal that judges of federal and provincial courts be no longer disqualified in provincial elections.[62]

## VOTERS' LISTS

As the past few pages have demonstrated, universal suffrage has never meant, and has never been intended to mean, that everyone shall vote. Although there has been a gradual reduction in the classes of statutory non-voters, some classes will always remain. However wide the extension of the franchise it is certain that there will remain some barriers of age, citizenship, residence, and mental capacity.

But even among those who possess the necessary statutory qualifications, the right to vote is not automatic. There are then various administrative barriers to be overcome, the first and most important of which is registration on some form of voters' list. There are all kinds of individual exceptions and special cases, but the general rule in all advanced democratic political systems is that only those who are registered or are in some way listed as eligible voters shall be entitled to cast ballots. It is at this level of the preparation of lists of voters that the first form of administrative disfranchisement appears. It is here that individual carelessness, inefficient administrative procedures, overly rigid formalities, or deliberate manipulation of rules for partisan advantage, can operate to deprive hundreds of citizens of their right to vote.

The preparation of the voters' lists is thus one of the most important stages in an election and every study of the reform of the election system as a whole will devote a great deal of time to this question. The registration systems can be classified in several ways, with permutations possible among the different classification schemes. One can, for example, begin by considering the time at which lists are prepared, and here there are two basic principles. A list may be prepared only when an election has been called: a list which will apply solely to that election and which will be discarded as soon as the election is over. This can be called a "temporary list," and it is the system which operates in federal and most provincial elections in Canada. Or there may be a list which is prepared at some fixed interval of time, independently of whether or not an election is to be held. The annual British Register of Electors is a typical example of such a system. One variation of this scheme requires that a new list be drawn up every few years and that in the interval between the preparation of lists, the one in force be kept up-to-date by a continuous process of additions, amendments, and deletions. Such a list, called, obviously, a "continuous" list and the British type of periodic list are both varieties of a "permanent" list.

Registration can also be looked at from the point of view of the responsibility for compiling the list. Under one system the responsibility for preparing voters' lists is assumed by the state and various paid officers (temporary or permanent) go out and collect the names of every available voter. This is the procedure followed in the enumeration of voters in Canada. Under another procedure the state provides facilities — registration offices and officials — and leaves it to the initiative of the citizen to become a registered voter. This initiative may be a completely voluntary action in which it is entirely up to the individual to decide whether or not to register. This system is found in many of the American states. Finally, there may be, as in Australia and New Zealand, a legal obligation on the citizen to register himself.[63]

A third classification, which is particularly important where there are permanent lists prepared perhaps some time before an election, categorizes lists as "open" or "closed." An open system is one in which names can be added after the list is printed or which permits people to vote, under certain specified circumstances, even though their names are not on the lists; while a closed list confines the right to vote to those formally registered as voters.

From these three two-part classifications it is possible to derive eight basic systems of voter registration, although it should be noted that in practice most actual registration laws will combine the elements of more than one system.

There is, first of all, the periodic list, compiled by election officials, and subject to constant updating until close to election day. Secondly, there is a similarly compiled list, but one that is closed off at a specified date so that no new names may be registered until the new list is prepared. The British permanent Register of Electors is of this type.[64] A third system is that in which there is a temporary list, prepared for a particular election by a set of state employees (including temporarily appointed enumerators), but which, after some specified period for revision or correction, is closed so that only those listed may vote. This system applies at the federal level for urban polls. The fourth system, a variation of the third which applies to rural polls at federal elections, is the open list under which those eligible voters whose names are not on the list may still vote after the completion of certain formalities. The four remaining systems are similar to those already described except that, in each case, the responsibility for adding a person's name to the list falls on the individual voter. Experience in many American states indicates that unless there is some degree of compulsion, or a scheme of intensive publicity campaigns, reliance on voter initiative is unlikely to produce a very complete list. In practice many countries use a combination of systems, placing the primary responsibility on the voters to register themselves, but also introducing a considerable measure of follow-up action by election officials to ensure that the greatest possible number of voters do, in fact, exercise their rights. This is, effectively, what is done in New Zealand and Great Britain.

Federally and provincially Canada has experimented with several of these systems. In his 1926 *Report*, the Canadian Chief Electoral Officer noted that several systems were, even at that time, in use. Provincial lists for Nova Scotia, New Brunswick, Quebec, and Ontario were prepared periodically by administrative officers. British Columbia offered a continuous, permanent list in which the initiative for registration lay with the individual. Manitoba, Saskatchewan, and Alberta all prepared lists specially for each election and adopted both the voluntary registration by citizens and the enumeration by official procedures. Prince Edward Island used no provincial lists at all. The federal scheme combined several elements, although a new list was still prepared for each election. For rural polls official registrars compiled lists without any direct intervention on the part of the electors, while urban registrars based their records either on the provincial lists, or on direct application by eligible voters whose names were not on the provincial lists.[65]

Canada has had one brief experiment with permanent lists for federal elections. The *Dominion Franchise Act* of 1934 authorized a system of permanent lists and one was created for the 1935 election. The innovation, however, was apparently not well received. The Chief Electoral Officer noted that ". . . it cannot be said . . . that the new list-making procedure proved to be an improvement upon the old."[66] When, in 1938, the *Dominion Franchise Act* was repealed and the voter registration procedures were incorporated in the new *Dominion Elections Act*, the permanent list was abandoned and what was essentially the present system of pre-election enumeration was adopted.

Debate on the relative merits of different registration procedures can take place at two levels: at the first level one considers the criteria by which a registration system is to be judged, and at the second level one assesses the effectiveness of each procedure in the light of the ends which it is supposed to achieve. At the first stage one is essentially making value judgments, setting objectives for the registration plan. Such objectives may be simply to reduce the costs of registration to the lowest possible level, or they may be designed to minimize the voting opportunities for transients, the very poor, or the uneducated. Since argument at this level would involve extensive examination it is perhaps best here simply to state the criteria one might use to evaluate a registration procedure. The criteria could be defended convincingly if space here permitted.

In the first place the best registration process will result in a list which, on election day, contains the greatest possible number of names of eligible voters and the least possible number of the ineligible. These are the overriding criteria, but they are not the only ones. Costs are important and once any given level of registration is achieved, one would have to weigh the advantages of ever greater accuracy against the rising cost of each additional name added. Inevitably there will be a diminishing return on investment and there will come a point where further outlay would be unjustified. Again, the lists should be compiled and published in a manner that gives the voters confidence that they are indeed accurate and honest. One could also require that the procedure for compiling lists should not be so cumbersome or time-consuming as to unduly prolong the election campaign. At another level, voters' lists are important to campaign workers and it is highly desirable that candidates, their agents, and their helpers should receive sufficient copies of lists early enough in the campaign for them to be of some real practical use in canvassing. A less important by-product of the publication of lists is that they be in a form facilitating their preservation for historians, archivists and political science researchers. The final, and to the author's mind the least important, criterion is that the registration process be sufficiently leisurely to permit the careful checking of occupations, addresses, and the spelling of names.

By these standards the permanent open (continuous) list with compulsory registration by voters has much to recommend it, although it fails most strikingly in cost. The findings of a recent study (1968) by the Canadian Representation Commissioner are most significant:

> The system of Continuous Electoral Rolls currently in use in the Commonwealth of Australia, including the method of compulsory registration on the part of the electors, can be adapted for use in federal elections in Canada, to reduce the time required for the holding of elections and to provide improved facilities for voting by electors. . . . However, it is my belief that the adoption of such a system would prove to be very costly. The setting up of a permanent office in each electoral district, the recruitment of a great many permanent and casual employees, and an annual house-to-house canvass by review officers in order to purge and update the existing lists of electors, would be the major items of expense.[67]

It is worth noting that when a Special Committee of the House of Commons raised the same general topics in 1937, it reached essentially the same conclusion.[68] Rough estimates indicate that the annual cost of maintaining a continuous roll would be slightly greater than the cost of producing a single list for a particular election under the present scheme. This would mean, in effect, that the cost of producing an electoral roll would increase from some $12,000,000 every three or four years to some $14,000,000 every year, which is a very high price to pay for what can, in the circumstance, be only a slight increase in the accuracy of the lists. The additional advantages of continuous lists for absentee or postal voting or for reducing the length of the campaign period are another matter which will be raised again later.

The permanent closed list of the British pattern has little except administrative convenience and tidiness to recommend it. The British roll does not come into effect until it is four months out-of-date, and by the time it is replaced it is sixteen months old.

Experience has shown that registration systems which place the entire responsibility for becoming registered on the individual citizen are unsatisfactory. The 1937 Special Committee of the House of Commons concluded that rolls based on voluntary registration could be brought to some satisfactory level of accuracy only through the costly, time-consuming efforts of political parties, members of parliament, and parliamentary candidates.[69] Such knowledge as we have of political apathy would seem to confirm this general proposition. In the absence of legal compulsions or strong political pressures, there are very large numbers of people who would not take the initiative to register themselves as voters. This appears to be the situation in British Columbia. Indeed it seems from experience in some of the southern states of America that it is often in those areas where it is desired to perpetuate a high level of political apathy and low voter registration among certain sections of the community that voluntary registration systems, unsupported by official get-out-the-vote campaigns, are the most determinedly preserved.

There remains to be considered the typical Canadian pre-election enumeration in effect at the federal level and all but one of the provinces. The enumeration procedure produces what is surely the most up-to-date list of voters possible. It is achieved at relatively low cost and appears to have a high degree of reliability. Such limited evidence as there is suggests that the main source of error on the lists is not so much the omission of the eligible as the inclusion of the ineligible, especially the under-age and the non-citizens (Americans in particular). If the enumeration lists have any faults, they lie principally in areas of secondary importance. They are produced in great haste by enumerators who go from door to door collecting names. Inevitably there are a great many spelling errors, although the act makes it quite clear that such clerical errors shall not deprive the elector of his vote.[70]

The present highly effective system of registering voters did not, of course, just happen. It is the result of many years of trial and error, with much intense argument and debate. The historical development of the modern enumeration system is beyond the scope of this book, especially as it has already been adequately covered (at least at the federal level) elsewhere.[71] One or two particularly relevant points are, however, worth mentioning. Since in the first federal elections a property qualification applied, lists of voters were simply and easily compiled from local or municipal assessment rolls. These lists were closed in the sense that once the formal revision period was over no further changes or additions could be made. It was absolutely necessary for the voter not only to possess the requisite qualifications, but also to be formally listed as a voter. It was only with the abandonment of, or extension of exceptions to, the property qualification that more elaborate systems of registering voters became necessary. The first experiments with the preparation of lists by enumerators were made in 1908, but the procedure applied only to territory in Ontario not municipally organized.[72] The system was gradually extended so that by 1921 it applied to all towns with a population of less than 2,500. In 1925 the limit was raised to 5,000, and in 1929 to 10,000. The obligation of electors in large towns to register themselves was abolished in 1929 and all subsequent lists were prepared by enumerators.[73] The 1930 general election was conducted on the basis of lists prepared entirely by the enumeration process. After a brief and unhappy experience with permanent lists in the 1935 election, the Chief Electoral Officer reported in favour of returning to door-to-door enumeration. "I have been connected with the administration of the last eight general elections and I have no hesitation in saying that in my opinion the system for the preparation of lists adopted in the 1930 election was by far the most satisfactory system used during that period."[74]

The present system was introduced in the *Dominion Elections Act*, 1938[75] and has remained substantially unaltered since then. The present enumeration procedure is set out in the *Act* in great detail designed to maximize accuracy and minimize carelessness or fraud. It is described in section 17 which, with its two schedules, takes up 24 pages in the *Act*. The essential stages are these: as soon as possible after receipt of the writ the returning officer will appoint two enumerators for each urban polling division and one for each rural polling division. Of course, as soon as it appears that an election is likely to be called, the returning officer will proceed informally to prepare his lists of enumerators although none can be officially appointed until after the issue of the writ. Each enumerator must take on oath, swearing that he will act faithfully in the capacity of enumerator "without partiality, fear, favour or affection."[76] As far as possible the returning officer tries to ensure that the urban enumerators will represent "two different and opposed political interests." (Rule 2) He does this by approaching the candidate who won the previous election and also the candidate for the party which came second. The right to nominate enumerators, who are then paid by the state, is an important source of minor patronage to the two largest parties and is of great assistance in recruiting campaign workers. The single rural enumerator is appointed by the returning officer and it is required that, if possible, he be a resident of the polling division as well as of the electoral district.

The two urban enumerators must commence their duties on the forty-ninth day before polling day (section 17 (1)) — a stipulation which sets the minimum period for a Canadian election campaign at about two months, for, before the forty-ninth day, enumerators must be selected, appointed, and sworn in. One obvious effect, therefore, of the introduction of permanent voters' lists would be to make possible a shorter campaign period.

The *Act* itself, and the instruction booklets which all enumerators receive, stress that urban enumerators are to work in pairs and that they must agree to every name added to their list. It is argued, probably correctly, that if the two enumerators do indeed represent the two strongest opposing parties in the constituency, then each will act as an effective check on any inclinations the other might have to falsify the list. The enumerators are to proceed to every dwelling place in their polling division, making return calls where necessary, and jointly compile a register of qualified voters. Unfortunately, individual enumerators, in defiance of their instructions, will sometimes divide the labour instead of working together. In such cases fraudulent padding of lists may pass undetected. While most of the list will be prepared from this house-to-house visitation, enumerators may fill out their records from "such other sources of information as may be available to them," (Schedule A. Rule 7) which means in effect that if a voter is out the enumerators can ask the next-door neighbour about him. They must leave a copy of the registration form, signed by both enumerators, with each elector. For a rural polling division only one enumerator is appointed. The general rationale for this is that rural areas have a much more stable population so that padding lists with false names or deliberately leaving names off the list is more easily detected. The actual enumeration must be completed by Saturday, the forty-fourth day before polling day and by the following Monday the enumerators must deliver to the returning officer copies of their lists in correct order (geographic for urban polls, alphabetical for rural). The returning officer is then responsible for having these preliminary lists printed, a task which must be completed no later than the twenty-sixth day before polling day (section 17 (5)). Since these substantial official printing orders are added to a mass of party propaganda all of which is wanted in a hurry it can be appreciated that local printing firms favour frequent elections.

All officially nominated candidates and persons "reasonably expected to be officially nominated" receive copies of these lists as soon as they are available. They are, of course, a basic source of information for canvassing and parties and candidates would be severely handicapped without them. It is one of the virtues of the enumeration process that campaign workers receive lists of voters which are as up-to-date as it is possible to make them. One copy of the preliminary list is also sent to every family in the polling division.[77] This mailing of a list to every household is, in itself, part of the machinery for minimizing fraud. Except perhaps in the anonymity of a high-rise apartment block most people are sufficiently concerned about their neighbours' affairs to comment if any unknown names are listed as living next-door to them.

The next stage in the enumeration of voters is the revision of the lists and here the procedure differs markedly between rural and urban polls. As a first step the urban polling divisions are regrouped into a series of revisal districts such that no more than about thirty-five polling divisions are included in one revisal district. The number is not defined and can vary according to circumstances. For each constituency there is an *ex officio* revising officer who is a judge as defined in section 2 (13) of the *Act*. The *ex officio* revising officer may, or may not, actually act in any revisal district within his constituency since he has the power to appoint such substitute revising officers as he thinks fit. All that is required of the substitute revising officer is that he be a qualified elector within the constituency and that he swear the appropriate oath.

In each revisal district a revisal office is established and is opened during well-defined hours of business (Schedule A. Rule 28) from Thursday to Saturday, the eighteenth to sixteenth days before polling day and, in special circumstance (Rule 40) on Tuesday the thirteenth day before polling. At the sittings for revision, the revising officer will consider, and dispose of, applications for additions to the list made either by the elector concerned or by any of several other people acting on his behalf — an officially appointed revising agent, a volunteer worker usually part of a candidate's campaign team who designates himself an "agent" of the elector, a relative, or an employer. Applications will also be considered for the correction or deletion of names already on the preliminary list. It is for the purpose of responding to charges that a name be deleted that the revisal office is open on the Tuesday following the normal revisal hearings. Elaborate procedures are detailed (in Rules 30 and 31) to protect any elector, properly enumerated, from having his name unjustly deleted at the revisal hearings. Part of Rule 31 is worth quoting here:

> . . . the onus of substantiating sufficient **prima facie** ground to strike off any name from the preliminary list shall be upon the elector making the objection, and it shall not be necessary for the person against whom objection is made to adduce proof in the first instance that his name properly appears on the pre-liminary list; the absence from or non-attendance before the revising officer, at the time the objection is dealt with, of the person against whom an objection is made does not relieve the elector making the objection from substantiating a **prima facie** case by evidence that, in the absence of rebuttal evidence, is con-

sidered by the revising officer sufficient to establish the fact that the name of the person objected to improperly appears on the preliminary list."[78]

Immediately after the completion of the revision hearings, and not later than the twelfth day before polling day, the revising officer will prepare, for each polling division, a statement of changes and additions to the preliminary list. Each officially nominated candidate is entitled to receive five copies of these and the returning officer receives three, one of which is kept on file while the other two, together with the preliminary list, form the official list of voters at the advance and ordinary polls.

Rural revision is a much simpler process in that the single enumerator himself acts as the revising officer and makes all the necessary changes and additions. The detailed procedures he must follow are set out in Schedule B, Rules 12 to 24 and they do not need to be explained here.

The enumeration procedure has been described here at some length because, in urban polling divisions, the official list, which is the preliminary list together with the changes and additions made during the revision, is a closed list. To vote it is not only necessary that one possess all the required legal qualifications, it is also essential that one's name be recorded on the official list. Voters are those who are listed as voters, not merely those who possess the qualifications of voters. There are only two exceptions to this rule in urban areas. The first is to protect those who, although properly enumerated and who can produce in evidence a copy of the enumeration form left by the enumerator, are through some clerical or printing error left off the list. The second is to protect those who, although properly added during the revision procedures, are again omitted from the list through some clerical error. Both groups, after completing certain formalities, may vote.

Rural lists are open lists. This means that no great disadvantage follows from omission from the preliminary list, and there is no great pressure to ensure that all corrections are made during the revision. An elector in a rural polling division may vote if (1) he takes an oath swearing that he is duly qualified to vote in that division and (2) he can be vouched for by another elector whose name properly appears on the official list for the division (section 46). This formality involves some inconvenience and most rural electors therefore find it more satisfactory to be correctly listed on the appropriate roll. No records are kept, apart from the entries in some 21,000 individual rural poll-books, as to the number of rural electors, not on the voters' lists, who vote after being vouched for.

At the provincial level the basic procedure in all provinces except British Columbia is patterned on the federal system. There is a process of house-to-house enumeration in the period immediately following the issue of the writ, with a time set aside for revision and objections. Of course there are a great many variations in detail, in the time allowed for enumeration, in the number of enumerators and the method of their appointment, and in the revision procedures. But these are all no more than details, adapted to the special needs of the province, and they do not raise any great fundamental issues.

In addition to these general uniformities we should note the alternatives which are allowed in some cases. In three provinces, Alberta, Manitoba, and Newfoundland, enumeration is the regular but not the only means of preparing a list of voters for an election. In Newfoundland, once a list is prepared it may be used for any election held within the next twelve months and, indeed, on an order by the Lieutenant-Governor-in-Council, a list may remain in effect for as long as five years.[79]

In Manitoba there is a somewhat similar provision, although it is even stronger in its effect. There, if a new election is called within two years of the previous one, then, "unless otherwise directed by the Lieutenant-Governor-in-Council" a new list will not be prepared.[80]

As between Newfoundland and Manitoba the difference appears to be that whereas in Newfoundland there is an option that the old list be retained, in Manitoba the normal procedure would be to use the old list for the new election, although there remains the option of adopting a new one. Insofar as they both open up the possibility of conducting an election with a list of voters that is seriously out-of-date and therefore both violate what was earlier stated as the first criterion for a registration system, neither has very much to recommend it.

In Alberta quite a different principle operates. The familiar enumeration procedure is carried out before each election in all polling divisions but, in city constituencies, and only in city constituencies, there is in addition a permanent Register of Electors. "Any qualified elector of a city constituency may register himself, during the regular office hours of the public service of Alberta, by appearing at the place where the register is maintained for the constituency in which he resides and showing to the satisfaction of the official in charge of the registry thereat that he is qualified as an elector residing in that constituency."[81] The Register is not a substitution for enumeration but is really a supplement to it, providing a check on the accuracy of the enumeration and giving an opportunity for the elector, who, through error, is not enumerated, to vote. Once an election is called the Register is closed and an enumeration is made. Subsequently a comparison is made between the enumeration lists and the Register and all discrepancies are checked out.

At another level, on the question of whether the list will be open or closed, one can recognize much more fundamental differences among the provinces in the law regarding voters' lists. Here there are three distinct patterns. First of all, in two provinces, Quebec and Prince Edward Island, both rural and urban lists are closed after the formal revision. Secondly, in three provinces, New Brunswick, Ontario, and Alberta, the rural lists are open, and the urban are more or less rigidly closed. Finally, in four provinces, Nova Scotia, Manitoba, Newfoundland, and Saskatchewan, both urban and rural lists are open.

The requirements of the nine provinces using an enumeration system are summarized in Appendix One.

British Columbia alone does not prepare lists by enumeration, maintaining instead a continuous electoral roll in which prime responsibility for registration rests with the individual elector.[82] The official Registrar of Voters appointed for each electoral district maintains a permanent office at which voters register. There is no annual or pre-election registration period although there is an intense campaign immediately before an election to persuade voters to register themselves.

Once an elector is registered his name remains on the electoral roll for as long as he continues to reside in the constituency and to vote. (There are provisions for the periodic cancellation of some or all of the rolls and for a complete re-registration of electors.) The rolls are kept up to date in response to applications for new registrations and notifications of changes of address. In both cases the initiative lies with the individual person and if he does not act to place his name on the list he will not be able to vote. The names of the deceased are removed from the rolls from information supplied by the Registrar of Vital Statistics.

After each general election, the poll books are checked. Each person who did not vote is sent a postcard informing him that if the reason that he did not vote was that he no longer resided in the constituency, his name will be removed from the list of voters. If any card is returned to the Registrar as undeliverable, the name is deleted from the roll.

Only those who are properly registered may vote and the only people who are not on the list who may vote are those who can prove that they have completed registration procedures and that their names have been omitted through clerical error.[83]

For the 1966 general election an intensive registration campaign was conducted throughout the province. All registered electors were sent a card which read, "You are presently registered as a Provincial voter at the address shown on this card. Your name will remain on the voters' list for the electoral district indicated unless any change of status or of address comes to my notice before close of registration for any Provincial election. If there is no change, it will not be necessary for you to re-register. Registrar of Voters." Advertisements in the newspapers and over the radio drew attention to the card and urged all who did not receive one to report to a registration centre. In larger districts, "a greater number of registration places were set up. In the Greater Vancouver area, use was made of department stores, supermarkets, drug stores and other similar places. In smaller places, local gas stations and various stores which were available were used for registration centres. Those wishing to do so could, by mail, request registration forms from the Registrar and, also by mail, return them completed."[84]

Despite this intensive effort it is quite clear that voluntary registration schemes of the type in use in British Columbia produce far less satisfactory results than the enumeration procedure used elsewhere in Canada. To this general criticism one qualification ought perhaps to be added. If the continuous roll were more widely used in Canada, so that the procedure became more familiar, then it might be more successful. As it is, people moving to British Columbia from other provinces will have been enumerated in the past and will in many cases continue to expect to be enumerated. Similarly, electors within the province itself will have been enumerated for federal elections and not all will be fully aware that something more is expected of them in provincial elections. Table 1: 5, which shows the percentage of voting-age population registered for the provincial election closest to the 1966 census date, makes the point quite clear. The differences between the numbers of registered voters and the total voting-age population will be made up in part by changes in population

## Table 1: 5

### A COMPARISON OF THE PERCENTAGES OF THE TOTAL VOTING-AGE POPULATIONS WHO ARE REGISTERED ON OFFICIAL VOTERS' LISTS

| Jurisdiction | Voting Age | Voting Age Population According to 1966 census | Number of Electors on Voters' Lists | Election Date | Registered Electors as a Percentage of Voting-Age Population |
|---|---|---|---|---|---|
| New Brunswick | 21 | 319,052 | 314,996 | May 1967 | 98.7 |
| Nova Scotia | 21 | 415,257 | 405,704 | May 1967 | 97.6 |
| Newfoundland | 19 | 249,572 | 239,616 | Sep 1966 | 96.0 |
| Saskatchewan | 18 | 580,317 | 549,256 | Oct 1967 | 94.6 |
| Alberta | 19 | 848,926 | 795,034 | May 1967 | 93.7 |
| Quebec | 18 | 3,494,538 | 3,222,302 | Jun 1966 | 92.2 |
| Manitoba | 21 (a) | 552,960 | 509,469 | Jun 1966 | 92.1 |
| Canada | 21 | 11,260,202 | 10,274,904 | Nov 1965 | 91.2 |
| Ontario | 21 | 4,051,603 | 3,685,755 | Oct 1967 | 90.9 |
| Prince Edward Island | 18 | 64,001 | 56,941 | May 1966 | 89.0 |
| British Columbia | 19 | 1,172,849 | 873,927 | Sep 1966 | 74.5 |

(a) The voting age in Manitoba was lowered to 18 in October, 1969.

figures between the census date and the election date, by the number of those who have not met provincial residential qualifications, and by the number of non-British subjects. Major discrepancies will also be explained in part by inefficient registration procedures.

Within British Columbia itself there have been numerous criticisms of the voter registration system. Prior to the 1963 provincial elections, for example, the following report appeared in *The Vancouver Sun* under the headline: "Thousands of Unlisted Voters Have Only a Week to Register."

> British Columbians have only a week to ensure their right to vote in the Sept. 30 provincial general election. Deadline for the voters' list is next Saturday and anyone not registered by then will go voteless.
> Opposition party leaders are protesting that the electoral machinery is not geared to meet the deadline, and that thousands will go voteless. Opposition leader Robert Strachan said today New Democratic Party workers in Vancouver were refused a supply of forms with which to seek registration. Provincial Deputy Registrar of Voters, Ken L. Morton said, in Vancouver, the criticism was unfair.
> He said there would be no door-to-door enumeration for the election and the 1960 election list, so far updated only in ridings where there have been by-elections or known deaths, will be used. He added that it is the responsibility of each elector to get his name on the list.[85]

It should be added that while opposition critics appear to assume that they are the principal victims of the inadequacies of the registration system, there is no actual evidence to support this, and nothing substantial to indicate that Social Credit voters are more efficient than other voters in getting themselves registered.

## ADVANCE POLLS, ABSENTEE BALLOTS, AND PROXY BALLOTS

At one time it was customary for elections to be held over a period of several days, or even weeks, a practice which increased the opportunities for bribery and intimidation. In this more enlightened age it is the general practice for the election in each constituency to be concluded within the time limits of one day and within all constituencies on the same date. It is also generally required that voters must attend one specified polling place and vote there and nowhere else. But, as in any general practice, there are special cases requiring special provisions to meet them.

Inevitably there will be some electors who will be unable to be in their polling division on election day and one measure of the efficiency of an election system is the extent to which it can extend voting rights to such people without excessive increase in cost and without unduly furthering the opportunities for fraud.

There are three principal ways of dealing with the problem: electors may be permitted to vote on a day other than and prior to election day (an advance poll), they may be permitted to vote somewhere else and to have their ballot mailed to their home constituency (an absentee ballot), or they may be permitted to authorize someone else to vote on their behalf (a proxy ballot).

Of these three the commonest is the advance poll which is found in some form or another in the federal and all provincial election acts. This is surprising for this method is the most cumbersome and the least satisfactory way of providing for absent electors. The principal disadvantages of the advance polls are: there is no provision for the person who is absent from his constituency on both the regular polling day and the days of the advance poll (and as the advance poll must normally be held within a very few days of the regular poll there must be considerable numbers in this position), there is no provision for the person whose absence on election day was not anticipated in time for the advance poll, and the procedures for voting at an advance poll are sufficiently complex and cumbersome to discourage some potential voters. Unfortunately there do not seem to be any accurate figures available on the number of non-voters who might have voted had there been some more convenient alternative to the advance poll and criticisms of its effect on disfranchising voters must remain at the level of intelligent speculation.

In the *Canada Elections Act* the advance poll provisions are covered in sections 92 to 97. Very simply put, they provide that normal polling divisions will be grouped in larger units known as advance polling districts, that the advance polls will be open between 8 a.m. and 8 p.m. on the Saturday and Monday, the ninth and seventh day before polling day, that any elector on the list of electors for any of the polling divisions comprised in the advance polling division "who has reason to believe that he will be absent from and unable to vote in such polling division on the ordinary polling day" may vote at the advance poll, that any elector voting at an advance poll must swear (or affirm) a special affidavit, and that the ballots in an advance poll may not be counted until after the close of the polls on the ordinary polling day. The extension of the right of voting at advance polls to all electors who believed they would be unable to vote in their regular polling places on election day was one of the major improvements made by the 1960 *Act*. Prior to that time only certain specifically listed classes of people could vote in an advance poll — commercial travellers, fishermen, those "employed upon railways, vessels, airships, or other means or modes of transportation," members of the reserve forces of the Canadian Forces, and members of the RCMP — whose occupations took them away from their polling places.[86] Even these few restricted groups could vote at the advance poll only if their prospective absence on ordinary polling day was in the course of their employment.

The federal election of 1962 was the first in which the more liberal provisions applied and their unfamiliarity introduced a new difficulty. ". . . at some advance polling stations one vote or so few votes were cast by electors for the same candidate that the secrecy of the ballot cast by such electors was not for such reason achieved."[87] It appears today that this danger is no longer as significant, although even in the 1968 elections there were slightly more than fifty advance polling stations in forty constituencies in which fewer than six electors voted, and in thirteen of them there was only one voter.

Nova Scotia, New Brunswick, Ontario, and Saskatchewan all have advance poll regulations very similar to those at the federal level, with slight variations in the days and hours on which the advance polls will be open. Prince Edward Island follows the same pattern except that the poll is open on one day only — the fourth day before polling day. This latter arrangement would seem to introduce one of the worst defects of the advance poll system in that the probability of a person absent on polling day also being absent four days earlier must be fairly high.

Until recently Manitoba and Alberta were alike in extending advance poll privileges from those who expected to be necessarily absent on election day to those who were invalids.[88] Presumably this was intended to protect invalids from the crowds and confusion of an ordinary polling place. Manitoba also provided special advance poll facilities for mariners. An amendment to the *Manitoba Election Act* in October, 1969, further facilitated voting by the physically incapacitated by providing that such persons could apply in writing to the returning officer at least ten days before polling day to vote by mail.[89]

In Quebec the restrictive, limiting provisions of the earlier federal legislation are still in force. The only persons entitled to vote at an advance poll, or, as it is termed in Quebec, a special polling-station, are

railway, post-office and express company employees, navigators, missionary priests, commercial travellers and all other persons whose ordinary employment obliges them to absent themselves from the place of their domicile and who have reason to believe that their ordinary employment will necessitate their absence on the general polling-day from the municipality in which they have their domicile and prevent them from voting at the current election.[90]

It appears from reading this section that the only electors entitled to vote at advance polls in Quebec elections are those employed in occupations which take them away from home as a matter of routine. Unusual business trips, travel for pleasure, or travel arising from such family occasions as weddings and funerals can all cause a loss of one's vote in Quebec.

The Newfoundland *Act*, while it does make specific reference to "members of the Armed Forces of Canada, fishermen, sailors, persons employed on a railway, vessel, airplane, or other means of transportation," extends also to all whose work is likely to take them away from home on election day.[91] This is much more generous than the Quebec act although it still does not give the right to vote at an advance poll to those who are likely to be away for any reason other than that their occupation demands it. Once the necessary mechanics for an advance poll are established it is difficult to see what advantages there are in so restricting its use. The costs of operating an advance poll would not be greatly increased by allowing some additional number of voters to cast their ballots there, and it is difficult to see what principle is served by denying the vote to a man whose annual holidays begin on election day and who would like to go away.

One of the great advantages claimed for the permanent voters' list printed sometime before an election is that it facilitates the opportunities for voting in places other than the assigned polling division. This claim would seem to be substantiated in British Columbia which does have very generous provisions for the conduct of an advance poll. Any elector "who has reason to believe that he will be unable to attend at a polling-place on ordinary polling-day" may vote at the advance poll. Further, he may, without any additional formality, vote at any advance polling station set up within the constituency.[92] In addition, it is provided that any voter "who has reason to believe that he will be unable to attend at a polling-place on ordinary polling-day, and who is unable to attend at a place in the electoral district in which he is registered where advance poll certificates are issued," may, after the completion of certain formalities to reduce the opportunities for fraud or double voting, "vote on a special ballot-paper at any polling booth within the Province."[93] This would seem to remove one of the major objections to the advance poll as operated in the other provinces, in that it makes provision for recording the vote of a person absent from his constituency on ordinary polling day and on the days of the advance poll.

The procedure in British Columbia whereby the voter, under certain circumstances, can cast an advance ballot at any poll in the province resembles in many ways the procedure for an absentee ballot and it is only in British Columbia that any wide use is made of the absentee ballot. Two sections of the *British Columbia Election Act* grant extensive absentee voting rights. Section 117, which would presumably apply mainly to the more scattered rural areas, provides that "any voter whose name is on the list of voters for one polling division of an electoral district, and who is absent from that polling division on the day on which the election is held," may, on the completion of certain formalities, obtain a ballot and record his vote at any other polling division within the same electoral district. Section 118 is generally similar in its wording, but provides that the elector who is absent from his electoral district may obtain a ballot and vote at any other electoral district within the province. Table 1: 6 indicates the use made of these special voting regulations.

## Table 1: 6

### VOTES CAST IN ORDINARY POLLS, ADVANCE POLLS, AND BY ABSENTEE BALLOTS IN THE BRITISH COLUMBIA GENERAL ELECTIONS OF SEPTEMBER, 1966*

| Kind of vote | Total Vote cast | Rejected Ballots | Rejected Ballots as % of total vote | Total Valid Votes | % of Valid Votes |
|---|---|---|---|---|---|
| Ordinary Poll | 723,746 | 4,338 | 0.6 | 719,408 | 95.68 |
| Section 114 — Advance Poll | 11,621 | 65 | 0.6 | 11,556 | 1.54 |
| Section 115 — Absentee Advance Ballot | 904 | 47 | 0.5 | 857 | 0.11 |
| Section 117 — Absentee Ballot within Electoral Division | 5,950 | 306 | 5.4 | 5,644 | 0.75 |
| Section 118 — Absentee Ballot in another Electoral Division | 12,997 | 1,912 | 17.2 | 11,085 | 1.47 |
| Miscellaneous Sections 115, 117, 118, and 80 votes | 93 | — | — | 93 | 0.02 |
| Section 80 — Voters† | 3,621 | 388 | 1.2 | 3,233 | 0.43 |
| Total | 758,932 | 7,056 | 0.9 | 751,876 | 100.00 |

* All figures are from British Columbia, **Statement of Votes, General Election, Sept. 12, 1966**, Victoria, Queen's Printer, 1967.

† A Section 80 voter is a person whose name does not appear on the list of voters and whose original application for registration is not on file in the polling division. Such a person is permitted to vote and his ballot is placed in a separate envelope until the validity of his application to vote is verified.

Every elector who wishes to vote under the provisions of section 80, 115, 117, or 118 of the B.C. *Provincial Election Act* must complete and sign an affidavit which is attached to a special envelope containing the ballot. At the time of counting the votes the returning officer will examine the affidavit and if all appears in order he will open the envelope and place the ballot, still unfolded, in a special ballot box for all such votes.

> If the Returning Officer finds that the affidavit is not signed by the deponent and the Deputy Returning Officer before whom it was sworn, and that the name of the deponent does not appear on the list of voters for the electoral district named in the affidavit, or that some person has in fact voted as such voter at the poll held in the electoral district, or if the signatures (on the affidavit and the voter's original application for registration) do not appear to the Returning Officer to be identical, he shall not open the ballot-envelope, but shall write in ink on the face thereof the word 'unopened' together with the reason therefor.[94]

This is a fairly normal kind of precaution against fraud and one would expect that it would be necessary to leave unopened only a few ballots. However, it would appear from the figures in the 1966 election that either there was an extremely heavy incidence of attempted election fraud in British Columbia, or that the returning officers were extraordinarily meticulous in comparing signatures, or that large numbers of absentee electors cast ballots in good faith on the mistaken assumption that their names were entered on a register of electors in the districts they had named.

In the 1966 general elections, 45,937 people cast ballots under the terms of section 80, 115, 117, or 118. Of these, 17,969 (39.1%) were "unopened" and so were not counted, a further 7,056 (15.4%) were "rejected" as improperly completed, and only 20,912 (45.5%) were accepted as valid votes.[95] Since there was no evidence to support either the proposition of an exceptionally high incidence of election fraud in British Columbia or that of unduly meticulous returning officers one can only conclude that the registration system, in this case at least, was quite inadequate for its purpose and that a substantial number of British Columbian electors were deprived of their vote by reason of this inadequacy.

Since one might wonder if the unopened ballots in this election had affected the outcome, it is worth noting that despite the substantial numbers of unopened ballots (as many as 828 in one single-member district) there were, in the 1966 elections, only five individual members who might have been defeated had all, or an overwhelming majority of, the unopened ballots gone to their leading opponents. Three of these five were members of the New Democractic Party opposition and two were members of the Social Credit government party.

The details of these ballots are given in Table 1: 7, page 36.

Despite the obvious difficulties, the regulations in British Columbia are

**Table 1: 7**

**VOTERS, NON-VOTERS, AND WOULD-BE VOTERS IN THE 1966 ELECTIONS IN BRITISH COLUMBIA**

| | Total | % of Total Registered Voters | % of Total Voting-Age Population |
|---|---|---|---|
| Total voting-age population (age 19 or over) at 1966 census | 1,172,849 | — | 100.0 |
| Disfranchised as: non-citizens, residents in B.C. for less than six months, or otherwise disqualified under section 4, **or not registered** | 298,922 | — | 25.5 |
| Registered voters | 873,927 | 100.0 | 74.5 |
| Number of voters attempting to cast ballots | 614,685* | 70.3 | 52.4 |
| Number of ballots unopened | 17,969 | 2.1 | 1.5 |
| Number of ballots opened and rejected | 7,056 | 0.8 | 0.6 |
| Number of valid ballots counted | 589,660 | 67.5 | 50.3 |

* The discrepancy between the figures for the number of voters attempting to cast ballots, as shown above, and the number of votes cast, as shown in Table 1: 6, arises from the fact that in B.C.'s two-member constituencies each voter may, if he chooses, cast two votes.

most generous provisions and go a long way towards meeting the criterion postulated earlier — that one of the marks of a good election system is the facility with which any eligible voter can record his vote. It is unfortunate that the absentee-voting laws of British Columbia, which are far superior to those found in any other province, are offset by an inefficient voter-registration system which excludes from the vote more people than are included by the advance poll and absentee-voter rules. Combined with an adequate registration procedure the British Columbia absentee-voting system would provide an opportunity for a turn-out higher than any in Canada.

Except for British Columbia, the only province which appears to make any provision for absentee voters, other than for members of the Armed Forces, is Alberta where there are special regulations allowing students at a "designated educational institution" to cast a ballot for their normal home constituencies.

The provisions in the *Canada Elections Act* and most of the provincial acts for absentee ballots by members of the Armed Forces will be discussed later. Here, one need note only that there was also a brief experiment with absentee-voting in the 1935 federal elections, but as the privilege was extended only to a fisherman, lumberman, miner, or sailor, actually engaged in one of these occupations at a distance of not less than twenty-five miles from his normal polling division, it was not a great success. Only 5,334 absentee ballots were cast throughout the whole of Canada and of these 1,533 were rejected as improperly completed. The cost per vote of the 3,801 valid votes was so high that the experiment was not repeated.[96] The possibility that the cost per vote might be considerably reduced by broadening the categories that could take advantage of the absentee ballot was not apparently seriously considered.

Proxy-voting, too, is a fairly rare phenomenon in Canadian elections. At the federal level there are, at present, no opportunities for voting by proxy. There is, however, a modern precedent. Under the provisions of *The Canadian Prisoners of War Voting Regulations, 1944*[97] the next of kin of a prisoner-of-war was entitled to cast a proxy vote on behalf of such war prisoner. When preparations for the first use of proxy votes were begun in March of 1945 there were some 8,000 Canadian prisoners-of-war in enemy hands. However, by election day 1945 (June 11) the only prisoners on whose behalf proxy votes could be exercised were 1,306 still held by the Japanese. According to the Chief Electoral Officer, "In every case the operation prescribed by the Regulations worked out in a most satisfactory manner."[98] At the time of the general elections of 1953 there were eighteen Canadians who were prisoners-of-war (in Korea) and, the proxy-voting provisions having been applied again, their next-of-kin voted on their behalf.[99]

At the provincial level there are, as far as one can ascertain, only two provinces which make provisions for votes by proxy. Ontario law makes special rules for mariners, allowing any such person to "appoint in writing a proxy who shall be the wife, husband, parent, brother, sister or child of the mariner, of the full age of twenty-one years and an elector entitled to vote in the electoral district in which the mariner is qualified to vote."[100] Presumably a mariner who has no close relations, or none within his own election district, cannot exercise a proxy vote. Unfortunately there appear to be no records available of the number of voters who have exercised proxy votes at recent elections, but it is doubtful if there were very many.

Nova Scotia is the only province having any extensive proxy-voting. The opportunity to vote by proxy is extended to several groups of electors: fishermen or mariners (provided their ship is of British registry — a fine patriotic touch), patients in hospitals or in licensed nursing homes, full-time members of the armed services, and unmarried full-time students at "an educational institution."[101] The main effect of such legislation is that the votes of the specified groups will be counted in their home constituencies and not in the places where they happen to be on election day.

With the growing size of universities, proxy-voting by students could be a very important consideration, especially in those provinces where the voting age has been lowered to eighteen or nineteen.

The principal administrative barriers to voting are those we have already discussed: the efficiency of the voter-registration procedures and the voting opportunities for those who are away from their own districts on election day. There are others which are, or have been, important from time to time, both in Canada and elsewhere, and which should not be ignored. The right to vote can be rendered meaningless if the hours during which the polls are open are such that the great mass of working men are unable to attend. Table 1: 8 details the present hours of voting throughout Canada.

### Table 1: 8
### HOURS OF VOTING AT FEDERAL AND PROVINCIAL GENERAL ELECTIONS

| | Polls are open |
|---|---|
| Federal elections | 8 a.m. to 7 p.m. standard time. section 31 (5) |
| British Columbia | 8 a.m. to 8 p.m. section 89 |
| Alberta | 9 a.m. to 8 p.m. section 65 (1) |
| Saskatchewan | 9 a.m. to 7 p.m. section 81 |
| Manitoba | 8 a.m. to 8 p.m. section 70 |
| Ontario | 8 a.m. to 7 p.m. section 76 (1) — but under special conditions polls in some municipalities may be opened as early as 6 a.m. section 76 (2) |
| Quebec | 9 a.m. to 7 p.m. if the election is on a weekday; 10 a.m. to 8 p.m. if the election is on a Sunday. section 216 |
| New Brunswick | 8 a.m. to 6 p.m. — but if for any reason opening time is delayed, the poll will remain open the full 10 hours. section 59 (5) |
| Nova Scotia | 8 a.m. to 6 p.m. section 72 |
| Prince Edward Island | 9 a.m. to 7 p.m. section 65 |
| Newfoundland | 8 a.m. to 8 p.m. section 51 |

Generally these are fairly reasonable hours although in any metropolitan area where people may need an hour or more to travel home from work, 6 p.m., and probably even 7 p.m., is too early to close the polls. The importance of a too-early closing can be better appreciated if it is noted that while every election act contains a clause requiring employers to give employees time off of up to three or four hours without loss of pay to facilitate voting[102] nowhere does it seem that there is any insistence on the enforcement of these sections. As a consequence, experience shows that many workers who have not had time off have in some cases not voted. Yet it does not appear that there have been any prosecutions of employers in any province on this issue.

Some slight amelioration of the effects of a too-early closing is found in the provision, common to the Canadian *Act*, and the *Acts* in British Columbia, Saskatchewan, New Brunswick, Nova Scotia, Prince Edward Island, and Newfoundland, that those who have arrived at the polling station before closing time may be permitted to vote, although no late arrivals may join a queue. The remaining provinces do not specifically forbid this practice, but simply make no mention of it.

While it is possible that there may be some electors who have not voted because they have been unable to find the polling place, there is nothing to suggest that in Canada, or in any of the provinces, polling places have been deliberately hidden or made difficult to get at. Indeed, the general practice of setting up a separate polling subdivision for every three hundred or so voters, which is a much smaller unit than is commonly found in other countries, must increase the ease with which the polling booth can be found and reached.

One last class of electors referred to earlier ought to be mentioned here. These are the members of the Canadian Armed Forces. For the most part the provisions for servicemen are generous and every facility is given to ensure that the vote of the serviceman is recorded and counted in the total votes in the serviceman's home constituency. At the federal level the rules regarding service votes are contained in *The Canadian Forces Voting Rules*. As far as the right to vote is concerned, servicemen are in a favoured position and little needs to be said about them in this chapter. More will be said in a later chapter on the mechanics and administration of elections for it is here that the service vote raises more complicated questions.

This chapter began by asserting that even under universal suffrage not everyone is a voter. It should now be clear that not all people are eligible to be voters since there are statutory limits on the franchise. It should also be clear that even among the eligible there are many who, as a consequence of various administrative rules and practices, are unable to exercise their rights. There still remain those who could vote but who choose not to. A study of these people is beyond the scope of this present work although it is suggested that perhaps some of the administrative barriers described here may be factors in creating a climate of "non-voting."[103] It is possible that certain election procedures which do not prohibit voting are sufficiently complex and time-consuming to discourage the marginal voter, the one whose interest in politics is low and easily deflected. These are possibilities which can be explored only through a series of intensive studies into the behaviour of voters. The relationship between statutory and administrative non-voters, and between administrative and voluntary non-voters has been neglected for too long, but hopefully a careful analysis of the character of administrative barriers to voting will stimulate further research along these lines.

## FOOTNOTES

[1] See, for example, J. A. Laponce, "Non-Voting and Non-Voters: A Typology," *Canadian Journal of Economics and Political Science*, 33 (1), Toronto, 1967, 75-87.

[2] For a much fuller account see N. Ward, *The Canadian House of Commons: Representation*, Toronto, University of Toronto Press, 2nd edition, 1963, 211-232.

[3] Sec. 41 of the B.N.A. Act, 1867, provides that: "Until the Parliament of Canada otherwise provides, all Laws in force in the several Provinces at the Union relative to the following Matters or any of them, namely — the Qualifications and Disqualifications of . . . the Voters at Elections of such Members . . . shall respectively apply to Elections of Members to serve in the House of Commons for the same several Provinces." Reproduced with the permission of the Queen's Printer for Canada.

[4] N. Ward, *op. cit.*, 213. An exception was made for Ontario, where the provincial franchise as adopted in 1869 was found acceptable.

[5] British Columbia, *Qualification and Registration of Voters Act*, 1876, sec. 2, granted the franchise to all adult male natural-born British subjects.

[6] S.O., 1885, chap. 2, secs. 4-7.

[7] S.C., 1885, chap. 40.

[8] N. Ward, *op. cit.*, 218.

[9] It required more than 7,000 words to define the "Qualifications of voters in cities and towns" in secs. 3-10.

[10] S.C., 1898, chap. 14.

[11] *Ibid.*, sec. 6. Reproduced with the permission of the Queen's Printer for Canada.

[12] S.C., 1917, chap. 34.

[13] *Ibid.*, chap. 39.

[14] S.C., 1920, chap. 46.

[15] British Columbia, *Qualification and Registration of Voters Act*, 1876, sec. 2 provided that: "every male of the full age of twenty-one years, not being disqualified by this Act or by any other law in force in this Province, being entitled within this Province to the privileges of a natural-born British subject, having resided in this Province for twelve months, and in the Electoral District in which he claims to vote for two months of that period . . . shall be entitled to vote . . ." For details of the complex property and income qualifications in the other provinces the most convenient source is C. O. Ermatinger, *Canadian Franchise and Election Laws*, Toronto, Carswell & Co., 1886. This useful book contains extracts from all federal and provincial statutes relating to election laws in force at the time of publication. For a history of the franchise prior to Confederation see John Garner, *The Franchise and Politics in British North America, 1755-1867*, Toronto, University of Toronto Press, 1969.

[16] For a full account of the events leading to the adoption of adult suffrage

in Nova Scotia in 1920 see J. Murray Beck, *The Government of Nova Scotia*, Toronto, University of Toronto Press, 1957, 257-8.

17 The property qualification was abolished in Quebec in 1936. S.Q., 1936, 2d session, chap. 8, sec. 122.

18 Prince Edward Island has for many years operated with a Legislative Assembly of thirty members consisting of fifteen Councillors elected on a property franchise and fifteen Assemblymen elected on a popular franchise. As late as 1962 *The Report* of the provincial Royal Commission on Electoral Reform recommended not only that the property qualification be retained for the Councillors but also that it be raised from $325 to $1,000. This recommendation was not accepted and in 1963 the property qualification was abolished. The present *Electoral Act* provides a uniform franchise for both Councillors and Assemblymen. S.P.E.I., 1963, chap. 11, sec. 21.

19 S.C., 1948, chap. 46, sec. 14 (3).

20 S.C., 1960, chap. 39, sec. 14 (1), (b) and (c).

21 R.S.C., 1952, chap. 33, sec. 23 (3). Reproduced with the permission of the Queen's Printer for Canada.

22 R.S.Q., 1964, chap. 7, sec. 47 (4).

23 S.P.E.I., 1954, chap. 14, sec. 2 (1).

24 Catherine L. Cleverdon, *The Woman Suffrage Movement in Canada*, Toronto, University of Toronto Press, 1950.

25 Canada, *Debates*, 1918, I, 643, quoted in Cleverdon, 133. Reproduced with the permission of the Queen's Printer for Canada.

26 R.S.Q., 1964, chap. 7 provides, in sec. 48 (c), that, "Indians domiciled on land reserved for Indians or held in trust for them, whether or not such land is situated in a municipality," may not vote in provincial elections.

27 British Columbia, *An Act Relating to an Act to Make Better Provision for the Qualification and Registration of Voters*. sec. I.

28 S.B.C., 1939, chap. 16, sec. 4.

29 S.C., 1885, chap. 40.

30 S.C., 1960, chap. 7.

31 S.C., 1934, chap. 51, sec. 4 (1) (c) (vi).

32 S.C., 1962, chap. 17, *An Act to Amend the Registration Act*. sec. 3 defines the new boundaries of the Northwest Territories.

33 S.C., 1917, chap. 39, secs. 154 (g) and (h).

34 S.M., 1901, chap. 11, sec. 17 (e).

35 R.S.B.C., 1960, chap. 306, sec. 4 (1).

36 R.S.O., 1960, chap. 118, sec. 90. The election acts of the four western provinces all include virtually identical provisions: R.S.M., 1954, chap. 68, sec. 87; R.S.S., 1965, chap. 4, sec. 97; S.A., 1956, chap. 15, sec. 85; R.S.B.C., 1960, chap. 306, sec. 111.

37 S.N.B., 1967, chap. 9, sec. 85; S.N.S., 1962, chap. 4, sec. 108.

38 S.C., 1960, chap. 39, sec. 45 (11).

39 R.S.Q., 1964, chap. 7, secs. 251 and 252.

40 R.S.C., 1952, chap. 23, sec. 14 (2) (h). Reproduced with the permission of the Queen's Printer for Canada.

41 S.C., 1955, chap. 44, sec. 4.

42 S.C., 1960, chap. 39, sec. 16 (3) and (4). Reproduced with the permission of the Queen's Printer for Canada.

43 It should be noted that the residence requirement is for twelve months in Canada, and is not confined to any one particular place in Canada.

[44] S.C., 1960, chap. 39, sec. 16 (7) and (8).

[45] S.P.E.I., 1963, chap. 11, sec. 24 (3).

[46] S.N.S., 1962, chap. 4, sec. 28 (3).

[47] S.N.B., 1967, chap. 9, sec. 45 (3).

[48] S.C., 1960, chap. 39, sec. 16 (9); S.N.B., 1967, chap. 9, sec. 45 (5).

[49] R.S.Q., 1964, chap. 7, sec. 2 (f).

[50] Canada, Chief Electoral Officer, *Report to the Speaker of the House of Commons*, May 20, 1940.

[51] S.C., 1938, chap. 46, sec. 16 (6) — a provision originally enacted in 1929.

[52] S.C., 1948, chap. 46, sec. 7 (3).

[53] R.S.S., 1965, chap. 4, sec. 32 (10); S.P.E.I., 1963, chap. 11, sec. 24 (5).

[54] *Ibid.*, (11).

[55] S.A., 1956, chap. 15; Fifth Schedule: Absentee Student Voting Rules.

[56] S.N.S., 1962, chap. 4, secs. 28 (5) and 93 (d).

[57] S.N., 1954, chap. 79, sec. 65 (4) (a).

[58] S.C., 1960, chap. 39, sec. 16 (11) and (13). Reproduced with the permission of the Queen's Printer for Canada.

[59] R.S.Q., 1964, chap. 7, sec. 2 (b).

[60] Canada, Chief Electoral Officer, *Report to the Speaker of the House of Commons*, Sept. 26, 1949, 7-14.

[61] S.C., 1960, chap. 39, sec. 16 (10). Most provincial election acts contain basically similar provisions.

[62] Ontario, Select Committee on Election Laws, *First Report*, February 1969, par. 15 (iv).

[63] Both Australia and New Zealand have compulsory registration, but only Australia has compulsory voting.

[64] The list for, say, the year 1969, is a list of those qualified to vote on the 10th October 1969 (including, as a special category, those who will be 21 on or before June 15th 1970). Amendments or corrections to this list must be made before December 16th, 1969, and it comes into force on February 15th 1970. It will remain the sole list of registered voters for all elections held between February 15th 1970 and February 14th, 1971.

[65] Canada, Chief Electoral Officer, *Report to the Speaker of the House of Commons*, Dec. 1, 1926, Appendix 2, par. 11.

[66] *Ibid.*, Feb. 3, 1936, I.

[67] Canada, Representation Commissioner, *Report on Methods of Registration of Electors and Absentee Voting*, 1968, 63. Reproduced with the permission of the Queen's Printer for Canada.

[68] Canada, House of Commons, Special Committee on Elections and Franchise Act, 1937, *Second and Final Report to the House*, April 6, 1937.

[69] *Ibid.*

[70] S.C., 1960, chap. 39, sec. 41 (1) provides that, "Where there is contained in the official list of electors a name, address, and occupation which correspond so closely with the name, address, and occupation of a person by whom a ballot is demanded as to suggest that the entry in such official list of electors was intended to refer to him, such person is . . . entitled to receive a ballot and vote." Reproduced with the permission of the Queen's Printer for Canada.

[71] See N. Ward, *op. cit.*, chap x, and Canada, Representation Commissioner, *Report on Methods of Registration of Electors and Absentee Voting*, 1968, 3-7.

[72] Canada, Representation Commissioner, *Ibid.*, 5.

[73] *Ibid.*, 7.

[74] Canada, Special Committee on Elections and Franchise Acts, *Minutes of Proceedings and Evidence*, 1937, 194. Reproduced with the permission of the Queen's Printer for Canada.

[75] S.C., 1938, chap. 46.

[76] Form of oath on Form 6, sec. 17, Schedule A, Rule 1.

[77] Actually there are some exceptions and qualifications to this general distribution scheme, but the details do not concern us here. They are contained in sec. 17 (7), (8) and (9).

[78] S.C., 1960, chap. 39, sec. 17, Schedule A, Rule 31. Reproduced with the permission of the Queen's Printer for Canada.

[79] S.N., 1954, chap. 79, sec. 30 (1).

[80] R.S.M., 1954, chap. 68, sec. 34 (1). This applies to by-elections as well as general elections.

[81] S.A., 1956, chap. 15, sec. 20, Third Schedule, Division Two, Rule 12. See also Rules 10-18 for additional details.

[82] Most of the detailed procedures are contained in R.S.B.C., 1960, chap. 306, secs. 6-32.

[83] *Ibid.*, secs. 79-80.

[84] Canada, Representation Commissioner, *Report on Methods of Registration of Electors and Absentee Voting*, 1968, 11. Reproduced with the permission of the Queen's Printer for Canada.

[85] *The Vancouver Sun*, Aug. 24, 1963, 1.

[86] R.S.C., 1952, chap. 23, sec. 95.

[87] Canada, Chief Electoral Officer, *Report to the Speaker of the House of Commons*, October 1962, 3.

[88] R.S.M., 1954, chap. 68, sec. 67 (1); S.A., 1956, chap. 15, sec. 63 (1).

[89] S.M., 1969, chap. 38, which adds new secs. 91 (4) to 91 (11) to the original *Act*. These sections detail the procedure for voting by mail.

[90] R.S.Q., 1964, chap. 7, sec. 283.

[91] S.N., 1954, chap. 79, sec. 157 (1).

[92] R.S.B.C., 1960, chap. 306, sec. 114 (1).

[93] *Ibid.*, sec. 115 (1).

[94] *Ibid.*, sec. 122 (1) (d).

[95] Figures from B.C. *Statement of Votes, General Election*, Sept. 12, 1966.

[96] Canada, Chief Electoral Officer, *Report to the Speaker of the House of Commons*, Feb. 3, 1936, 2: "The cost of the application of the absentee voting provisions is not yet available, but it is estimated that it will be close to a quarter of a million dollars. In my opinion, therefore, the result of the last general election shows that absentee voting is a costly, ineffective and complicated procedure which should not be resorted to at any future Dominion election." Reproduced with the permission of the Queen's Printer for Canada.

[97] S.C., 1944, chap. 26, Schedule B.

[98] Canada, Chief Electoral Officer, *Report to the Speaker of the House of Commons*, Sept. 15th, 1945, 7.

[99] *Ibid.*, Nov. 13, 1953, par. 4.

[100] R.S.O., 1960, chap. 118, sec. 78 (2).

[101] S.N.S., 1962, chap. 4, sec. 93. The actual mechanics of proxy-voting are described in secs. 94-98.

102 In Prince Edward Island the time mentioned is only one hour, and in a number of provinces there are specific exceptions for those engaged in the running of trains and/or aircraft.

103 For further information on voters and non-voters in Canadian elections see, for example, J. A. Laponce, "Non-Voting and Non-Voters: A Typology," *Canadian Journal of Economics and Political Science*, 33 (1), 1967, 75-87, and H. A. Scarrow, "Patterns of Voter Turnout in Canada," *Midwest Journal of Political Science*, 5 (4), 1961, 351-364. See also John Wilson and David Hoffman, "The Nature of Conservative Dominance: An Essay on the Position of the Liberal Party in Ontario Politics," a paper presented to the annual meeting of the Canadian Political Science Association, Toronto, 1969.

# TWO
## FOR WHOM?

A completely open election would, presumably, be one in which anybody could vote for anybody. But, outside some very small groups and associations, such free-wheeling procedure is not a serious possibility. The choice of electors must, for all practical purposes, be confined to some more or less formally recognized "slate" of candidates.[1] This chapter deals with the procedures, legal and customary, by which some individuals come to be formal candidates.

It is not enough to ask who may legally be a candidate, for the answer to this question is usually a population not very much smaller than that of the eligible electors. One must also ask what are the economic, social, and political restraints that will reduce this population to the four, five, six or so whose names actually appear on the ballot in each constituency. The basic questions are: "Who are, in fact, the potential candidates?"; and "who, among these, can reasonably expect to be nominated?"

These are vitally important questions to the health of a democracy. If the mass of electors are reduced to choosing from among a set of candidates pre-selected by a small unrepresentative elite, then the democracy is a fake and its electoral institutions a mere facade. Again, if the social and economic pressures of candidacy and membership are such as to discourage or bar all but the chosen few then the reality of democracy is restrained and inhibited.

On the other hand, if there were no winnowing process, if there were to be hundreds or thousands of candidates for every elective position, then representative government would likely collapse in anarchy.

The question of candidacy can usefully be considered under three headings: the legal, the political, and the socio-economic. The legal heading

45

subsumes both the qualifications a person must possess to be eligible as a candidate — age, residence, citizenship, property, absence of a criminal record, or whatever else may be demanded — and the procedures which must be followed to make candidacy official — nomination formalities, and so on. Under the political heading, one can consider both the processes by which the parties select their candidates and the extent to which the customary political practices make formal endorsement by a recognized party a virtual necessity. The third heading, the socio-economic, which becomes inseparably intertwined with the political, concerns those factors which increase or decrease the chances that one will be either selected as a candidate or, if nominated, elected. They will include occupational status, ethnic origin, sex, independent financial resources, age, political apprenticeship, religion, and other related factors.

## LEGAL QUALIFICATIONS OF CANDIDATES

A very simplified version of the provisions common to the federal and provincial election acts might read: "Anyone who is qualified as an elector is also qualified as a candidate, unless otherwise provided in this or any other act." It is the "unless otherwise provided" phrase that is the source of all the complications and difficulties.[2]

The commonest source of disqualification is conviction for "corrupt or illegal practices"[3] as defined or specified in the election act. It is important that there be such a disqualification but, today, it has little immediate application. There have been no recent cases of candidates disqualified because of shady dealings in a previous election. The point now is not a controversial one and it does not really require elaboration.

A second and much more important category is that of government contractors. Here the principle is quite clear. No person who is "holding or enjoying, undertaking or executing" any contract or agreement with the Government of Canada "or with or for any of the officers of the Government of Canada, for which any public money of Canada is to be paid" may be a candidate at an election "during the time he is so holding, enjoying, undertaking or executing."[4] The rationale is a straightforward attempt to minimize the conflicts of interests between the Members of Parliament as guardians of the public interest, and contractors doing business with the government for a profit. The problem is that the restriction is too inclusive and could legally disqualify a great many otherwise acceptable candidates. Common sense demands that there be exceptions and it is here that one can find an enormous variety among the eleven election systems being examined. A complete province-by-province catalogue would be tedious, repetitious, and ultimately pointless, but a few random illustrations might add life and meaning to what might seem a rather sterile remark.

Thus, while individual contractors are disqualified, it is usual to allow directors or shareholders of incorporated companies doing business with the government to be candidates or members. This is a sensible provision to which there is generally added a further exception to the exception: if the incorporated company is engaged in the "building of any public work" then the shareholder or director may not be a candidate. The Saskatchewan *Legislative Assembly Act* has a lengthy list of exceptions: of persons who, although they are in receipt of government money for services rendered, are not disqualified from seeking office as members of the legislature. They include members of the Law Society of Saskatchewan who receive legal-aid fees from the government, those who contract to teach with the Northern Educational Committee, those who contract for the "construction or installation of water or sewage works upon a farm-stead" under the *Family Farm Improvement Act*, and those who receive compensation for livestock killed by hunters.[5] In Ontario, among the many receivers of public money who are not disqualified as candidates are the owners of newspapers which contain government advertising, trustees for the estate of a contractor, and those who are in receipt of payment for the burial of indigents.[6] New Brunswick allows employees of a "patriotic committee or organization whose funds may be contributed wholly or in part by the Province," doctors being paid out of public funds for their work with the cancer and rehabilitation programme of the government, coroners, justices of the peace, and notaries public, to be parliamentary candidates.[7] Alberta law makes it clear that those who receive fees as witnesses for the Crown in any proceedings, or perform a postmortem examination at the request of a coroner, or those who receive "goods, services, pensions or allowances made available, pursuant to an Act of the Province, to residents of the Province by reason of age, incapacity or unemployment," may all freely stand as candidates and, if elected, sit as Members of the Legislative Assembly.[8]

It would be a fascinating study to examine the peculiar set of circumstances which led to the specification of each of these exceptions to the general rule that receipt of public money renders one ineligible as a candidate. All, however, are motivated by the same considerations: while in general it is not desirable that Members of Parliament should be in receipt of public money, the expansion of government activity has meant that an ever-increasing number of people do receive some portion of their income from the public treasury and it is a matter of practical common sense that not all of these people be barred from Parliament.

A third related, and equally complex, disqualification concerns what are termed "offices of profit under the Crown." This is a question which, in turn, is deeply involved with that of the independence of Parliament, and especially independence from the executive. A 1941 Select Committee of the British House of Commons in a detailed study of the subject,[9] found that there were three major issues involved: (1) Certain salaried offices of the Crown are incompatible with membership of the House of Commons and thus the holders of such offices should be barred from the House. This principle disqualifies civil servants and members of the armed forces in peacetime.[10] (2) There is a need to limit the control of the executive government over the House by restricting the proportion of office-holders who may be members of the House. This is the rationale of legislation defining or limiting the number of cabinet posts. It is an important constitutional point, but is outside the scope of a study of the election process and it is enough simply to mention it here. (3) Parliamentary government, by its nature, demands that a certain number of Ministers must be members of the House of Commons, hence some, if not all, Ministers of the Crown must be exempted from the disqualification of holders of offices of profit under the Crown.

Canadian law from the beginning followed British precedents and the position of office-holders was set out quite clearly in the *Independence of Parliament Act*, of 1868:

> 1) Except as hereinafter specially provided —
> 1. No person accepting or holding any office, commission or employment in the service of the Government of Canada, at the nomination of the Crown, to which an annual salary, or any fee, allowance or emolument in lieu of an annual salary from the Crown is attached, shall be eligible as a Member of the House of Commons, nor shall he sit or vote in the same during the time he holds such office, occupation or employment.[11]

Some difficulties arose from the wording of this statute and especially from the reference to an annual salary, which seemed to exclude payment on a weekly or monthly basis, but the details of these great historical controversies do not concern us here.[12] The strange and awkward position of ministers does, however, merit some discussion. Statutes of the Province of Canada, re-enacted virtually word for word after Confederation,[13] provided that a Cabinet Minister who held a portfolio as a head of a department could sit as a Member of Parliament only if he was elected while holding the portfolio. This meant that a Cabinet Minister re-elected at a general election could continue to sit in the House. If, however, a Member was appointed to the Cabinet after his election he would have to resign his seat and seek re-election as a Minister. In effect the electors were asked to confirm the position of their Member as a Minister of the Crown. This was a cumbersome, inconvenient, and sometimes expensive procedure and successive prime ministers exercised considerable ingenuity in evading its consequences.[14] It was finally accepted that the disadvantages of the regulation outweighed whatever merits it still retained and in 1931 an amendment to the *Senate and House of Commons Act*[15] freed Ministers appointed after election from the necessity of vacating their seats and seeking re-election.

A further exemption from the disqualification of office-holders is for "a member of Her Majesty's Forces while he is on active service as a consequence of war."[16] The normal intention of the office-holder's disqualification is that permanent members of the armed forces should not be involved in politics and so should not be parliamentary candidates. At the same time, however, it is recognized that in wartime there will be many, including some who are already Members of Parliament, for whom military service is hopefully a brief interruption of normal life. The law does not wish to exclude such people from politics.

The position of civil servants reveals an interesting contrast in attitude. The normal practice in Canada is not only that a civil servant may not be a Member of Parliament, which is a universal and very sensible provision, but also that a civil servant may not even be a candidate without resigning his position. There are also strong sentiments, in part enforced by legal requirements, that civil servants, even at relatively junior ranks, should not participate in overt political activity of any kind, except voting. Most government employees do not feel they are free to participate actively in election campaigns except in the most discreet "backroom" capacities.

There are some exceptions to this general principle. In Saskatchewan, under provisions first enacted in 1947, a member of the provincial public service who wishes to be a candidate for public office (presumably this would apply to federal as well as provincial politics) is entitled to leave of absence for the thirty days prior to the date of the election.[17] If the candidate is elected then "he shall be deemed to have resigned his office or place of profit under the Government or his employment in the public service of the province on the day immediately prior to the day on which he was elected."[18] The position of the civil servant is even further protected by the provisions that if he is apparently elected, and resigns, and his election is subsequently set aside or invalidated for any reason, then his resignation is automatically withdrawn and he is deemed to have been on leave until such time as the election is finally determined. In an age when so many competent people are in government employment, these are eminently reasonable propositions.

Amendments to the Ontario *Public Service Act* in 1963 considerably extended the rights of provincial civil servants. Under the new legislation, employees who wish to contest federal or provincial elections may be granted leave without pay. If elected they must resign from the civil service, but a successful candidate who remains a Member of Parliament for less than five years may be reinstated in the civil service.[18a]

The British approach begins by classifying civil servants under three headings: the politically free group, embracing the "industrial staff, and minor and manipulative grades"; the intermediate group which would include all civil servants up to the grade of executive officer; and the politically restricted group, which includes all the senior civil service, and then stipulates that those in the politically free group must resign on becoming parliamentary candidates, but are entitled to reinstatement if not elected, while those in the two other groups, who must also resign, have no automatic right to reinstatement. Those in the politically restricted group are expected to refrain from all overt partisan political activity other than voting.[19]

The British practice of defining a politically restricted group and limiting the political activity of such a group is an improvement on a policy which treats all civil servants alike, irrespective of responsibility or rank although the restraints on the politically free and the intermediate group seem unnecessarily restrictive. The Saskatchewan policy, if it were to exclude the senior ranks, would seem to be a very desirable innovation. The problem, which a compromise between the British and the Saskatchewan approaches might very well solve, is how to protect the political impartiality of the civil service as a whole without denying to any larger number of civil servants than is strictly necessary the normal rights of democratic citizenship, which rights include those of running for public office.

It might be argued that if the tradition is that the bulk of the civil servants are patronage appointments of the government of the day, then political activity by civil servants, especially if directed against the government, is both unwise and undesirable. But as the civil service becomes more a permanent career this argument loses some of its strength. If civil servants, at least in junior and intermediate ranks, may freely run for public office without endangering their careers, there is much to be gained in removing from the civil service the stigma that they are second-class citizens.

There is, of course, no disputing the proposition that a civil servant, once elected to the legislature, must resign from the service.

The whole question of candidates and members receiving payment from government funds, whether as contractors or as a salary or in any other form, raises issues that become more and more significant as the functions of government continue to expand. If the prohibition on elected members receiving government money were enforced rigidly then members would be unable to take advantage of government programmes for the benefit of all citizens. Members would find that, simply because they were members of a legislature, they would be denied their rights as ordinary citizens. One recent example illustrates the point. Members of the Alberta legislature are not permitted to negotiate loans through the Treasury Branch of the Government. A Member of the Alberta Legislative Assembly, who was also a member of a Farmers' Co-operative, was therefore unable to participate in a programme of the Co-operative because it was negotiating a loan which would be funded through the Treasury Branch.[20] Amendments to the *Legislative Assembly Act* of Alberta have been increasingly concerned with measures to preserve the Member's rights as an ordinary citizen, without disqualifying him, and without sacrificing the principle that a Member should not be paid out of government funds if such payment is in any way likely to compromise his independence.

A fourth type of disqualification, which prohibits dual membership in a federal and a provincial legislature, was at one time a live political issue[21] but it is now dead. The federal act prohibits any member of a provincial legislature from standing as a candidate in a federal election[22] and it is standard practice in provincial acts to bar federal Members of Parliament from contesting provincial seats. It is not necessary for a province to specifically disqualify a member of another provincial legislature, as a minimum qualification for candidacy in every province is eligibility as an elector in that province, and every province makes formal residence in the province a necessary qualification for an elector.

There are, or have been, other disqualifications. In 1867 a property qualification was normal and existed in some form in all provinces. It was, however, never very strictly enforced. The main difficulty arose from the fact that the qualification applied only to candidates and not to elected members so that it was possible for a man to be elected on borrowed property which, after the election, would revert to the original owners. It was abolished as a federal qualification in 1874.[23]

Members of the House of Commons have never been obliged to meet a residence qualification, either in their own constituency or even in the province. Indeed, before 1948, candidates and members did not have to be residents of Canada. The change was brought about not by requiring that a candidate be a resident but that a candidate possess, as a minimum, the qualification of a voter, which involves residence in an electoral division. In the provinces, of course, the residence qualifications demanded of electors apply also to candidates so that all candidates for provincial legislatures must be legal residents in their own provinces. Apart from the legal obligation, residence is in fact enforced by a very strong social and political custom. There are, in every parliament, many exceptions, especially in the metropolitan areas, but residence in the constituency, at least after election, is still the norm.

The British Columbia *Election Act* requires not only that the would-be candidate possess the qualifications of an elector in the province, but demands also that he be *registered* as an elector.[24] In view of the peculiar British Columbian process for registering electors it is possible that a potential candidate could mistakenly assume, until too late to do anything about it, that he was on the register of electors and thus disqualify himself. There appears to be no evidence of this happening as yet.

There are now three provinces where the age qualifications for candidates are more restrictive than for voters. The voting age in Prince Edward Island is 18, and in Newfoundland and Alberta it is 19, but in all three provinces candidates for election must be at least 21.[25] In the other four provinces where the voting age is less than 21 (Quebec, Saskatchewan and Manitoba (since October 1969) 18; and British Columbia, 19) candidates are not required to be more than the minimum voting age. There do not seem to be any examples of candidates under the age of 21 contesting elections in any of these provinces.

Women may now be candidates on terms legally equal to those for men, although this legal right has by no means conferred actual political equality. Women in some provinces waited many years from the date of the removal of legal disabilities to the date on which the first woman member was actually elected. Women in Prince Edward Island waited until May 1970. Table 2: 1 outlines, first of all, the dates on which women first became legally entitled to be candidates and, secondly, the date on which a woman was first actually elected.

## Table 2: 1
### THE LAW AND THE FACT OF WOMEN MEMBERS OF CANADIAN LEGISLATURES

| Administration | Women Obtain the Legal Right to be Candidates | First Woman Elected |
| --- | --- | --- |
| Canada | July 7, 1919 | Dec. 6, 1921 |
| British Columbia | April 5, 1917 | Jan. 24, 1918 |
| Alberta | April 19, 1916 | June 7, 1917 |
| Saskatchewan | Mar. 14, 1916 | June 29, 1919 |
| Manitoba | Jan. 28, 1916 | June 29, 1920 |
| Ontario | Apr. 24, 1919 | Aug. 4, 1943 |
| Quebec | Apr. 24, 1940 | Dec. 14, 1961 |
| New Brunswick | Mar. 9, 1934 | Oct. 10, 1967 |
| Nova Scotia | Apr. 26, 1918 | June 7, 1960 |
| Prince Edward Island | May 3, 1922 | May 11, 1970 |
| Newfoundland | May 13, 1925 | May 17, 1930* |

* A by-election result

## NOMINATION FORMALITIES

The would-be candidate must not only possess the requisite legal qualifications, but he must also complete certain formalities before the law will recognize his candidacy. There is no provision in any Canadian administration for a write-in vote so the electors must choose from among the officially nominated candidates.

In all systems the candidate must be nominated by fellow electors in the constituency he wishes to contest. Table 2: 2 summarises the details. In

## Table 2: 2
### NOMINATION REQUIREMENTS

| Administration | Nomination Papers to be signed by | Deposit Required |
|---|---|---|
| Canada | 25 or more electors qualified to vote in the district. sec. 21 (5) | $200.00 sec. 21 (10) |
| British Columbia | In an electoral district with fewer than 10,000 registered voters, nomination is by not fewer than 25 registered voters. In a district with 10,000 or more registered voters, not fewer than 50 registered voters must sign the nomination. sec. 56 | No deposit |
| Alberta | 4 or more electors. sec. 33 | $100.00 sec. 34 (1) (f) |
| Saskatchewan | Any 4 or more electors. sec. 49 (1) | $100.00 sec. 50 (1) |
| Manitoba | 25 or more voters of the electoral division. sec. 37 (1) | $200.00 sec. 37 (2) |
| Ontario | At least 100 duly qualified electors of the district. sec. 49 (2) | No deposit |
| Quebec | Any 25 electors of the district. sec. 143 | $200.00 sec. 147 (1) |
| New Brunswick | Any 10 or more electors qualified in the district. sec. 51 (1) | $100.00 sec. 51 (5) |
| Nova Scotia | 5 or more qualified electors in the district. sec. 60 | $100.00 sec. 60 |
| Prince Edward Island | 2 or more persons qualified to have their names on the list of electors in the district. sec. 54 | $100.00 sec. 54 |
| Newfoundland | Any 2 or more electors qualified in the district. sec. 42 (1) | $100.00 sec. 42 (4) |

any organization nomination is an essential preliminary to election and one can, therefore, reasonably expect that in a parliamentary election a candidate should be nominated by a fellow elector. One might ask, however, what is gained by requiring that there be five, or ten, or even twenty-five nominators. The only purpose in requiring any additional number of names on a nomination paper should be to ensure that the candidate does have some measure of support, that some number of electors want him as their representative. The requirement that the candidate be nominated by a substantial number of fully qualified electors in his own district would impose no burden at all on the serious candidate who has some organized support behind him, but at the same time it could be more effective than a token deposit in discouraging crank candidates. Nevertheless, a couple of dozen names would not achieve this latter aim, especially as there is no obligation on the nominator to support or vote for the candidate. The point is that if two names are not enough, then there is nothing to be gained by setting the limit at anything less than a hundred or so.

Table 2: 2 also summarises the position on deposits. Federally, and in all provinces except British Columbia and Ontario, the candidate must submit with his nomination papers a deposit of $100 or $200. This is returned to him if he is elected, or if he gets at least half as many votes as the winning candidate. An amendment to the Nova Scotia *Election Act* in 1969 provides that the deposit will be returned to any candidate who receives at least 15 percent of the total number of valid votes polled.[26] The ostensible purpose of requiring a deposit is to discourage frivolous candidates, yet there is no evidence that it achieves this purpose. There is nothing to indicate that the number of candidates, or even the number of candidates unassociated with any major party, is any greater in British Columbia and Ontario than in some other provinces.

Under today's cost of living the sum required as a deposit is not sufficient to discourage anyone who has ambitions in politics, or who merely wishes to use the electoral system for a little personal publicity. At the same time, the deposit is a source of annoyance and inconvenience to many serious candidates. In any system where it is usual for three or more parties to contest the majority of seats, it is to be expected that many candidates will not get 50 per cent of the votes of the winner. All the parties now put up candidates who are not expected to win in their local constituency, and in this sense they are "frivolous" candidates. But their main purpose is not to win, but to encourage the supporters of the party wherever they live, to add votes to the party's grand total, to demonstrate the strength of the party throughout the whole territory, and in this sense such candidacies are far from frivolous. They play a very important role in the total context of national or provincial party politics.

Under the rules as they are presently constituted it is not only the cranks or the silly candidates who are penalized, but also the spokesmen of serious, organized parties. In the 1968 federal election, for example, there were 8 candidates for the Liberal party, the party which formed the government, who lost their deposits. Yet it cannot seriously be argued that a candidate for the government party, a party which has elected representatives from all regions of Canada, is a frivolous candidate wherever he might stand. At the same election there were 88 Progressive Conservative candidates, and 185 from the New Democratic Party who surrendered $200 each to the Treasury. In all 433 candidates, or 44.8 percent of the total of 967, lost deposits in the 1968 elections. This is not an exceptional figure. It was 483 in 1965, 509 in 1963, 461 in 1962, and 369 in 1958.[27] In elections held in 1966 and 1967 in the eight provinces with deposit requirements, a total of just over 500 candidates forfeited their deposits.

There is a certain advantage in discouraging the merely silly candidates. There is no great advantage in penalizing candidates who represent substantial bodies of opinion. Two alternatives are available. One is to increase considerably the size of deposit, to perhaps $1,000, which would discourage the hopeless case and, at the same time, make it a good deal easier to recover. Any candidate who can gather, say, 10 percent or 12½ percent of the total vote is not a frivolous candidate and ought not to be penalized for running. The second alternative is to abolish the notion of a deposit altogether and require instead that the nomination papers be signed by a substantial number of qualified electors, say 500, as evidence of significant support within the constituency.

There are other nomination formalities which do not need to be examined here, although it should be noted that in every election there is inevitably the odd candidate who is disqualified because he fails to observe all the rules — principally because he arrives at the place of nomination after the times at which nominations are officially closed or because the deposit is not properly made. (Federal law, for example, requires that the deposit be made either in cash or by a *certified* cheque).[28]

## THE NEED FOR A PARTY LABEL

Federal election law makes no mention of parties, except insofar as enumerators are supposed to represent "two different and opposed political interests."[29] The ballot paper contains simply the names of the candidates, in alphabetical order, with the address and occupation of each. The absurdity of ignoring partisan affiliation has been noted by the federal Committee on Election Expenses, which remarked in its *Report*: "A study of the legislation would lead one to believe that those who drafted the legislation envisaged contests in each constituency among a series of independent candidates. . . . (But) it has become increasingly difficult to continue the myth that political parties do not exist and are not a vital part of our form of government."[30]

Three provinces (Manitoba, Ontario, and Newfoundland) follow the federal lead in refusing to recognize political parties on the ballots and other election documents. In Nova Scotia the decision to add the party label to the candidate's name on the ballot was reached only in 1969.[31] The major argument against the inclusion of the party name is that this would involve the election administration in the internal affairs of the political parties and that this is an unwise thing to do. It is an argument that has much to commend it, especially in the circumstances where election officials might be called upon to adjudicate the claims of rival candidates to be the official representative of a party. On the other hand, in the seven provinces where the election law now gives official recognition to parties and requires that candidates declare their affiliation on the ballots, there is nothing to suggest that this factor has of itself led to any deterioration in the impartiality of the election administration.

The simplest procedure is in Prince Edward Island where it is provided that "the name of every candidate on each ballot shall be followed by his address, occupation and political affiliation."[32] The names are arranged on the ballot in alphabetical order. This is a fairly simple system and one which is of some assistance to the voter. However, possibly because the situation has not yet arisen, the *Act* says nothing about challenging the right of a candidate to adopt a particular party label, nor does it determine by whose authority a political affiliation may be used.

Saskatchewan goes one stage further. First of all a political party is defined as "a group of electors comprised in a political organization by which money is expended in support of a candidate,"[33] a definition which would allow for the existence of a party nominating only one candidate. The *Act* then requires that the political affiliation of the candidate be entered on the ballot, but in an abbreviated form. The official abbreviations to be used are specified in the *Act*.[34] On the ballot itself the names appear alphabetically, unless the candidates have themselves agreed that they shall be otherwise arranged.

The Alberta system seems to have found a way round some of the difficulties in determining party affiliation. On the nomination paper the nominators state the political affiliation of the candidate and this is the affiliation that is apparently accepted by the returning officer.[35] This political label is then printed on the Notice of Grant of Poll[36] and on the ballot.[37] This places the whole responsibility for determining the political affiliation on the nominators. Alberta also makes an attempt, unique in Canada, to solve the problem, if it is a problem, that there might be some unfair advantage for the candidate whose name appears first on the ballot. In city constituencies the ballots are printed in batches of one hundred, with the ordering of names different on each batch. In other constituencies the names appear alphabetically on every ballot.[38]

Insofar as there is any merit in a varied order of names, and the election law seems to acknowledge that there is some merit by making it possible in certain circumstances, it is hard to understand why it is confined to the city constituencies. It is not firmly established that there is any clear advantage in being first named on the ballot, particularly when there are only three or four names there, but it is almost certainly no disadvantage. A varied order of names, therefore, if it does nothing else, demonstrates a willingness to make the election system as impartial as possible; and positive indicators of the integrity of the system may be important in minimizing the level of political alienation.

In Quebec a "recognized party" means "the party of the Prime Minister or of the leader of the official opposition, and a party which at the last general elections had ten official candidates" or a party which indicates that it will have at least ten official candidates at the election in progress. In the latter case if, after the close of nominations, the party has in fact fewer than ten official candidates, it ceases to be a recognized party.[39] Basically similar provisions, described more fully below, now apply in New Brunswick and Nova Scotia. To be qualified as a recognized party is important in the election process of these three provinces since the candidates of recognized parties are very precisely distinguished from other candidates. On the ballot papers the names of candidates of recognized parties appear before those of Independents. Non-party candidates are thus clearly placed in a subordinate position, not only as a fact of political life, but with the full force of the election law. In Quebec this position is even further emphasized by the requirement that the candidate who does not represent a recognized party shall have only two choices as to how he shall describe himself on the ballot. He may simply put his name without any designation at all, or he may enter his name, followed by the description "Independent."[40]

The effect of this kind of legislation is to give formal acknowledgement to what are facts in all parts of Canada: first, that the official party candidates are, in almost all cases, the important ones, the only ones with any real chance of winning; and second, that the most important piece of information most voters wish to know about a candidate is his party affiliation. It goes further and recognizes that, in the meaning of party politics, a party candidate is a representative of some more or less formally organized group which is nominating several candidates, and is not merely an individual who might like to attach some ideological label to his name. For Quebec election purposes a man is, for example, a Liberal, not because he declares himself to be a Liberal, but because he is a member of a formal, structured political organization called the Liberal Party. A candidate who does not have this association is simply an "Independent" and is relegated to the bottom of the ballot paper.

The position of the party and, even more important, the authority of the party leader, is given added weight by the requirement in all three provinces that the candidate of a recognized party, "must deliver, at the same time as his nomination-paper, a letter from the leader of such party declaring that he is its official candidate."[41] Such a requirement confers tremendous authority on the official leaders of the parties. A would-be candidate cannot declare himself to be anything other than an independent unless he is a candidate for a recognized party, and he cannot be a candidate for a recognized party without the written consent of the leader of that party.

In a sense one could say that in Quebec, New Brunswick and Nova Scotia there is simply a very realistic and practical acceptance of the fact that the concept of the representative as the voice of his constituency has lost much of its relevance in an age of mass parties. It accepts that most candidates are chosen, not by the electors as such, but by groups of electors organized in parties, and that the majority of electors are limited to choosing between the candidates nominated by the parties. Also, insofar as it is valuable to minimize the charge that the election process, or any other part of the broader political process, is a fraud, a facade, it is wise to make the formality of the election law conform to the reality of the election practice. But the Quebec law goes a good deal further than is likely in a province such as Ontario, in that it places the authority for the determination of the candidate's rights to wear the party's colours, not on the local constituency organization, nor on any provincial organization, but directly and personally on the leader of the party.

Especially striking in New Brunswick is the strong emphasis placed on the fact that an election is basically a contest between parties in which candidates are important largely to the extent that they are representatives of parties. First of all, the ballot paper is arranged, not by some ordering of candidates, but by order of party;[42] and it is the name of the party that takes precedence on the ballot: "The name of a recognized party shall be printed on the ballot paper *preceding and in larger type than the names of the candidates* of the party and separated from them by a solid black line. . . ."[43] Under this arrangement it is not so much that the party label is a piece of supplementary information about the candidate, perhaps useful in helping the voter give an accurate expression of his opinion, but it is the party that dominates, and the candidates appear to have little importance other than as members of parties. In all multi-member districts (and this covers the majority of districts in New Brunswick) the names of the candidates are arranged alphabetically under each party label.

The parties themselves are not treated equally on the ballot. The candidates for the government party always appear first, followed by the party of the official opposition, followed by all other recognized parties in alphabetical order of party names, and, last of all, independent candidates, grouped under the label "Independent" or "Independents."[44] This strongly party-oriented ballot, which is unique in Canada, is a recent innovation in New Brunswick, although the system it replaced was no less unusual. Until 1967 a voter in New Brunswick entering a polling booth would find a stack of blank pieces of paper, and perhaps several other stacks each with the names of one or more candidates printed on them. He could either choose one of the printed ballots supplied by the parties or write the names of his favoured candidates on one of the blank sheets of paper. The ballot was then placed in an official envelope and deposited in the ballot box.[45]

The definition of a political party in British Columbia is somewhat looser than in Quebec or New Brunswick. For election purposes a political party "is an affiliation of electors comprised in a political organization which has expended money in the support of any candidate in the election."[46] This eliminates any attempt to define a party in terms of the number of candidates it runs (a quantitative definition) and instead concentrates on the criterion of an organized group of candidates spending money in support of a candidate (a functional definition). On the ballot papers, as in New Brunswick, the candidate for the government party appears first (but with his party affiliation in smaller print after his name), followed by the candidate for the official opposition party, followed in turn by the candidates for all other parties in alphabetical order of party names.[47]

Both New Brunswick and Britsh Columbia, in marked contrast with Alberta, seem to take the view that if there is any advantage to be gained from being first on the ballot, then it should go to the government party. There is no substantial evidence as to the actual number of additional votes gained by government party candidates in the two provinces through the use of this device and it may very well be totally irrelevant. What is more important is, first, that the governments which have sponsored such provisions seem to argue that there may be something to gain and there is certainly nothing to lose and, second, that the political culture still tolerates the proposition that the election system may legitimately be manipulated (within limits) to strengthen the position of the party in power.

## SELECTION BY PARTIES

Seven provinces, by requiring that the candidate state his party affiliation on the ballot, make explicit the fact that elections today are basically contests between organized parties. They focus attention on the candidate's party label, and thus correspondingly de-emphasize his individuality. The candidate unblessed with official party recognition is reduced to some second-class status as an independent.

In the other three provinces the primacy of party is no less real for being ignored on the nomination papers and ballots. Effectively an election is still a contest between parties and although the elector is officially offered a choice among a set of individuals, an enormous amount of money, time, and effort are devoted to ensuring that as he enters the polling booth the elector will mentally attach the appropriate party labels to the candidates listed in front of him. Independent candidates are in fact accorded a subordinate position from which they only rarely rise to electoral victory. Irrespective of the format of the ballot, and despite what the law may say about the recognition of parties, it requires very little effort to demonstrate that, with only occasional exceptions, the winning candidate will be a party man.

Given then that in all but the most special cases the electors will be confronted with the task of choosing among a small group of candidates who have been endorsed by the political parties, it becomes vitally necessary to know more about the process by which parties select their standard-bearers. Yet this is possibly the one area of Canadian politics on which there is the least amount of systematic and coherent information, possibly because the process itself is neither coherent nor systematic.

All parties, in all provinces and federally, have constitutions, many supplemented by local constituency constitutions, or regional constitutions for small groups of ridings. Almost all of these will lay down the formal rules for selecting a candidate to represent the party at an election. But even a superficial acquaintance with the operation of any constituency association confirms the proposition that such constitutions are only poor guides to actual practices.

Constitutions naturally say little about the processes by which a potential candidate is chosen for presentation at a nomination meeting. Constitutions may presuppose a degree of efficiency and organization beyond the limits of some local associations, in which case constitutional requirements become "adapted" to local conditions. Then, too, the degree of competitiveness within the constituency will to a large extent influence the care with which nomination procedures are followed. A party which has no hope of winning does not need to be too precise about observing all the constitutional niceties, while groups within winning parties may be tempted to override or sidestep constitutional restraints.

Writing on the 1957 General Elections, John Meisel noted that one could gather only general impressions about party selection procedures across Canada, and that no evidence was available as to the frequency with which various selection procedures were adopted.[48] Howard Scarrow has agreed that little is known about the nomination process in Canadian elections.[49] However, we can draw from various sources, hints and clues which let us postulate a number of apparently quite reasonable, although still tentative, propositions.

The first of these is that good candidates are hard to find. Because of what Professor Scarrow has called the "natural" selectors, which include in his phrasing, "societal values and prejudices, as well as the economical realities associated with running for, and accepting a seat in Parliament,"[50] the party leadership must often be more concerned with finding suitable people willing to accept a nomination, than with setting up procedures to control competition for it. This has been especially true for a party that has been long in opposition, or in constituencies where it is acknowledged that only one party has any hope of winning. Engelmann and Schwartz, for example, write that even "one of the major parties may be in a truly hopeless competitive situation in several constituencies. Minor parties are in this position in a majority of constituencies, but they still often nominate in most of them. In such circumstances, many of the candidates literally have to be found."[51] In his paper, "Recent Changes in Canadian Parties," Professor Meisel referred to the inability of the Conservatives to find good candidates in areas where they were not strong: "During the long sojourn of the Conservatives out of office, from 1935 to 1957, they found it increasingly difficult to attract able young people as candidates. Few promising and ambitious men were willing to run for a party which appeared to have little chance of election."[52]

Again, in Nova Scotian provincial elections, during the long period of Liberal domination, we find evidence that the minority Conservative party had great difficulty in securing any candidates at all, especially in those counties which had the strongest Liberal forces.[53] The Liberals in Ontario between 1905 and 1934 experienced similar difficulties.

Of course the reverse is also true. When it appears that the fates have decreed a resurgence in the party's fortunes, would-be candidates, anxious to share in the benefits of victory, begin to gather. Professor Beck has described how this happened to the Conservative Party in Quebec before the 1958 federal elections. In contrast to the old days when only a few perennials were available to ease the problem of finding any candidates at all, "the party's central organizations were deluged with aspirants for nomination, included among them municipal leaders and lawyers of considerable standing in their communities."[54]

The general proposition is understandable. A man needs either a great sense of loyalty to the party, or be possessed of an inordinate desire for publicity, to devote all the time, energy, and money necessary to wage even a token campaign for a hopeless cause. Some, of course, may agree to run because secretly they feel that perhaps the cause is not really lost after all, and they never completely give up hope. The democratic process owes a great debt to such optimists.

The second proposition is that local constituency associations have considerable autonomy, not only in the actual selection of candidates, but also in adopting procedures for selection. This is less true, of course, for the New Democractic Party[55] than for the two older parties, largely because each local New Democratic riding association must have its constitution approved by the Provincial Office, but even here the circumstances in which local parties find themselves require adaptations. Thus the formal procedure in the Ontario New Democratic Party requires that a nominating convention shall be called for the purpose of selecting a candidate and that all those entitled to vote at such a convention shall receive fourteen days' written notice.[56] There is also the custom that the nominating meeting shall be a major public event, with a key party figure as speaker, at which the candidate is presented to the public. It has been the practice in at least one local party to confine the formalities of nomination to a Saturday afternoon business meeting, which naturally attracts a minimum of attention, and then present the candidate, now safely adopted, to the public at a widely advertised dinner meeting in the evening.

Within the Progressive Conservative Party, the desirability, or perhaps it is the necessity, of flexibility at the local level is officially recognized. The Constitution of the Progressive Conservative Association of Canada requires of constituency associations only that they adopt a constitution "which shall contain definite rules and regulations for the conduct of a nomination meeting for the purpose of selecting an official Progressive Conservative candidate."[57] It requires only that there shall be a nomination meeting and leaves it up to the local associations to devise their own rules. It is difficult to see how anything much more rigid could be uniformly imposed on Conservatives in every one of Canada's provinces. The comment in Engelmann & Schwartz that, at least among Liberals and Conservatives, "the decision as to what kind of procedure to employ may be within the discretion of the constituency association, acting through the annual meeting or the executive,"[58] is fully consistent with the official attitude of the two parties.

The same is true at the provincial level. For example, after describing the conventions adopted by both the Conservative and Liberal parties in Prince Edward Island for the selection of candidates for the legislature, Frank MacKinnon acknowledged that the procedure varied considerably and was often "highly informal." His account includes such phrases as "on many occasions," "some polls include," "in most cases," "in some districts," and so on.[59] The general picture is that there is a recognized format for choosing candidates by delegates at a convention, but that individual districts have considerable discretion in adapting the pattern to local needs and usages. Murray Donnelly's study of Manitoba confirms that similar flexibility is found in the West. Writing on nominating conventions within the Conservative party, he said that for provincial elections the rules "on who is entitled to attend and vote vary."[60]

A third proposition is that the executive of a local association will normally, but not quite always, succeed in having its favourite candidate nominated. John Meisel has described the process:

> In most instances the executive agrees beforehand on a candidate who then secures the nomination. Many cases are known, however, of executive-sponsored candidates being turned down by the constituency organization. Considerable maneuvering and in-fighting concealed from the public, may, in any event, precede the decision of the executive. In the majority of cases, the executive's favourite will be one of a number of persons nominated. Most of them turn out to be individuals who have no intention of running. . . . Usually more than one name remains and a vote is taken. Invariably the person receiving the second-highest vote moves that the election be made unanimous.[61]

As a more concrete illustration we can turn to Denis Smith's study of the 1962 campaign in Eglinton, which details the contest for the Liberal nomination between the Executive's choice, Mr. Mitchell Sharp, and a challenger, Dr. Russell Taylor. Mr. Sharp was chosen by a vote of more than three to one.[62]

In Winnipeg North Centre in the 1962 federal elections there does not appear to have been any opposition to the nominations proposed by the executives of any of the parties. "All the nominations were virtually foregone conclusions. Decisions were prearranged by small groups at the provincial or national level, with the formal votes being little more than ritual concessions to grass-roots democracy."[63]

On the other hand things do not always go as planned. In the 1968 federal elections many Liberal nominating conventions were apparently swamped by the "mini-skirted teeny-boppers" infected with what was, for a time, called "Trudeaumania." "In Toronto Davenport, where the membership of the riding association rose from 150 to 5,445 in a few weeks, . . . the outcome may have been determined by non-residents and ten-year-olds who, under the rules, could not be debarred from voting."[64] But these upsets are the exceptions which add life and uncertainty to politics. They make wonderful anecdotes for the historians, but they do not give a true picture of the way in which things are normally done.

Proposition four is a fairly obvious one and it would be much more a matter for lengthy comment if it did not apply. It is simply that the incumbent who wishes to be renominated will nearly always get his wish. The corollary of the "nearly always" is that he sometimes will not. On the affirmative side it has often been reported how, under the Taschereau regime in Quebec, both the Liberals and Conservatives automatically renominated all sitting members as candidates.[65] Requests for nomination meetings within individual constituency associations were apparently rejected unceremoniously. Scarrow has also referred, although incidentally, to the "rather automatic renomination of incumbent MP's."[66]

In his memoirs, C. G. Power talked of the selection of Liberal candidates for the 1935 elections, noting that in many constituencies "sitting members were allowed to run, and were chosen as candidates without much opposition and without anything in the way of a formal convention."[67] In a later period, Denis Smith referred to the "unanimous and uncontested" renomination of Mr. Donald Flemming as Progressive Conservative candidate for the federal constituency of Eglinton in 1962.[68]

On the other hand, it is well to remember that sitting members, even when they hold Cabinet appointments, do not always have their own way. In May of 1968 the Veterans Affairs Minister in the Liberal Government, Roger Teillet, was rejected as Liberal candidate by the St. Boniface Liberal constituency association, although Mr. Teillet had represented the riding since 1962. This was, of course, an exceptional case. A somewhat similar fate, also in 1968, befell Mr. Maurice Sauvé, who lost the nomination in the Montreal constituency of Gamelin, although Mr. Sauvé was not an incumbent in Gamelin, having lost his own constituency in the 1966 redistribution.

Proposition five, which suggests that in provinces in which the democratic tradition has been less fully developed, the procedure for nominating candidates will be even less democratic than in other parts of the country, is harder to document.

We note to begin with the point already made about the automatic renomination of sitting members under the Taschereau administration in Quebec, where the requests of local associations for nominating conventions were simply overruled. Then it is appropriate to recall the provision of the Quebec *Election Act* which requires that a candidate for a recognized party be endorsed by the leader of that party. Professor Meisel, in his study of the 1957 general election, has noted further that in many Quebec constituencies it was the provincial organization, rather than the local association, which nominated or confirmed the federal Liberal candidates.[69] Later in the same book he referred to the practice, fairly widespread among Quebec Conservatives, by which selection committees have appointed candidates without bothering to confirm their selection at a meeting of the constituency association.[70]

Professor Beck has an account of the Progressive Conservative nomination in Quebec East before the 1958 federal elections, which lasted from 8 pm to 6 am and featured such episodes as women changing "their hats, their coiffure, or even their clothing" and returning to vote again. He concluded, "All in vain! The scandal of the convention was such that its nominee withdrew and was replaced by a newcomer, allegedly after the personal intervention of Mr. Duplessis himself."[71]

Turning from Quebec to Newfoundland one cannot neglect George Perlin's footnote to his study of the 1962 election in St. John's West, which has already been quoted in several places. He reported that:

> The method of selecting Liberal candidates for both federal and provincial elections is revealing of the nature of the Newfoundland Liberal party. Although a general nominating convention was held in 1949, candidates since then have been appointed by the party. In fact this has meant that the selection of candidates has been entirely the prerogative of Mr. Smallwood. There is nothing covert about the use of this process for the names of candidates always are announced either in personal statements by the Premier or in statements issued by his office.[72]

Perlin's assessment, never challenged, has been further confirmed in a more recent paper by Peter Neary which stated that even in 1968 the Liberal Party of Newfoundland had "evolved no democratic procedure at the constituency level for the democratic selection of candidates."[73]

These accounts are not meant to suggest that Quebec and Newfoundland are the only undemocratic parts of Canada, or that pure democracy prevails throughout the rest of the country. They are, however, among the most extreme examples of the blatant disregard of democratic procedures. Although the cases are more difficult to document, it is commonly accepted that nominations in Ontario rural ridings are firmly controlled by a few executive members and this is almost certainly true elsewhere. For the most part, however, this lack of popular participation seems to be due more to apathy than to deliberate manipulation.

It is also unfortunately true that there is little information available about nomination procedures within the different parties in British Columbia, or Alberta, or Manitoba, or the Maritimes. As with all the propositions in this section, a great deal more evidence is needed and there is urgent need for a whole series of studies of nomination practices in different constituencies and in different parties.

A sixth proposition, to which there will again be many exceptions, is that as the party's chances of winning the election increase in any constituency, so will its nomination procedures become more formalized and more carefully controlled. This is a matter of fairly obvious common sense. If a party is almost certain to win the election, the competition for the nomination may well be keen, and the party will take great care to ensure that the nomination procedure is kept carefully under control. If, on the other hand, a party has no chance, if it is merely putting up a token candidate for the purpose of showing the flag, it can afford to be more relaxed, more casual, about the whole process.

Meisel, for example, has described in some detail the carefully structured procedure in the Progressive Conservative Party in the then safe Conservative seat of Carleton.[74] And Scarrow, in describing the open convention system used for the adoption of the Liberal candidate in his "Urban" riding, remarked that it was not the procedure one would have expected in a party which had controlled the seat for a long period of time. The main argument in its defense, apparently, was that it had become the customary procedure and any attempt to change it would have been regarded with suspicion.[75]

What emerges, then, from a survey of the rather sparse literature on the selection of candidates by the parties, is a picture of a basic pattern of selection by some kind of meeting of "members" of the party, either in open convention, or as carefully selected delegates. But this basic pattern allows for wide variations in detail and in adaptation to local needs and usages. The procedure is not particularly democratic, and it quite clear that only a very small segment of the electorate has any effective say whatever in determining who the candidates will be. It is not, however, completely autocratic and, periodically, revolutions, coups, and grass-root uprisings upset the best-laid plans of party machines. It is also recognized that some party executives must spend a great deal of energy searching for a candidate prepared to act as the party's standard-bearer. It is not possible to say anything precise about a process which is itself no more precise than this.

## THE SOCIO-ECONOMIC CONSIDERATIONS

It is clear that certain socio-economic variables influence the availability of individuals as political candidates, in the sense that while some considerations may dissuade some individuals from putting themselves forward others may dissuade parties from accepting them. Beyond this rather obvious statement, it is difficult to say anything that is concise and meaningful.

There have been no in-depth studies of the motivations that have led some people to allow their names to be entered on a ballot or, what is perhaps an even more important question, have led others to decline the opportunity. Innumerable surveys have asked voters why they have preferred this candidate to that. Only a very few have sought to examine the motives of candidates in running for public office. Perhaps for candidates whose election seems assured, the candidates for the "top" party in the safe seats, it is easy to ascribe motives of power, fame, honour, monetary gain, influence, and so on, but what of the candidate who has no hope? One can only speculate about the combination of motives — including probably vanity, public service, loyalty, and the desire for personal recognition, that leads a man to set aside his occupation and his normal family life in order to spend a great deal of time, physical and emotional energy, and money, contesting an election which he knows, and all who work with him know. he cannot win. It is an interesting question that one day may be answered.

Most of that which is known about candidates and their characteristics must be gathered from an after-the-fact examination of the biographies of those who have actually become candidates. Even in this regard information is hard to come by and what there is is largely incomplete. This, while also partly true for successful candidates, it especially true for independents and defeated candidates. There is even less information about those who have not come forward as candidates at all.

The main sources of information about successful candidates are, first of all, the annual publication, *The Canadian Parliamentary Guide,* which contains brief biographies of all elected members of the House of Commons and of the provincial legislatures. At the federal level there is *The Canadian Directory of Parliament 1867-1967*[76] which has consolidated and filled out from other sources the biographical details of the *Parliamentary Guide*. Even these works are incomplete as they are, for the most part, based on information supplied by the members themselves. Not all members have chosen to give details of the date or place of their birth, their education, their religion, their occupation, or prior political experience. So there are very incomplete data, which apply only to elected members. For defeated candidates the position is very much worse and there is little by way of official information about them. The reports of the Chief Electoral Officer for Canada and some of the provinces do include summaries of the names, addresses and occupations of all candidates, but the details are sketchy and far from complete.

In addition to these official sources there is a small amount of published academic material, the most notable of which is Norman Ward's study of "The Personnel of Parliament."[77] This summarises and tabulates data about the members of the House of Commons in the period from 1867 to 1945. Under such subheads as The Turnover of Members, The Ages at which Members Enter the Commons, The Pre-Parliamentary Experience of Members, The Birthplaces of Members, The Age-Composition of the Commons, The Occupations and Economic Interests of Members, The Parliamentary Experience of Members, and The Post-Parliamentary Careers of Members, Professor Ward presents a reasonably clear picture of the kind of representatives the people have had in Ottawa over the years. It is admitted that the data are weak, but Professor Ward concludes by citing J. F. S. Ross to the effect that although there are omissions and errors, in such an analysis they are not such as to impair the general accuracy of his conclusions.

At the provincial level we are less well served and we have reasonably full data on only two provinces. Professor David Smith has done in briefer form for the Saskatchewan legislature what Ward did for the House of Commons, with additional information and tables on the religious affiliation, the ethnic origin and the educational background of members.[78] There is also prepared for publication a study of Ontario politics which will include the results of a survey of the socio-economic background of all candidates, elected and defeated, who ran in the 1967 Ontario provincial election.[79]

Apart from these studies, other information can be gathered from the several constituency election reports, most of which have already been mentioned. It is customary in an election study to pay some attention to the candidates and their backgrounds, but these are isolated cases and only a very few constituencies have been subjects of this kind of analysis. There is nothing to indicate how typical are these few selected examples.

From all these sources it would be possible to compile a series of tables comparing the different variables at the federal and provincial levels. But such tables, being based on far-from-complete data, would be misleading. At the same time they would, by their format, give an air of scientific authenticity to what would remain simply a set of broadly based generalizations. It is, perhaps, safer merely to state the generalizations as generalizations, supportable in broad terms by the data available, but not presented in a form which would make the data appear harder than they really are.

In the first place, it is quite obvious that women are at a great political disadvantage. The parties do not welcome women as candidates because it is believed that the voters will not elect them as members. At the time of writing, a check of the *Parliamentary Guide* for 1968 indicated that of some 903 members of the federal and provincial parliaments only 12 are women.

It is, secondly, equally clear that neither the House of Commons nor any of the provincial legislatures is a perfect mirror of the population at large. "Parliament is, and always has been, recruited from particular groups in the country to the detriment of other groups."[80] The professional and managerial segments of the population, and especially the lawyers, are clearly grossly over-represented. In the House of Commons in 1968, 26 percent of the members were classed as lawyers, although lawyers represent far less than half of one percent of the working population. Professional men, including lawyers, accountants, doctors, clergymen, professors, teachers, and other professions made up 50 percent of the membership of the House, and only 8 percent of the working population.

At the other end of the scale it is easy to demonstrate that manual workers, trade unionists, agricultural labourers, and semi-skilled white-collar workers are not proportionately represented. There will be variations in statistical detail in the different provinces, with a slight decline in the number of lawyers here and an increase in the number of farmers there, but the general pattern will remain basically the same. This is not to suggest that representation ought to be proportional over all sections of the population, but merely to state the fact that members of certain occupations are more likely than others to be adopted as candidates and so become elected.

On the question of age there will again be considerable variation, especially in the extremes, from election to election, among the parties, and from province to province. But the broad generalization remains true: the great majority of members have been between 35- and 50-years-old when first elected. A would-be candidate who is under 35 or over 50 when he first seeks nomination needs some added advantage to overcome the age constraints — the principal advantage often being that he is the only candidate available. A party which, in a given constituency, has little hope of winning may be more inclined, or compelled, to adopt either an enthusiastic young man running for the fun of running, or an older, retired person who can contest an election without taking time out from a more profitable business.

Religion raises even more complicated questions in that we live in a culture in which there are certain strong, but far from universal or binding, social pressures to make some formal declaration of adherence to some religious denomination. The pressures are less strong in requiring a person to behave in complete consistency with the social and theological tenets of the declared faith. A person's statement of religion therefore is only a very approximate indication of his actual religious beliefs or practices.

Perhaps the most striking aspect of religion as a qualification for a candidate is the marked party orientation of some religious faiths. Numerous voting behaviour studies have confirmed, for example, the strong tendency for Roman Catholics to vote Liberal or for Anglicans to vote Conservative. These tendencies, and they are no more than tendencies, are to be found also among members of the various legislatures. A Roman Catholic member is more likely to be in the Liberal party than any other single party, and an Anglican is more likely to be in the Conservative party. From the point of view of the selection of candidates, all that can at this stage be said is that either the parties themselves will tend to favour candidates of particular religions, in the belief that this religious affiliation will win a few more votes, or that members of any one faith, if they have political ambitions, will be inclined to seek fulfilment of those ambitions in one particular party.

The importance of religion has varied from province to province. As long as the federal constituency of Halifax was a two-member seat it was customary for all parties to nominate both a Catholic and a Protestant. This meant that once, say, the Liberal party had chosen one Catholic or one Protestant a second Catholic or a second Protestant had no chance of being nominated. In the Newfoundland legislature a practice which is only just beginning to lose some of its force has been to base provincial constituency boundaries around areas of denominational concentration.[81] In any such officially recognized scheme for the representation of religious communities *per se* it would, of course, be a virtual necessity for the would-be candidate to be a member of the dominant religion. Elsewhere one seems to perceive, with little detailed or precise confirming data, that the "major" religions — Roman Catholic, Anglican, United Church, Presbyterian, Baptist, and so on, are well represented in all legislatures, while the minor faiths and sects are significantly under represented. David Smith noted that in Saskatchewan the most under-represented religions were the Greek Orthodox and the Ukrainian (Greek) Catholic.[82]

At the level of education it is perhaps gratifying to see that the legislatures are not representative of the total population, that the level of education among legislators is considerably higher than that of the represented. In the House of Commons in 1968, for example, 72 percent of the members had university education, compared with 7 percent of the population. From the point of view of candidate selection all this means is that most parties will normally prefer to nominate a man whose education indicates a high level of articulateness and administrative capacity over a working man with no more than Grade Eight schooling.

Finally, there is the cost factor. An election is an expensive business, although no one seems to know for sure just how expensive it is. "The money is somehow gathered (no one knows quite how) and spent (no one quite knows exactly how much for what specific items)."[83] Harold Angell, the author of the preceding quotation, in summarizing what others, who should have been able to speak with authority on the subject, had written, commented simply that estimates had varied widely. There seemed to be only one firm piece of data, and that was that election campaigns were a great deal more expensive to run in Quebec and in the Maritimes than in the rest of the country.[84]

At the federal level, a summary of responses of 454 candidates who returned questionnaires which had been addressed to all 1,011 official candidates in the 1965 federal elections indicated an average *declared* expenditure of $6,835 per candidate.[85] The range from which this average was computed extended from less than $500 to nearly $50,000.

It must be stressed that these figures are based on officially declared expenditures. This is important for, as the Committee on Election Expenses politely noted, "Other evidence produced before the Committee indicates that candidates' declarations give only a partial picture of their total expenditures."[86] Earlier, in the main body of the *Report* the Committee, after noting that there were 255 candidates in 1965 who made no official return of election expenses, although required to do so by law,[87] commented that, of the returns that were received, "examination suggests that many are incomplete and misleading. The Committee has no exact statistics on the inaccuracy of these reports, but the evidence indicates that the election expense returns are not taken as seriously as they should be by all candidates."[88] It is safe to assume, therefore, that the cost of an individual election campaign, not taking into account the benefits the candidate might receive from national or provincial party campaigning, will on the average be considerably in excess of the reported figure.

The candidates who spend this money must raise it from somewhere and again we run into a situation where wide variations in practice make simple generalizations impossible. Within the Progressive Conservative and Liberal parties it is common for the constituency organizations handling individual campaigns to draw on the resources of either the national or the provincial office of the party, with the amount of direct subsidization being roughly based on the resources already available to the candidate, and on his prospects of winning. Candidates for the New Democratic Party, and its predecessor the Co-operative Commonwealth Federation, traditionally were forced to rely more heavily on the resources of their own constituencies and, indeed, were also committed to contribute a portion of their campaign funds to the provincial office. This is still to some extent true, but the increasing resources of the party have made it possible for the provincial office, in Ontario at least, to subsidize campaigns in key constituencies.

Whatever the outside sources available, however, the candidate himself must carry some significant share of the cost. Although he was writing exclusively about the Liberal party, Professor Regenstreif's remarks have broader application: "More often than not, the candidate is forced to spend a great deal of his own money in order to get elected. . . . The candidate may have local sources such as personal friends or some area business establishments to which he can appeal but it is a certainty that his constituency . . . is usually unable to help very much."[89]

A general study of political party financing is beyond the scope of this book, although some more will be said about the subject in Chapter Four. Here, it is necessary to consider only those factors which affect the selection of some individuals as political candidates. Obviously the costs involved must be one of these factors.

> So long as the heavy cost of fighting an election falls on the candidate and his supporters, so long will finance play a role in the selection of candidates that should be played by different considerations. Worse consequences may follow than the preference for poorly qualified but wealthy candidates rather than well

qualified but poor candidates. So long as candidates must invest, to be elected, much more than they can hope of recouping from salary as an M.P.P., so long will the unscrupulous search for loopholes in the best legislation against "patronage" and the sale of influence.[90]

The reference to the salaries of M.P.P.'s introduces another dimension into the element of cost. The costs of being a candidate stop with the end of the campaign only for the defeated. For the victor the costs are even higher. He must set against his salary and expense allowances as a member, first, the additional costs that go with being a member and, secondly, the loss of other income not earned while serving in the legislature. The first dimension is easily measurable. The salaries of members of the provincial legislatures and of the House of Commons are summarised in Table 2: 3. Nowhere are they excessively high, and in most provinces they are disgracefully low. The figures are the basic remuneration of an ordinary member, and so do not include the sums paid to cabinet members or for other special duties.

## Table 2: 3
### INDEMNITY OF MEMBERS OF THE HOUSE OF COMMONS AND OF THE PROVINCIAL LEGISLATURES (1969)

| Administration | Total Indemnity including tax-free expense allowance $ | Administration | Total Indemnity including tax-free expense allowance $ |
|---|---|---|---|
| Canada | 18,000 | Quebec | 18,000[iv] |
| British Columbia | 8,000 | New Brunswick | 7,500 |
| Alberta | 7,200 | Nova Scotia | 6,000 |
| Saskatchewan | 9,000[i] | Prince Edward Island | 4,000 |
| Manitoba | 7,200 | Newfoundland | 8,500 |
| Ontario | 11,000[ii] | | |
| | 12,000 | | |
| | 18,000[iii] | | |

[i] Representatives from the three most northerly districts in Saskatchewan receive an additional expense and indemnity allowance of $835.

[ii] Members from metro Toronto receive $1,000 a year less in expenses than members outside metro.

[iii] Increases in the indemnity of members of the Ontario legislature were approved by the cabinet in November 1969.

[iv] Indemnities of members of the Quebec legislature were increased to $21,000 in December 1969.

The other variables are more tenuous. Each member will be able to estimate for himself how much it costs him to be a member — how much he spends in serving his constituents and how much in maintaining an image that will help his subsequent re-election. And only the individual member will know what he might otherwise have earned had he chosen not to serve the community as a member of the legislature. All that can be said is that for the conscientious member who is genuinely interested in public service, not simply seeking new opportunities for graft and patronage, the bargain is, in financial terms, a poor one.

Certainly, financial considerations are such as to discourage a great many otherwise attractive candidates. Only a small percentage of the population have the resources to run a meaningful campaign, the type of campaign that might actually bring victory. Of those who could perhaps afford to run only another smaller segment could afford to win.

Of all the provinces, Quebec and Nova Scotia alone seem to make any kind of realistic assessment of the responsibilities and costs of serving in the legislature. Quebec generally pays its members a higher remuneration than any other province[91] and initiated the scheme, which may eventually be copied more widely, of reimbursing certain candidates for part of the cost of running an election campaign. The *Election Act* first of all sets limits on the election expenses that may be incurred by either a recognized party or by individual candidates.[92] This in itself is a major step forward and one that could well be imitated elsewhere. It is then provided that the returning officer will reimburse a portion of the election expenses actually incurred and paid by the official agent of each candidate who has been elected, or who has obtained at least 20 percent of the valid votes cast in the constituency, or who represents a party that received the highest or second highest number of votes cast in the last election.[93] In order to receive reimbursement the official agent must, of course, make returns of expenses with proper documentation and there are quite elaborate provisions to minimize the opportunities for fraud.

These seem to be very reasonable provisions. The province is not going to be faced with an excessive bill for election expenses from hundreds of quite silly candidates, for the only ones entitled to reimbursement are those who can obtain a minimum of 20 percent of the total vote cast, or who are members of a major party and who can therefore be considered serious candidates even though they may personally suffer total defeat in their own ridings.[94]

There are also quite specific directions as to what are and what are not legitimate election expenses eligible for reimbursement. The initial definition of "election expenses" is quite broad and is taken to include, "all the expenditures incurred during an election period to promote or oppose, directly or indirectly, the election of a candidate or that of the candidates of a party or to propagate or oppose the program or policy of a candidate or party or to approve or disapprove the steps recommended or opposed by them or the things done or proposed by them or their supporters."[95]

Then, in the same section of the *Act*, there are the exceptions, the listing of expenses which may be incurred during an election but which are not deemed to be "election expenses" within the meaning of the *Act*. Such excluded expenses are, first of all, not part of the limitation on election expenses as defined in section 379 and so add to the overall cost of a campaign, and secondly, they are not subject to reimbursement under the terms of section 380. The expenses of an election which are not legally election expenses include: the cost of publishing regular news items, editorials, letters, etc., and normal radio or television broadcasts of news or comments for which no payment is made and which are treated by the newspaper or the broadcasting station in the same manner as similar items outside the election period; within defined limits, the necessary expenses of a nomination convention; the cost of food and lodging incurred during a journey for election purposes by the candidate or any other person if such expenses are not reimbursable by the campaign organization; the candidate's transportation costs and the non-reimbursable transportation costs of any other person; the candidate's deposit; the costs of publishing various non-partisan comments and explanations of the *Election Act*; and the costs incurred by a recognized party in maintaining permanent offices in Montreal and Quebec City. The main point of these definitions is to separate out actual campaign promotion costs, the propaganda of the election, and to provide for the reimbursement of these and, at the same time, to distinguish these from the incidental administrative and other costs which necessarily arise during an election.

One other province has given serious formal consideration to the question of reducing the cost of elections to the individual candidate. A Nova Scotia Royal Commission, set up in July 1968, reported in February 1969. Its recommendations were basically similar to those already enacted in Quebec: precise definition of what is and is not to be regarded as an election expense, limitations on the amounts candidates may lawfully spend on election expenses, and provision for the reimbursement of a proportion of these expenses, up to certain limits, for candidates who received more than a minimum share of the total vote cast.[96]

These recommendations were adopted, with some variation in detail, in an amendment to the Nova Scotia *Elections Act* in April 1969. The essential features of the new legislation centre around two issues: the limits on expenditures and the reimbursement of expenses incurred. As to the first point, the new *Act* provides that the election expenses of a candidate shall not exceed the aggregate of:

(a) one dollar per elector in respect of not more than five thousand electors;

(b) eighty-five cents per elector for the number of electors between five and ten thousand; and

(c) seventy-five cents per elector for all electors in excess of ten thousand.[97]

The actual election expenses incurred, to a maximum of twenty-five cents an elector, are reimbursed to all candidates who are elected, or who receive at least fifteen percent of the total votes cast in the constituency.[98]

The reimbursement of all, or a fixed portion, of the actual election expenses incurred up to certain limits is a practice which will probably gradually become more widespread. There are advantages in it for all parties and if candidates were relieved of the immediate burdens of campaign financing the pool of available candidates of high quality might be significantly increased. But, as already mentioned, the campaign is only the first and the most drastic of the costs involved in serving as a Member of Parliament.

The loss of other earning power by the member who, if salaried, must usually take leave without pay or resign or, if self-employed, must devote less time to his own business, is far less widely publicized and attracts much less popular sympathy. Legislators who raise their own salaries must expect a great deal of public criticism and often a quite intemperate level of abuse. Yet it is an undeniable fact that until legislative salaries can be raised to a competitive level there will remain many talented, worthy persons who will be discouraged from seeking public office.

If we exclude that small group always found on the fringes of political life in a democracy — the independents who gather no more than a few hundred votes, the seekers after publicity or a brief moment of fame, the zealots for some newly discovered universal truth, the earnest and persistent advocates of lost causes, and the exuberant to whom running for office is fun, merely another experience — that is, if we confine our attention to the candidates who run, either to win in their local constituency, or to swell the grand total of votes for their party, we find that the opportunities for candidacy are severely constrained by a number of factors. Some of these are statutory, imposing greater restrictions upon the right to run than upon the right to be a voter. Others are economic, discouraging many from putting their names forward. But the most important are the combination of the political and the socio-economic. With very few exceptions, to be a successful candidate one must be endorsed by a political party, and the political parties set their own criteria for extending such endorsement. The selection of parliamentary candidates, which implies the rejection of others who might wish to run, by the parties is invariably made by a minority group, representative neither of the electorate at large, nor of the particular party.

Candidates are chosen by, at worst, one man or, at best, by a relatively small group of men. In some areas and in some parties it is better than in others, but nowhere is it particularly democratic. Candidate selection seems to be one area of Canadian party politics which departs widely from the democratic ideal and is, at the same time, an area about which there is only patchy and incomplete knowledge. Perhaps the two factors are related? This is a vital question. It is appropriate to recall the words of a petition from the electors of Middlesex in defense of their choice of John Wilkes: "If any power on earth can dictate our choice, and prescribe who shall and who shall not become candidates to represent us in Parliament, we may talk of our rights, and take pride in our freedom, but in fact we have none."[99]

## FOOTNOTES

[1] Write-in candidates — unknown in Canada, but quite common in the United States — are something of an exception to this principle. We could say, however, that insofar as there is an organized campaign to encourage write-in votes for a particular candidate, then that person is a formal candidate even though his name does not appear on the official ballot.

[2] Sec. 19 of the *Canada Elections Act* is a model for all provincial acts. It reads: "Except as in this Act otherwise provided, any person, man or woman, who is (a) a Canadian citizen or other British subject, (b) a qualified elector under this Act, and (c) of the full age of twenty-one years, may be a candidate at an election." The main variation is that in most of the provinces the exceptions are specified, not in the provincial *Election Act*, but in a *Legislative Assembly Act* or its equivalent.

[3] The federal *Act* carefully distinguishes between corrupt and illegal practices. See S.C., 1960, chap. 39, sec. 20 (1) (a) and (b).

[4] The phrasing here is from S.C., 1960, chap. 39, sec. 20 (1) (c), but there are similarly worded sentiments in the provincial statute books.

[5] R.S.S., 1965, chap. 3, sec. 15.

[6] R.S.O., 1960, chap. 208, sec. 10.

[7] S.N.B., 1967, chap. 9, sec. 49 (3).

[8] R.S.A., 1955, chap. 174, sec. 12.

[9] Great Britain, House of Commons, Select Committee on Offices or Places of Profit Under the Crown, *Report, with Minutes of Evidence*, House of Commons Paper 120, October 1941. Much of the Canadian history of the topic is to be found in N. Ward, *The Canadian House of Commons: Representation*, Toronto, University of Toronto Press, 2nd edition, 1963, chap. v.

[10] The army in wartime is another matter and more will be said about it shortly.

11 S.C., 1868, chap. 25, sec. 1. Reproduced with the permission of the Queen's Printer for Canada.

12 See N. Ward, *op. cit.*, 85-86.

13 See, for example, *Statutes of the Province of Canada*, 20 Vict., chap. 22, sec. 6, 1857.

14 N. Ward, *op. cit.*, 92-96.

15 S.C., 1931, chap. 52.

16 S.C., 1960, chap. 39, sec. 20 (2) (b).

17 R.S.S., 1965, chap. 9, sec. 52 (2).

18 *Ibid.*, (3) (a).

18a S.O., 1962-3, chap. 118. See also W. D. K. Kernaghan, "The Political Rights and Activities of Canadian Public Servants," in his *Bureaucracy in Canadian Government*, Toronto, Methuen, 1969, 95-104.

19 Great Britain, Parliament, *The Servants of the Crown (Parliamentary Candidates) Order*, 1960, and "Parliamentary Candidates and the Civil Service," — A Treasury Memorandum submitted to the House of Commons, both contained in House of Commons Paper, 262, June 1963.

20 This problem was raised in a letter to the author from W. C. Graves, Clerk Assistant to the Executive Council of Alberta.

21 N. Ward, *op. cit.*, 65-69.

22 S.C., 1960, chap. 39, sec. 20 (1) (d).

23 S.C., 1874, chap. 9, sec. 20.

24 R.S.B.C., 1960, chap. 306, sec. 55 (a).

25 S.P.E.I., 1963, chap. 11, sec. 53; S.N., 1954, chap. 79, sec. 41; and S.A., 1956, chap. 15, sec. 32.

26 S.N.S., 1969, chap. 40, sec. 3.

27 Figures are all compiled from the *Reports* of the Chief Electoral Officer which are issued after each election.

28 S.C., 1960, chap. 39, sec. 21 (10) (b).

29 *Ibid.*, sec. 17, Schedule A, Rule 2. But note that federal legislation does not entirely ignore parties. Sec. 16 of the *Canadian Forces Voting Rules* reads:
(1) As soon as possible after the nominations of candidates at the general election have closed, on the fourteenth day before polling day, the Chief Electoral Officer shall transmit a sufficient number of copies of a list of the names and surnames of the candidates officially nominated in each electoral district to every special returning officer.
(2) Upon the list referred to in subparagraph (1) shall be inserted after the names and surname of each candidate the designating letters currently used to indicate his political affiliations.
(3) The designating letters shall be ascertained from the best sources of information available to the Chief Electoral Officer.
Reproduced with the permission of the Queen's Printer for Canada.

30 Canada, Committee on Election Expenses, *Report*, 1966, 38. Reproduced with the permission of the Queen's Printer for Canada.

31 R.S.M., 1954, chap. 68, sec. 63 (6); R.S.O., 1960, chap. 118, sec. 63 (8); S.N.S., 1962, chap. 4, sec. 77 (but in Nova Scotia there is a provision — in sec. 64 (2) — that in two-member districts the candidates may agree to an arrangement of names on the ballot paper "otherwise than alphabetically"); S.N., 1954, chap. 79, sec. 58 (1) — Here it might be worth noting that although the *Act* requires that the names be arranged alphabetically, on the

sample ballot printed in the office consolidation of the *Act* — Form 30 — they are not in correct order.

[32] S.P.E.I., 1963, chap. 11, sec. 71 (10).

[33] R.S.S., 1965, chap. 4, sec. 2 (1) (v).

[34] *Ibid.*, sec. 20 (5). After giving the abbreviations for the well-known parties, the section adds, "such abbreviations *as may be designated by the Chief Electoral Officer* with respect to other political affiliations." (my italics).

[35] S.A., 1956, chap. 15, sec. 33 and Form 16.

[36] *Ibid.*, sec. 41 (1).

[37] *Ibid.*, sec. 59 (2).

[38] *Ibid.*, sec. 59 (3) and (4). The rearrangement is not random and follows precise rules set out in the *Act.*

[39] R.S.Q., 1964, chap. 7, secs. 2 (20) and 375 (3).

[40] *Ibid.*, sec. 193 (2).

[41] *Ibid.*, sec. 147 (3). Similar phrasing is found in S.N.B., 1967, chap. 9, sec. 51 (3) and S.N.S., 1969, chap. 40, sec. 2 (3). This provision is new in Nova Scotia.

[42] S.N.B., 1967, chap. 9, sec. 63 (9). It is only in the multi-member districts that candidates' names are arranged alphabetically *within their party blocks.*

[43] *Ibid.*, sec. 63 (12). (Italics added)

[44] *Ibid.*, sec. 63 (9) and (13).

[45] R.S.N.B., 1952, chap. 70, secs. 55 and 67.

[46] R.S.B.C., 1960, chap. 306, sec. 177 (2).

[47] *Ibid.*, sec. 86 (4).

[48] J. Meisel, *The Canadian General Election of 1957*, Toronto, University of Toronto Press, 1962, 121.

[49] H. Scarrow, "Three Dimensions of a Local Political Party," in J. Meisel (ed), *Papers on the 1962 Election*, Toronto, University of Toronto Press, 1964, 53.

[50] *Ibid.*

[51] F. C. Engelmann and M. A. Schwartz, *Political Parties and the Canadian Social Structure*, Toronto, Prentice-Hall of Canada, 1967, 164.

[52] J. Meisel, "Recent Changes in Canadian Parties," in H. G. Thorburn (ed), *Party Politics in Canada*, Toronto, Prentice-Hall of Canada, 4th ed, 1967, 38, and see also 51.

[53] J. M. Beck, "The Nomination of Candidates in Nova Scotia," *The Dalhousie Review*, 36 (4), 1957, 367.

[54] J. M. Beck, "Quebec and the Canadian Elections of 1958," *Parliamentary Affairs*, 12 (1), 1958, 93.

[55] See, for example, F. C. Engelmann & M. A. Schwartz, *op. cit.*, 166, where it is noted that the CCF/NDP nominations in Saskatchewan "are carefully structured and representative of every poll in the constituency."

[56] New Democratic Party of Ontario, *Constitution*, Article 10.

[57] Progressive Conservative Association of Canada, *Constitution*, Rule 9 (e).

[58] F. C. Engelmann & M. A. Schwartz, *op. cit.*, 165.

[59] F. MacKinnon, *The Government of Prince Edward Island*, Toronto, University of Toronto Press, 1951, 255-6.

[60] M. S. Donnelly, *The Government of Manitoba*, Toronto, University of Toronto Press, 1963, 68.

[61] J. Meisel, *The Canadian General Election of 1957*, Toronto, University of Toronto Press, 1962, 121.

[62] D. Smith, "The Campaign in Eglinton," in J. Meisel (ed), *Papers on the 1962 Election*, Toronto, University of Toronto Press, 1964, 71.

[63] T. Peterson & I. Avakumovic, "A Return to the Status Quo: The Election in Winnipeg North Centre," in J. Meisel (ed) *Papers on the 1962 Election*, Toronto, University of Toronto Press, 1965, 95.

[64] J. M. Beck, *Pendulum of Power: Canada's Federal Elections*, Toronto, Prentice-Hall of Canada, 1968, 401.

[65] R. M. Dawson, *The Government of Canada*, Toronto, University of Toronto Press, 4th edition, 1963, 482.

[66] H. Scarrow, *op. cit.*

[67] N. Ward (ed), *A Party Politician: The Memoirs of Chubby Power*, Toronto, Macmillan of Canada, 1966, 336.

[68] D. Smith, *op. cit.*, 72.

[69] J. Meisel, *The Canadian General Election of 1957*, Toronto, University of Toronto Press, 1962, 63.

[70] *Ibid.*, 122.

[71] J. M. Beck, "Quebec and the Canadian Elections of 1958," *Parliamentary Affairs*, 12 (1), 1958, 93.

[72] G. Perlin, "St. John's West," in J. Meisel (ed), *Papers on the 1962 Election*, 7 n.

[73] P. Neary, "Democracy in Newfoundland: A Comment," *Journal of Canadian Studies*, 4 (1), 1969, 37.

[74] J. Meisel, *The Canadian General Election of 1957*, 122.

[75] H. Scarrow, *op. cit.*, 54.

[76] J. K. Johnson (ed), *The Canadian Directory of Parliament 1867-1967*, Ottawa, The Public Archives of Canada, 1968.

[77] N. Ward, "The Personnel of Parliament," chap. viii in his *The Canadian House of Commons: Representation*, 115-149.

[78] D. E. Smith, "The Membership of the Saskatchewan Legislative Assembly: 1905-1966," in N. Ward & D. Spafford (eds) *Politics in Saskatchewan*, Toronto, Longmans of Canada Ltd, 1968, 178-206.

[79] J. M. Wilson & J. D. Hoffman, "Ontario: A Three-Party System in Transition," in a volume of essays of party politics in the Canadian provinces forthcoming from Prentice-Hall of Canada Ltd.

[80] N. Ward, *op. cit.*, 135.

[81] G. O. Rothney, "The Denominational Basis of Representation in the Newfoundland Assembly, 1919-1962," *Canadian Journal of Economics & Political Science*, 28 (iv), 1962, 557-570.

[82] D. E. Smith, "The Membership of the Saskatchewan Legislative Assembly: 1905-1966," in N. Ward & D. Spafford (eds), *Politics in Saskatchewan*, 197.

[83] H. M. Angell, "The Evolution and Application of Quebec Election Expense Legislation 1960-66," chap. vii in Canada, Committee on Election Expenses, *Report*, 1966, 279.

[84] *Ibid.*, 280 and 281-2.

[85] Canada, Committee on Election Expenses, *Report*, 1966, 411.

[86] *Ibid.*, 426.

[87] S.C., 1960, chap. 39, sec. 63. No legal action appears to have been taken in recent years against those who failed to file returns, or against those whose returns were clearly inaccurate.

[88] Canada, Committee on Election Expenses, *Report*, 1966, 30.

[89] S. P. Regenstreif, *The Liberal Party of Canada: A Political Analysis*, unpublished Ph.D. thesis, Cornell, 1963, reissued by University Microfilms Inc. Ann Arbor, 1965, 164-5.

[90] H. M. Angell, *Report on Electoral Reform in the Province of Quebec*, Montreal, 1961, unpublished manuscript prepared for the Quebec Liberal Federation, Oct. 1961, 14-15.

[91] In 1969 Ontario increased the remuneration of its members to match Quebec, but Quebec indemnities were further increased in December, 1969.

[92] R.S.Q., 1964, chap. 7, sec. 379. Election expenses of each candidate must not exceed:
60¢ per elector in the constituency up to 10,000 electors
50¢ per elector over 10,000 and up to 20,000
40¢ per elector for each elector over 20,000
In by-elections the foregoing sums are increased by 25¢ per elector. In the electoral districts of Abitibi East, Isles de la Madeleine, Duplessis, and Saguenay there is an additional allowance of 10¢ an elector.

[93] *Ibid.*, sec. 380. Amounts reimbursable are the actual expenses up to 15¢ per elector, plus 20 percent of the actual expenses over 15¢ per elector, plus the total expenses of actual expenses over 40¢ per elector, up to the maximum limits permitted under sec. 91. The 25¢ extra allowed to be spent on by-elections is not reimbursable.

[94] For a detailed analysis of the history, operation, and costs of the Quebec election expense reimbursement scheme see H. M. Angell, "The Evolution and Application of Quebec Election Expense Legislation 1960-66," in Canada, Committee on Election Expenses, *Report*, 1966, 279-319.

[95] R.S.Q., 1964, chap. 7, sec. 372.

[96] Nova Scotia, Royal Commission of Election Expenses and Associated Matters, *Report*, Halifax, 1969, 11-3.

[97] S.N.S., 1969, chap. 40, new sec. 164A (3). There are special provisions for multi-member districts.

[98] *Ibid.*, new sec. 164B (1).

[99] As quoted by P. Paterson, *The Selectorate: The Case for Primary Elections in Britain*, London, MacGibbon & Kee, 1967, 184.

# THREE

## WHERE?

The relationship of the represented (as examined in the first chapter) and the representatives (as examined in the second) appears at first sight to be fairly simple — simple, that is, in recognizing which individuals fall into which category — although not in determining the powers, authorities, or role expectations of each category. Even the basic relationship, however, leads into more complex matters, one of which is the concern of this chapter. The main question is how to organize groups of represented around individual representatives.

Suppose, for example, that there are 1,000,000 people whose interests in the legislature are to be cared for by 100 representatives. Leaving aside the possibilities of multi-member districts or elections at-large, suppose further that each representative will speak for 10,000 represented. In the absence of any further criteria it can be seen that the number of possible ways of combining 1,000,000 individual units into 100 lots of 10,000 each is astronomical. Still, without any further criteria, any one of these extremely large number of combinations would be as defensible as any other.

But any one given arrangement will confer, or will appear to confer, advantages on one set of candidates seeking to become representatives, and corresponding disadvantages on another set. No system of distribution of constituencies is neutral in its effects. The question of selecting an appropriate division of represented among the representatives ceases immediately therefore to be one of random mathematical choice and becomes a hard practical political issue on the settling of which a great deal can depend. The how and why of apportioning representatives among constituents may be a difficult problem, but at any point of time there must exist at least some temporary solution to it. The problem is further complicated by the fact that the environment, the setting for these constituencies, is not static, but is subject to constant variation.

Within a democracy a great deal depends on the establishment of an equitable basis for representation, and a machinery for regularly adjusting it to this changing environment. Representative government implies, as a necessary condition for its continued existence, that there shall be some rational relationship between the represented and the representatives; rational, not only in a strict logical sense, but also in terms of democratic values. While the question is not a new one, it has today acquired a greater relative significance and urgency. Because the environment is changing more rapidly than ever before, the review machinery needs to be more elaborate, operating regularly, or automatically, and not only when mounting external pressure finally forces drastic and convulsive change. In a healthy democracy change is accomplished when necessary with minimal disruption, which would seem to mean that so long as the environment continues to change through population movements, varying social structures and major economic shifts, the parallel changes in the political structure must proceed as frequent small adjustments rather than as infrequent upheavals.

Then, too, the increasing role of government makes it essential that those who claim the authority to make decisions affecting the economic, social and, indeed, private life of every citizen, on the grounds that they are the chosen spokesmen for those citizens, should be required to justify that claim. They should be able to demonstrate that they are chosen through a machinery which ensures that they will be as genuinely representative as human ingenuity will allow.

The impact of the constituency structure on the balance of party power is one of the most effective measures of the adequacy of that structure. In a democracy there should be some form of direct relationship between majority popular opinion and the authority to make decisions. This need not be a direct one-to-one relationship and, indeed, the plurality voting system will so exaggerate the number of seats won by a party with a plurality of the popular vote that the relationship will more closely approximate a cubic function.[1]

However, a fairly minimal requirement of a truly representative system is that if Party A has more votes than Party B, then it should not normally have fewer seats than Party B. A corollary is that if any party has some more or less significant share of the popular vote it should also find meaningful representation in the legislature. Another requirement is that any significant swing in the popular vote should be reflected in a significant, but not necessarily exactly equal, swing in the number of seats held by the parties in the legislature. A final minimal requirement is that although the mathematics of vote-counting might give a majority party more than a proportionate share of the seats, the system ought not to be so structured that one specific party will be given a permanent advantage in the manner in which votes are translated into seats.

Where there are gross inequalities in the population of constituencies some, or all, of these requirements will not be met. Wherever it is found, and it is in fact found in most parts of Canada, that one party, can normally draw a greater share of the rural vote, and another has better-than-even support in the cities, then, obviously, rural overrepresentation gives a built-in advantage to the rural-based party. Conservatives in Great Britain, the Country Party in Australia, the National Party in New Zealand, the Republicans in the northern and midwestern states of the U.S.A., and the Progressive Conservatives in Canada, all expect more support from the rural areas and the small towns than do their opponents. Also, as each of these systems has, or has had until recently, a guaranteed rural overrepresentation, conservative interests in each case have had an automatic bias in their favour.

Perhaps as conclusive as any post-election analysis of votes, which may be confused by the multiplicity of influences at work, is each party's own perspective of the implications of redistribution schemes. The nature of any distribution system, and of its defenders and critics, can tell us much about the sources of strength of the various political forces. In Canada in 1964 most of the argument for greater latitude in the extent to which individual constituencies could vary from the average population, a latitude which would permit smaller rural and larger urban districts, came from the Progressive Conservative Party and the Ralliement Créditiste, which drew much of their strength from rural and small-town Canada, while the argument for narrower limits came from the Liberal Party, and, especially, the urban-based New Democratic Party. It is this alignment of proponents and opponents of special protection for rural interests (found also in almost identical form in Great Britain, Australia, and New Zealand) which provides the most convincing evidence of the partisan advantage of urban underrepresentation.

At this point we should note, however, that in the United States, and to a similar but lesser extent in Canada, the last decade or so has witnessed a decline in the population of the central city cores and an enormous growth in the surrounding suburban areas. This means that while the battle for redistribution has been fought largely in terms of an urban-rural rivalry, with the advocates citing evidence of the underrepresentation of urban interests and the opponents crying their fear of big-city dominance, in fact the "suburbs and, in the long run, only the suburbs will gain."[2] Far from being dominated by big-city interests, the new legislatures will see substantial increases in the representation of the suburbs which now sprawl across the counties around the old city boundaries.

## CRITERIA FOR CONSTITUENCIES

Generally one can recognize three broad classifications of constituencies — although too much significance should not be attached to the labels: the functional constituency, the community constituency, and the population constituency.

Of the three the least defensible in terms of democratic ideology and practice is the functional constituency. It is based on the proposition that the individual's most important political interests focus around his occupation or some other specialized group membership and it is as a member of an occupation or profession that the individual should be represented. The proposal is occasionally put forward, usually by members of small, highly organized professional groups such as bar associations, that voters should group themselves according to occupations, ignoring entirely their geographic places of residence, and that each occupation should elect its own representatives. Functional representation enhances the political role of professional and managerial associations, the only ones sufficiently small and tightly structured to profit from distinctive representation, and strengthens the oligarchic tendencies of these associations. The political voice of large mass-membership organizations is correspondingly weakened, while that of the unorganized is virtually silenced. It is thus essentially an anti-democratic device. Fortunately, functional representation has never seriously been considered in Canada, although it has had some influential advocates in Great Britain.[3]

The two most basic criteria for establishing constituencies are population, or numbers of people, on the one hand, and what might be variously termed geography, territory, or community on the other. There are many who will argue that the basic unit of representation should be the discreet geographic community recognized by law, or tradition, as having an independent entity irrespective of relative population, that it is the community as such which should have a voice in the legislature. The opposite approach, that constituencies should simply be composed of more or less equal numbers of people, can rarely be as strictly applied. For although it might be argued that geographic features, lines of communication, boundaries of subordinate political units, or community of interest must not be determining factors, they are never entirely irrelevant and, at very least, provide some administrative convenience.

The debate about the two concepts of representation has been a lengthy one, conducted at many levels. But although both sides have looked to history for authority and precedent, neither can *prove* its case from the historical evidence. There is no single true, valid tradition to be discovered from the perusal of old documents. Both traditions have solid historical antecedents; both have their roots far back in the past, although the weight of evidence is that time is on the side of representation of populations. Each extension of the franchise has been followed by a de-emphasizing of the role of the community and a stressing of the significance of numbers. Whatever may have been in the past, and whatever may be the merits of the change, we live today in an egalitarian democracy in which numbers, which can at least be counted and measured, are gaining influence over "other factors" which are often abstract, subjective, and unmeasurable.

In Britain, at the end of the 17th century it was still the community as such that was represented, but even then many were prepared to argue that movements of population ought to be taken into account in determining which communities should gain and which should lose representation. There is, for example, a striking passage in John Locke which in itself seems sufficient refutation to those critics who argue that equality of numbers has no part in the historical tradition of representation.

> Things of this world are in so constant a flux that nothing remains long in the same state. Thus people, riches, trade, power, change their stations; flourishing mighty cities come to ruin, and prove in time neglected desolate corners, whilst other unfrequented places grow into populous countries filled with wealth and inhabitants. But things not always changing equally, and private interests often keeping up customs and privileges when the reasons of them are ceased, it often comes to pass that in governments where part of the legislative consists of representatives chosen by the people, that in tract of time this representation becomes very unequal and disproportionate to the reasons it was at first established upon. To what gross absurdities the following of custom when reason has left it may lead, we may be satisfied when we see the bare name of a town, of which there remains not so much as the ruins, where scarce so much housing as a sheepcote, or more inhabitants than a shepherd is to be found, send as many representatives to the grand assembly of lawmakers as a whole county numerous in people and powerful in riches.[4]

The "gross absurdities" persisted unchanged for another century and a half, until the Reform Bill of 1832, a measure which was less significant for the changes it made than for the fact that it introduced the possibility of change into a system unchanged in many centuries, and whose main defense was that it had continued unchanged for many centuries. The Preamble to the Bill itself paid homage to the two concepts of representation: "It is expedient to take effectual Measures for correcting divers Abuses that have long prevailed in the Choice of Members to serve in the Commons' House of Parliament; to deprive many inconsiderable Places of the Right of returning Members; to grant such Privilege to large, populous and wealthy Towns. . . ."[5]

It was *places* that were to be deprived of the right to members, not units of population, and *towns* that were to be given this right, but the criterion for determining which places were to lose representation and which were to gain it was that of population. The place with too few people was to lose its franchise, the heavily populated towns were to gain theirs.

In British North America there was a similar awareness of the opposing bases of representation. For example, when, in 1872, the Canadian Parliament debated the first redistribution of seats since Confederation, the Prime Minister, Sir John A. Macdonald, recognized that population was a valid criterion in drafting constituency boundaries, although he chose to give it a subordinate role. Thus he stressed that while population was certainly to be considered there were also other factors which could not be ignored. In order to give proper representation to interests, classes and regions, "the principle of population should not be the only one" to be taken into account.[6]

A quarter of a century later, in 1899, Sir Wilfrid Laurier chose to ignore the dominant trend in Great Britain and reverted to the principle of constituencies based on communities — insofar as it can be argued that a county meets the tests of being a community. "We think," said Laurier, "it is a principle which will commend itself universally to public opinion, that the basis of representation in this House should be the municipal county organization."[7] In all further redistributions in Canada until 1966 "other factors" (principally the convenience of members and candidates) took precedence over the principle of population and there developed extreme inequalities between the largest and the smallest constituencies.

Even in the allocation of federal parliamentary seats among the several provinces the principle of population equality was sometimes subordinated to other interests. In the redistribution of 1952, for example, if population criteria had been uniformly applied, Saskatchewan's representation at Ottawa would have been reduced from twenty seats to fifteen. But of the twenty members from Saskatchewan, fourteen were Liberals and so the Liberal Prime Minister argued: "It is worthy for consideration, I think, to remember that although there has been a diminution in the number of people counted in Saskatchewan in the last census, there has been no diminution in the contribution of new wealth to the Canadian economy provided by the people of that province."[8] Special rules were devised to meet the situation, and Saskatchewan lost only three members.

The *Electoral Boundaries Readjustment Act* of 1964,[9] which provided the authority for the 1966 Canadian redistribution, did not disregard "community of interest" or other factors, but for the first time limited these through an approach to equality of population. It specified that no constituency could have a population which varied more than 25 percent above or below a quota, or average population for constituencies within any given province.

There were few, if any, who denied that the situation as it existed in March 1964 when the *Electoral Boundaries Readjustment Bill* was introduced was unsatisfactory. All members accepted that a structure of constituencies in which the population ranged from 12,479 in Îles-de-la-Madeleine to 267,252 in York-Scarborough, or which, even excluding the special cases of the Yukon and the Northwest Territories, permitted there to be twenty-five constituencies with a population of less than 40,000 and thirty-six constituencies with a population of over 100,000 (three of them over 200,000), was not defensible by any argument of theoretical principle or practical political necessity.[10]

At the same time, while there was general agreement that these grosser inequalities had to be elminated, there was even broader agreement that strict equality of population, however desirable in theory, was impossible to achieve in practice. The debate therefore centred around just how far, and for what reasons, one could tolerate, or even insist upon, a measure of inequality.[11]

## THE MEASUREMENT OF MALDISTRIBUTION

Phrased another way, the general acceptance that the structure of the constituencies as it stood in March 1964 was unsatisfactory meant agreement on the proposition that the constituencies were badly distributed. From this very general proposition a number of more specific questions arose: "How bad is bad? How is maldistribution to be measured? How do we compare one distribution scheme with another? How can we test the effectiveness of any reform proposals?" All these questions are related and all are reducible to the single question, which is that of establishing an acceptable measuring device for the level of maldistribution in any legislature.

Perhaps the commonest measure of all, and undoubtedly the least satisfactory, is that which simply compares the population of the largest district to that of the smallest, giving the extreme ranges within a given set of districts. The comparison between Iles-de-la-Madeleine and York-Scarborough made earlier is a measure of this kind. If it is expressed as a ratio (21.4: 1) it becomes a maximum population variance ratio, which sounds very technical, but actually tells us practically nothing unless we know further whether these extremes are isolated instances — special-case exceptions to a fairly normal distribution — or whether all districts are spread at more or less even intervals along a scale between the two extremes. It is misleading to draw too many conclusions from extreme cases without proper weighting for the number of instances that approach these extremes as against the number that conform more closely to some central point. The main attractions of the maximum population variance ratio are that it is simple to calculate, it is easily understood, and it makes good copy in arguments on the necessity for reform.

An improvement is the mean variance ratio, which is also commonly used, both to measure the extent of maldistribution and to establish a criterion for redistribution. The procedure for setting a criterion is to determine a "quota" or mean size for a constituency by dividing the total population by the total number of constituencies. Population in this sense may be any of several things: it may be exactly what it says, the total population; or it may be the voting-age population; or the population of eligible voters; or the population of registered voters. Any of these populations could be used. The only important points are that the universe be specified and that it be held consistent for any one set of calculations. The population of each district may then be compared with this mean or average district.

As a redistribution tool it may be required that no constituency may contain a population greater or less than a specified percentage of the mean. The *Electoral Boundaries Readjustment Act* thus provides that ". . . in no case . . . shall the population of any electoral district in the province . . . depart from the electoral quota for that province to a greater extent than twenty-five per cent more or twenty-five per cent less."[12]

However convenient these regulations may be in setting the terms of reference of bodies engaged in the readjustment of boundaries, the range of variation from the mean is in itself an inadequate measure of the actual distribution of population. It is possible for two countries with the same quota limitations to produce very different patterns of distribution. One of them might regard the mean as an ideal constituency to be approached as closely as possible in almost every case, with the outer limits to be a safeguard for those few exceptional cases where too strict an adherence to the mean would produce geographical absurdities. The other might regard the limits as discretionary variables to be used fully to perpetuate certain traditional patterns of inequality.

Australia falls into the first category. Although the *Commonwealth Electoral Act* allows a departure from the mean of plus or minus twenty percent[13], the redistribution following the 1955 census established only 8 out of 122 divisions which exceeded the mean by more than ten percent, and left more than ninety percent of the divisions within less than half the full limits of tolerance. This is achieved in a country in which the states vary enormously in population, area, and socio-economic background. The population of the smallest district in 1955 was some 30,500 and that of the largest was 46,500.

In Canada, by contrast, following the 1966 redistribution, less than half the constituencies were within ten percent of the mean, and nearly thirty percent exceeded it (plus or minus) by a margin of fifteen percent or more. Excluding the Yukon and the Northwest Territories, two of the remaining constituencies had populations of between twenty and twenty-five percent above the quota, and twenty-five were below it to a similar extent.

Table 3: 1 gives more complete details.[14]

## Table 3: 1
### DETAILS OF THE EXTENT TO WHICH CONSTITUENCIES ESTABLISHED IN 1966 VARIED FROM THE OFFICIAL QUOTA OF THEIR OWN PROVINCE

|  | No. | % |
|---|---|---|
| 20–25% above quota | 2 | 0.8 |
| 15–20%    ”      ” | 27 | 10.3 |
| 10–15%    ”      ” | 45 | 17.2 |
| 5–10%    ”      ” | 36 | 13.7 |
| 0– 5%    ”      ” | 23 | 8.8 |
| 0– 5% below quota | 39 | 14.9 |
| 5–10%    ”      ” | 28 | 10.7 |
| 10–15%    ”      ” | 16 | 6.1 |
| 15–20%    ”      ” | 21 | 8.0 |
| 20–25%    ”      ” | 25 | 9.5 |
| Summary |  |  |
| Number of constituencies within + or – 5% of quota | 62 | 23.7 |
| 10% | 126 | 48.1 |
| 15% | 187 | 71.4 |
| 20% | 235 | 89.7 |
| 25% | 262 | 100.0 |

(Totals and percentages do not include Yukon and Northwest Territories)

While it is true that a reasonably restrictive quota does limit the opportunities for excessive maldistribution, anything over about 15 percent still leaves room for considerable discretion. As a measure of maldistribution, mean variance limits are meaningless unless supplemented by information on the distribution of districts within the extreme limits.

Other measures have been devised from time to time[15] but the details of most do not need elaboration here. There is only one that deserves some closer attention, the so-called Dauer-Kelsay index.[16] The procedure, readily adaptable to any legislature, is to list all districts in rank order of their populations, from the smallest to the largest. If the legislature has multi-member districts, the number of representatives is listed beside the population of each, otherwise each entry would represent a single-member district. The median figure plus one for the number of representatives, that is, a majority of the legislature, is then determined, and the population of the minimum number of districts, counting from the smallest, necessary to elect the majority of the legislature is then computed and expressed as a percentage of the total population of all districts. This produces the theoretical minimum percentage of the population capable of electing a majority of the legislature.

The major criticism of the Dauer-Kelsay index is centred round the postulation of a minimum percentage of the population capable of exercising control. Two American critics, for example, wrote:

> Such an index . . . is so patently unrelated to the relevant political characteristics of both district populations and their representatives that we must consider what significance can be attached to the numbers that it produces, for any particular set of empirical data. The assumption (which necessarily underlies the Dauer-Kelsay index) that the representatives from the districts with the smallest populations — by no means necessarily rural districts — will frequently combine to vote in opposition to the remaining legislators who represent the districts with the larger populations is contradicted by all the recent empirical research in legislative voting behavior with which we are familiar.[17]

This criticism, of course, misses the whole point of the Dauer-Kelsay index which is intended to do no more than measure the disparity in population size between electoral districts. The index itself carries no implication that any group, be it a formal political party, or the collectivity of the most rural constituencies, gains any partisan advantage from the disparity. It is not, as Schubert and Press claim, a necessary assumption of the index that the smallest population districts should show any uniformity in voting behaviour. What the index does is to remove the emphasis from the extremes of the single smallest or largest district (which may be quite exceptional and justifiable special cases) and to place it on the whole set of the smaller half of the districts. The Dauer-Kelsay index demonstrates that a province in which one or two very small or very large constituencies were balanced by a majority closely approximating the norm would produce a less objectionable maldistribution than one in which there were no extreme cases but where the mean departure from the norm was significantly greater than in the first case. "The result is a reliable indicator of the general prevalence of inequalities in representation."[18]

The great advantage is the usefulness in comparative studies. The legislature in one province may be readily compared with others, and changes in the general representative character of a single legislature may be measured over a period of time.

The Dauer-Kelsay index also provides a useful tool to measure the over-all impact of redistribution. In the 1965 federal elections, for example, the constituencies were based on the 1952 redistribution. Leaving out the very special cases of the Yukon and the Northwest Territories, the Dauer-Kelsay index for a majority of the remaining 263 seats, calculated on the total population according to the 1961 census, was 34.3 percent, which means that the 132 least populated constituencies contained only 34.3 percent of the total population, while the 131 most heavily populated constituencies contained 68.6 percent of the population. By the time the 1966 census was taken, and immediately before the new redistribution, the index figure had declined to 31.4 percent. In the 1966 redistribution the Boundary Commissions were required to use the 1961 census figures and to work within specified tolerance limits (no constituency to exceed a provincial average figure by greater than or less than 25 percent). An application of the Dauer-Kelsay procedure to the new constituencies, and again excluding the Yukon and the Northwest Territories, produced an index figure of 44.3 percent, an index figure which dropped to 42.0 percent with the publication of the 1966 census. On either set of census data, therefore, the index shows a total "improvement" between the two redistributions of approximately 10 percentage points, which would seem to suggest that the 1966 redistribution, while significant and important, was less far-reaching and dramatic in its total effect than might be assumed from looking merely at extreme cases. The fact that 36 constituencies with populations of over 100,000 were broken up and a new maximum size of approximately 87,000 established, or that the number of constituencies with a population of under 40,000 was reduced from 27 to 6 very special cases[19] becomes less noteworthy in the context of the wide disparities still permitted.

Table 3: 2 compares the Dauer-Kelsay index values for each provincial legislature and for the House of Commons. Because it is not always possible to obtain total population figures for provincial electoral districts, the populations used throughout are the populations of registered electors. When estimates of population growth between the date of the 1966 census and the date of the most recent election were taken into account, a number of spot checks in situations where the information was available indicated that indices based on total population differed only very slightly from those based on registered voters, although in individual constituencies the variance was sometimes quite large.[20]

These figures show that while it is true that everywhere there exists a condition approaching that at "one man, one vote," it is not even approximately true that "one vote has one value." And, as shall be seen, it is commonly, but not exclusively, the urban interests which are underrepresented and the rural interests which are overrepresented. It is contended

Table 3: 2

## DAUER-KELSAY INDEX VALUES, BASED ON NUMBER OF REGISTERED VOTERS, AT RECENT FEDERAL OR PROVINCIAL ELECTIONS

| Election | No. of seats in the Legislature | Total number of registered voters | Minimum number of registered voters for 50% + 1 of seats | Dauer-Kelsay Index Value |
|---|---|---|---|---|
| Canada June 1968 | 262 (not including Yukon or NWT) | 10,839,522 | 4,370,284 | 40.4 |
| British Columbia Sept. 1966 | 55 | 873,927 | 346,903 | 39.7 |
| Alberta May 1967 | 65 | 795,034 | 233,732 | 29.4 |
| Saskatchewan Oct. 1967 | 59 | 549,256 | 211,022 | 38.4 |
| Manitoba June 1966 | 57 | 509,469 | 173,604 | 31.6 |
| Manitoba June 1969 | 57 | 522,032 | 228,971 | 43.9 |
| Ontario Oct. 1967 | 117 | 3,685,755 | 1,412,568 | 38.3 |
| Quebec June 1966 | 108 | 3,222,302 | 1,044,549 | 32.4 |
| New Brunswick Oct. 1967 | 58 | 314,996 | 123,733 | 39.3 |
| Nova Scotia May 1967 | 46 | 405,704 | 160,823 | 39.6 |
| Newfoundland Sept. 1966 | 42 | 239,616 | 90,119 | 37.6 |
| Prince Edward Island* | | | | |

* With only sixteen electoral districts, each returning one councillor and one Assemblyman, P.E.I. does not lend itself to this kind of calculation.

here that this unrepresentative character of our legislatures is the most serious defect in our total election system. Our legislators sometimes appear to be out of touch with the feelings and moods of their constituents because the majority of the legislators are chosen by a minority of the constituents, and that minority is largely a rural minority.

Thus, in the case of Alberta, where it may be noted that 33 of the 65 seats have less than 30 percent of the total registered voters, none of those 33 least populated constituencies are in the metropolitan areas of Calgary or Edmonton and Strathcona. Indeed, if all Alberta constituencies had had an equal number of registered electors in the 1967 election, these two metropolitan areas would have had 32 seats instead of their present 20.

## THE CASE FOR REDISTRIBUTION

While the actual measurement of maldistribution may be a complex, technical task which excites only a very few people and while there may be considerable disagreement about how equal constituency populations ought to be before any distribution scheme can be labelled "good," there were very few prepared to deny that by 1966 seats in the Canadian House of Commons were badly distributed. The same verdict could also have been passed on the structure of the provincial legislatures. The growth in population and its increasing urbanization had not been reflected in the restructuring of representative districts and had, indeed, simply exacerbated existing inequalities in distribution.

A Committee of the Alberta legislature, reporting in 1969, noted that no province "has adopted the principle of representation strictly by population, however, some Provinces have recognized the need to shift representation to reflect increased urbanization." As far as Alberta was concerned, the Committee noted "the marked shift in population distribution as between urban and rural areas of the Province and believes that a corresponding shift in representation is desirable. The Committee recognizes that in a Province such as Alberta which is characterized by large areas of sparsity of population there are limitations to the extent to which such a shift can properly be made."[21]

It is at this stage that the earlier discussion on philosophies of representation, on representation of communities *versus* representation of populations, ceases to be a purely academic point and becomes a matter of practical politics. The real problem is that of adapting legislative assemblies, established in a rural age, to the needs of an increasingly urban-industrial society. This is what lies at the core of the many debates on individual redistribution plans.

At various times when the question of redistribution has been raised in the House of Commons two major principles have been put forward as counters to the argument for a strict representation by population. Professor Dawson has summarized these:

> First, municipal and county boundaries should be followed when at all possible. It is considered wiser to over- or under-represent an area than to dismember districts which have established traditions, long history, and strong local pride and character. Secondly, rural areas should be more generously represented than urban, that is, the population of the rural constituencies should be definitely less than that of city constituencies.[22]

There is some administrative convenience in associating parliamentary constituency boundaries with county or municipal boundaries, although as the county or municipal government's main political contacts are likely to be with the provincial administration, it is an association of greater relevance to the provincial arena than to the federal. In part, however, the case is one of tradition.

> The federal riding and the county have been parallel in the past and ought, therefore, to remain parallel. Because redistribution in Canada is an infrequent process and because in the past it has been performed by politicians without any coherent philosophy other than that of causing as little upset as possible to government party politicians, the idea of preserving historic boundaries has acquired conventional authority.[23]

When the *Electoral Boundaries Readjustment Bill* was introduced in the House of Commons it was proposed that there be a tolerance of 20 percent above or below the quota within each province. The government made it clear that, while this was the lowest tolerance that would be acceptable, it would not resist if the House wished to raise the limits slightly and, indeed, the quota was eventually raised to 25 percent at which level it has remained.

> Whatever the basis of argument it was soon apparent that the great majority of those favouring a wide tolerance were those representing, or speaking on behalf of, rural constituencies and those who wished to narrow the limits were those from the urban areas. Here, undoubtedly, was the most significant variation of opinion, with the argument for or against the proposition that for some special reason or another the rural constituencies ought to have a lower population than the urban.[24]

The disproportionate weighting of urban and rural populations is a well-established convention of Canadian political life, at the provincial as well as at the federal level. While some Members of Parliament may decry it, most seem to accept it as part of the unchangeable order of things.

One line of defense in the protection of the overrepresentation of rural constituencies has been to stress the problems of accessibility, transport, and communications as obstacles to both effective representation and ease of campaigning. It was a recurrent theme in the parliamentary debate on the report of Canada's first independent Boundary Commissioners.[25]

This proposition that rural areas deserve special consideration because their populations are more dispersed has not gone unchallenged. Principally the objection takes the form of the argument that while there may have been some justification for special allowances for scattered rural areas in the past, the modern revolutions in transport and communications have weakened the argument. Thus, in Manitoba, where the task of redistribution is now undertaken by an independent Electoral Divisions Boundaries Commission, this was recognized when it was accepted that Greater Winnipeg would have to have more members:

> Consequently both the area and population of many rural electoral divisions in southern Manitoba are significantly increased. However, good roads and modern means of transportation and communication make it possible for candidates for election and members of the Legislative Assembly to keep in touch with and serve a wider area and more people than was the case in earlier days.[26]

Further, it is asserted that although the big-city representative may be able to travel across his district in a few minutes by car, he is no closer to his constituents than the rural representatives whose constituents may be many miles apart. There can be few groups among whom it is harder to establish contact, or a sense of community cohesion, than the shifting populations of anonymous thousands who pack the city's apartment blocks and tenements. This is especially true in the newer high-rise apartments where elaborate precautions are taken to isolate each person from his neighbours and from external instrusions on his privacy.

The argument has also been put forward that a rural member has greater responsibilities than a city representative. Because people in a rural riding often call upon their member for services which in a city would be provided by a government office, the rural member is "called upon to give more service per capita to his constituents than is a member representing an urban riding."[27]

These arguments are all founded on the proposition that constituencies are created largely for the convenience of those who must campaign in them. Certainly practical considerations of ease of transport and the responsibilities of members are relevant and ought to be taken into account, but none of those who have advanced these arguments has established any theoretical justification for placing the convenience of the politicians ahead of the equal rights of the electors. Constituencies are, after all, drawn as units of representation and not as units of party organization, and they exist for the satisfaction of the represented, not for the convenience of the representatives.

What is involved in the satisfaction of the represented is, of course, a difficult question. "While it is true that it is individuals rather than groups which are represented, the electoral machinery requires that individuals shall be grouped. This leads to the question: what groups or kinds of groups are significant for purposes of representation?"[28] Yet, although the answer to this is generally given in terms of community of interest, little attention is paid to what exactly constitutes a community of interest. Despite this vagueness, the defense of rural overrepresentation has been founded on the philosophy of representation of communities and not mere numbers of peoples. But the only communities for which this claim is ever seriously advanced are the rather amorphous and unconsolidated communities of those who happen to live on farms or in small towns. It is never applied to the ethnic, racial, religious, or economic communities which are to be found in the big cities. Indeed, if anything is clear it is that a federal constituency, however large or however small, does not meet any of the sociological criteria of a community. The county, for example, which is often cited as the logical foundation of the constituency, is an arbitrarily defined administrative unit which neither presupposes nor establishes any community of interest among those who live within its borders.

In 1966 there was established in British Columbia a Commission of Inquiry into the Redefinition of Electoral Districts which conducted a thorough and detailed inquiry, not merely into the specific details of redistribution proposals, but into public attitudes towards representation and the drawing of constituency boundaries. Its *Report*, unfortunately largely ignored by the British Columbia legislature, is one of the most complete documents of its kind yet published in Canada.

The Commissioners noted, first of all, "the ardent desire of some districts with small populations to preserve their historic identity,"[29] and saw this as a case of rural fear of dominance by the big city. This has also been a constant theme in the recent debates over reapportionment in the United States, where much of the opposition to increased representation to the cities was expressed in terms which echoed Thomas Jefferson: "Those who labor in the earth are the chosen people of God, if ever He had a chosen people, whose breasts He has made His peculiar deposit for substantial and genuine virtue. . . . The mobs of the great cities add just so much to the support of pure government, as sores do to the strength of the human body."[30] These sentiments, although of course entirely unfounded on evidence, are still very much part of rural mythology in Canada as well as the United States. The British Columbia commissioners were astonished to note that in the northern half of the province and in the Kootenays an "extraordinary belief seemed to exist that the people of the Lower Mainland were economic parasites, producing little wealth themselves, and intent on exploiting the people who live in the under-developed areas."[31]

It seemed clear to the commissioners that the concept of representation by population, of electoral districts with nearly equal populations, was neither widely understood nor appreciated. More importance was attached to the idea of representation as being the "advocacy of local interests" in which the prime responsibility of the member was to "service the district." There appeared to be a widespread opinion that "even in the Lower Mainland and Vancouver there was no popular demand for representation by population but merely an artificial campaign by Vancouver newspapers."[32]

The Commission itself did not share this attitude and, within the limits of its terms of reference, was clearly committed to the notion of "one vote, one value." "It must be constantly borne in mind," wrote the commissioners, "that the basic principle in a modern democracy is that every voter should have an equal share of political power and that, therefore, he should have a vote equal in value to every other vote. It follows that, unless some other considerations require some deviation from the principle of democracy, every Electoral District should comprise the same number of voters per member of the Legislative Assembly,"[33] although, of course, exact mathematical precision was neither possible, nor sought.

While they found that "lip-service" was paid to this concept of democracy, the commissioners discovered that it did not really correspond to the actual view taken by the majority of people. Again and again the member of the legislature was described as an "agent" for the people of his district. Thus, in the under-populated electoral districts people apparently feared that if the district were enlarged they would no longer have a spokesman for their particular interests. "No apology whatever was made for claiming an excessive share of political power in order to have this special representation by a devoted advocate."[34] Those in the most heavily populated districts seemed more concerned with retaining a single voice for the entire district than with the "sacrifice of voting power that was involved."

Taking all these considerations into account the commissioners then listed all those claims which, it is held, modify the principle of equal populations in electoral districts. These were the usual ones of geography, ease of transport and communication, preserving intact municipal and other local government units, special consideration for under-developed areas, and the necessity of urban districts being numerically larger than rural. "Every one of these claims calls for judgment as to how far it should prevail if it is in competition with other claims or with the dominant democratic principle of equality. Within limits each type of claim is valid but the Commission considers that the proper limits are much narrower than those that have usually been claimed."[35]

In 1963 a majority (27) of the 52 members of the British Columbia Legislature represented districts containing only 235,429 of 873,140 registered voters in the province — giving a Dauer-Kelsay index of 27.0. The Commission recommended a new structure of districts which, if it had been adopted in full, would have raised this index value to 43.2, the highest in Canada (until Manitoba in 1969). The government of British

Columbia took into account some of the recommendations, but chose to disregard or modify others. The result was that the redistribution did bring about a vast improvement in the representative character of the legislature — in 1966 it took 39.6 percent of the registered electors to account for the majority of legislators, but this figure still fell considerably short of the Commission's recommendations.

## THE MACHINERY OF REDISTRIBUTION

The situation in British Columbia, as described above, in which a Comission worked to produce a set of recommendations which could be accepted or rejected at the discretion of the legislature, which means in effect at the discretion of the government, raises the whole question of how distribution schemes are to be carried out. A quotation from an American source might be a useful introductory text for the topic: "Revising an outmoded pattern of representation is, to be sure, a difficult act for a legislative body, each of whose members has a vested interest in the *status quo*."[36]

Patterns of legislative distribution, even if initially satisfying the most demanding requirements of compactness, contiguity, and equality of population, eventually become outdated. Recognition of the need for periodic readjustment of electoral division boundaries introduces two closely related questions: "Who shall be responsible for drafting the new boundaries?" and "What criteria will guide them?" These are questions so closely related that they must be considered together. Indeed, the nature of the body charged with redrawing boundaries will, to a very large extent, limit the criteria it will use. A very broad generalization which retains some validity despite many individual exceptions is that the greater the degree to which the legislature itself is directly involved in redistribution the more flexible will be the criteria it adopts.

Norman Ward, for example, noted that in Canada before the first independent Boundary Commissions were set up in 1964, and while Parliament itself still assumed direct responsibility for the redistribution of federal seats, there were in effect no rules at all. The process was a "freelance operation in which any rational boundary drawing was likely to be the result of coincidence or accident."[37] Although even here there were often exceptions, the only general rule followed with any consistency was that which made urban constituencies more populous than rural.

Wherever and whenever the legislature assumes full responsibility for redistribution, either directly or through a legislative committee dominated by the government party, it can be shown that the first and overriding criterion will be that of causing as little inconvenience as possible to sitting members, and especially those of the governing party.

In the United States, where most states have a legal requirement that the legislator must reside in the district he represents, a change of boundaries can mean the loss of a seat. Because the American state legislator is so closely tied to his constituency his determination to retain control over the process of redistribution, and his general coolness or even aversion to independent boundary commissions becomes a matter of practical political self-defense.

In Great Britain, on the other hand, where permanent residence in the constituency is not demanded of the member, either by law or any strong custom, and where it is, at best, no more than an additional advantage in campaigning, loss of a constituency through redistribution is often an inconvenience, but it is seldom much more than that. The British Member of Parliament does not feel he is committing political suicide when he entrusts the task of redistribution to an outside independent body.

In Canada there is, as in Britain, no legal requirement of residence in the district,[38] but a long-established custom which, with some frequent exceptions, has almost the same degree of binding force as American law, ties most members to their home districts. The number of exceptions appears, on closer examination, to be a great deal higher than popular mythology would have suggested. In the Ontario elections of 1967, for example, with all three parties contesting 117 seats, there were 19 New Democratic Party candidates, 8 Liberals, and 4 Progressive Conservatives who had never lived in the districts in which they were seeking election. Nevertheless, the custom is still strong, and it took many years, indeed until 1964, before the House of Commons was prepared to entrust the responsibility of redistribution to a set of boundary commissions.

A number of informal "rules" have been devised to explain redistribution by legislatures.[39] Rule one is: "Save the incumbents," a rule which, in Canadian experience, has applied principally to party leaders. Before 1964 it appeared that the House of Commons was guided by the doctrine that the constituencies of party leaders, opposition as well as government, were not to be tampered with. It is a doctrine which is sometimes disregarded. Again we may note the more flexible practice of British countries (including Canada) as compared with the United States when a member loses his seat, for any reason, and must find another. There is thus the fairly recent instance where T. C. Douglas, leader of the New Democratic Party, who was defeated in his home riding of Regina City, Saskatchewan, in the 1962 federal elections, and then successfully contested a by-election in October of that same year in Burnaby-Coquitlam, British Columbia. Defeated again in the new riding of Burnaby-Seymour in the 1968 general elections, Mr. Douglas returned to the House of Commons in February 1969 after winning a by-election which made him the new member for Nanaimo-Cowichan-The Islands.

A second "rule" applied when legislators redistribute their own districts is "cut the retirees," *i.e.* if the number of districts is to be reduced, or if some districts in some parts of the area are to be amalgamated, then as far as possible eliminate the constituencies of members who are going to retire anyway. Professor Ward's paper on the Canadian redistribution of 1952 has a brilliantly succinct account of the application of this rule. The number of seats from Nova Scotia in the House of Commons was to be reduced from thirteen to twelve and "a sacrificial lamb was found in an ailing Liberal who had not been around the House of Commons for some time. Amid loud tributes to his distinguished record as a public man, and expressions of best wishes for his speedy recovery, he was subjected to one further operation."[40]

Rule three might be stated as "cut the minority party" and is so obvious that it requires no illustration. More will be said on the reduction of opposition strength when the topic of gerrymandering is taken up in closer detail.

A fourth "rule" is that if there is pressure strong enough to demand increased representation for heavily populated areas, it is better to increase the size of the House rather than to cut the representation of rural areas. In Ontario, for example, pressure for increased urban representation at the expense of rural districts has been resisted by the rural areas from which the governing Progressive Conservative party draws its greatest strength. The obvious solution has been to leave the rural areas alone as far as this is possible and to grant relief to the cities by increasing the size of the legislature, which in three elections in 1959, 1963, and 1967 has grown from 98 to 108 to 117 members. The present figure of 117 was arrived at when the Boundary Commission requested a group of architects to determine the maximum seating capacity of the existing legislative chamber. In 1965 Quebec also increased the membership of its legislature from 95 to 108, largely to accommodate new constituencies in Montreal. Indeed over the past forty years every provincial legislature has experienced some increase in membership.

The development of redistribution machinery at the federal level in Canada has been thoroughly documented by Professor Ward[41], and the historical details do not need to be repeated here. All redistributions prior to 1966 were carried out on an *ad hoc* basis, normally in great haste, with partisan motives dominating all other considerations, a procedure which, in Ward's phrase, "revealed the Commons at its worst."

The *British North America Act* contains the provision that the readjustment of representation shall be "by such authority, in such manner, and from such time as the Parliament of Canada from time to time provides. . . ."[42] This clause has generally been interpreted as giving Parliament full authority to readjust federal electoral boundaries as it sees fit — an interpretation which has never been challenged. Until 1966 it was Parliament itself which, either directly or indirectly, carried out each redistribution, and it was Parliament which, in 1964, established and set out the terms of reference of the independent Boundary Commissions which prepared the 1966 redistribution.

The concept of redistribution by non-parliamentary agencies is not new to Canadian political thinking, although it took a hundred years after Confederation to make a reality of the concept. The first draft of the *British North America Act* provided for readjustment by "an independent authority,"[43] and although the principle was dropped from the final version, it has been frequently revived and has always had its proponents.

In 1962 the Prime Minister, the Rt. Hon. John Diefenbaker, moved a resolution for the setting up of an electoral boundaries commission. The resolution passed, but the Parliament of 1962 was dissolved before action could proceed beyond the first reading.

The initiative then passed to the Liberal government and in March 1964 the *Electoral Boundaries Readjustment Bill* was introduced. This was a step of major political importance which not only made provision for the first redistribution of Canadian federal constituencies since 1952, but provided that, for the first time, this task of redistribution would be taken out of the hands of Parliament and entrusted to independent representation commissions. It also, again for the first time, specified certain rules and criteria to be applied in the process of redistribution. The various clauses of the Bill aroused a great deal of controversy with the debate being suspended for weeks at a time and it was not until November 1964 that it received a third reading.

In its final form the *Act* provided that there should be ten Electoral Boundaries Commissions (one for each province) to be appointed following each decennial census. Each Commission was to consist of four members: a chairman appointed by the Chief Justice of the Province from "among the judges of the court over which he presides," with provision for alternative arrangements if necessary; two members to be appointed by the Speaker of the House of Commons "from among such persons resident in the province as he deems suitable"; and the federal Representation Commissioner (a new office created in 1964) who was to be a member of all Commissions.[44] The insistence on involving a judge in the redistribution procedure is peculiarly Canadian and it seems rather difficult to understand the rationale for it. By contrast it is worth noting the composition of the New Zealand Commission. There are four *ex officio* members: the Surveyor-General, who has general knowledge and expertise on the technicalities of map-making and the proper recording of topographical features; the Government Statistician, who is responsible for the preparation of the census and for the projection of population trends; the Director-General of the Post and Telegraph Department, who is responsible for facilities of communication, existing and planned; and the Chief Electoral Officer, responsible for the registration of electors and the conduct of elections. There are, in addition, two unofficial members, who must be neither Members of Parliament nor civil servants, who are nominated by the two parties in Parliament, and who are chosen for their knowledge of party organization and of the practical difficulties of campaigning and representation. There is, finally, a chairman, chosen by the other six, who is appointed to form these six into a competent working group. This would seem to be an almost ideal combination which, with some variations, could be adapted to the Canadian scene.

The ten Canadian Commissions commenced work in January, 1965, and each was required by the *Act* to hold at least one public meeting after publication of a preliminary report. Representations made at these public meetings were to be considered by the Commission and dealt with as they saw fit. The criteria were set out principally in section 13 which required, first of all, that a quota be obtained for each province by dividing the total population of the province by the number of members assigned to the province. The population figures were to be those reported in the 1961 census. It should be noted, too, that the basis was to be total population, and not adult population, or eligible voter population, or anything else. They were then to proceed on the basis "that the population of each electoral district in the province . . . shall correspond as nearly as may be to the electoral quota for the province." But a commission could depart from a "strict application" of this rule where:

(i) special geographic considerations, including in particular the sparsity, density or relative rate of growth of population of various regions of the province, the accessibility of such regions or the size or shape thereof, appear to the commission to render such a departure necessary or desirable, or (ii) any special community or diversity of interests of the inhabitants of various regions of the province appears to the commission to render such a departure necessary or desirable.

This, however, did not give any commission unqualified discretion. Except in the case of a two-member constituency, the commission could not propose an electoral district in which the population departed from "the electoral quota for that province to a greater extent than twenty-five per cent more or twenty-five per cent less."

An important point in the legislation concerned the authority of Parliament over the Commissions' recommendations. Each Commission had a maximum period of one year to complete its report and preliminary maps. These were to be transmitted by the Representation Commissioner to the House of Commons through the Speaker. The House was given thirty days (later amended to forty-five sitting days) to object to any proposals. The

Commissions were given final authority to dispose of these objections as they saw fit and once their final reports were presented to the Speaker, the House could take no further action. That the new Commissions were, indeed, genuinely independent is evidenced by the fact that although there were many strongly worded objections to details of the preliminary reports, made by members of all parties,[45] in their final reports the Commissions made no changes to the preliminary reports of Alberta, New Brunswick, Nova Scotia, Prince Edward Island, and Saskatchewan, and only relatively minor changes to the preliminary reports for the remaining five provinces. Final reports were tabled in the House of Commons in June 1966 and the new districts came into effect for the elections of June 1968.

The *Act* contains one further provision which hopefully will avoid a repetition of the long, often acrimonious, debate on the establishing of the Electoral Boundaries Commissions. It is provided that the machinery established should be permanent and that automatically, within sixty days of each decennial census report, new Boundary Commissions will be established in each province.

Canada and Australia, both federal countries, have found very similar compromises between overcentralized control and state autonomy in the redistribution of federal seats. This is ignoring for the moment the problem of the allocation of the appropriate number of seats to each province, a question which will be taken up again shortly. In both countries much of the responsibility for the actual drawing of constituency boundaries is entrusted to the residents of the state or province who have local knowledge, but they are appointed under the authority of federal legislation, operate under terms of reference laid down by Parliament, and report finally to Parliament. Both countries have rejected the proposition that the drafting of federal legislative districts might be entrusted to state or provincial legislatures. The unhappy experience of the United States with state legislative control over Congressional districting, indicates the wisdom of this decision.

While the Boundary Commissions were enjoined to make the population of each electoral district "correspond as nearly as may be" to the mean, or quota, for the province, and while they did so much to remedy the serious underrepresentation of the urban areas, at the price of sacrificing some rural seats, it is quite clear that they were not prepared, or able, to carry this approach to its logical conclusions. The tolerance limits of plus or minus 25 per cent from the quota were used largely to soften the blow for the rural regions, to protect them from losing as many seats as they might properly have done, and to give to the expanding metropolitan areas no more than was strictly necessary. The consequence is that the redistribution which must follow the 1971 census must again produce a major upheaval in constituency boundaries. Logic, but not perhaps political expediency, would have suggested that the lower limits should have been applied to the rapidly expanding suburban districts surrounding the large cities and the upper limits to those rural areas where the population is declining. Given the extraordinary unbalance of rural and urban districts before the commissioners started work, such drastic surgery was a practical impossibility and again the cities were left with the largest populations and the farmlands with the smallest.

The original redistribution was based on the population figures for the 1961 census. The new districts applied for the first time in the elections of 1968, by which time the census figures for 1966 showed that a great many of them were already out of date. When the 1966 census figures are applied to the present electoral districts it is shown that by 1966 there were twenty-two districts with populations above the quota greater than the permissible margin of 25 percent and a further nineteen which were more than 25 percent below their provincial quotas. Table 3: 3 gives an analysis of the present constituencies in terms of the 1966 census as compared with the 1961 census.

Table 3: 4 gives a further breakdown of the redistribution of 1966 according to the 1966 census figures. It demonstrates that the constraint imposed on the Electoral Boundaries Commissioners, requiring them in 1966 to

### Table 3: 3
### AN ANALYSIS OF THE DISTRIBUTION OF POPULATION IN THE FEDERAL CONSTITUENCIES (EXCLUDING THE YUKON AND THE NORTHWEST TERRITORIES) ACCORDING TO THE 1961 AND 1966 CENSUS FIGURES

| Constituencies | 1966 redistribution according to 1961 census | | 1966 redistribution according to 1966 census | |
|---|---|---|---|---|
| | No. | % | No. | % |
| more than 25% above quota | — | — | 22 | 8.4 |
| 20–25% above quota | 2 | 0.8 | 17 | 6.5 |
| 15–20%   "      " | 27 | 10.3 | 20 | 7.6 |
| 10–15%   "      " | 45 | 17.2 | 12 | 4.6 |
| 5–10%   "      " | 36 | 13.7 | 16 | 6.1 |
| 0– 5%   "      " | 23 | 8.8 | 36 | 13.7 |
| 0– 5% below quota | 39 | 14.9 | 38 | 14.5 |
| 5–10%   "      " | 28 | 10.7 | 21 | 8.0 |
| 10–15%   "      " | 16 | 6.1 | 23 | 8.8 |
| 15–20%   "      " | 21 | 8.0 | 24 | 9.2 |
| 20–25%   "      " | 25 | 9.5 | 14 | 5.3 |
| more than 25% below quota | — | — | 19 | 7.3 |
| | 262 | 100.0 | 262 | 100.0 |

**Table 3: 4**

**THE RURAL-URBAN CHARACTER OF THE 1966 CONSTITUENCIES (ACCORDING TO THE 1966 CENSUS FIGURES) SHOWING THE EXTENT TO WHICH THEY ARE ABOVE OR BELOW PROVINCIAL AVERAGES, OR QUOTAS.**

| Urban-Rural Ratios (% of registered voters in urban and rural polling subdivisions) | No. of const-ituencies | Total population of constituency as a percentage of provincial average | | | |
|---|---|---|---|---|---|
| | | below 75% (below legal limits) | 75%–100% | 100%–125% | over 125% (above legal limits) |
| 100% urban | 85 | — | 19 | 50 | 16 |
| 50%–99% urban | 64 | 2 | 25 | 31 | 6 |
| 50%–99% rural | 94 | 12 | 62 | 20 | — |
| 100% rural | 19 | 5 | 14 | — | — |
| Totals | 262* | 19 | 120 | 101 | 22 |

\* excluding Yukon and Northwest Territories

work with 1961 census figures, meant that they were unable to give full recognition to the changes in population between the census dates. By the time of the 1968 elections the new boundaries were already largely out-of-date. But, as Table 3: 4 shows, it was principally the urban areas which suffered and were once again underrepresented and the rural areas which were overrepresented.

The figures used in the Table are not exactly analagous. The population figures as related to the provincial quotas are those of total population according to the 1966 census. It is necessary to use this figure because it is the one mentioned in the *Act* and it is the one on which quotas are based.

The urban-rural ratios, however, have been calculated on the basis of the number of registered voters in urban and rural polling subdivisions within each electoral district as shown in the report of the Chief Electoral Officer for the June 1968 elections. These will, of course, differ in total from population figures, but it is assumed that the percentage ratios will be basically the same. Total population figures for urban and rural polling subdivisions are not available.

## REDISTRIBUTION PROCEDURES IN THE PROVINCES

Manitoba became the first province to establish an independent agency responsible for the drafting of the boundaries of electoral districts when, in March 1957, royal assent was given to the *Electoral Divisions Act*.[46] The

*Act* provided that there would be a three-man Electoral Divisions Boundaries Commission consisting of the Chief Justice of Manitoba, the President of the University of Manitoba, and the provincial Chief Electoral Officer.[47] The Commission was to draw up its recommendations and report them to the Lieutenant-Governor who would transmit the Report to the legislature. Final authority rested with the legislature which would formalize the boundaries by an Act of the Legislature after considering the Commission's report.[48]

The 1957 *Act*, which has subsequently been amended, established the criteria to be followed by the Commission. First of all (in section 10) it divided the province into urban and rural electoral districts. The urban districts, precisely defined in the *Act*, consisted principally of Brandon and of Metropolitan Winnipeg. Two separate quotas were then set up: one for the urban districts and one for the rural districts, on a formula designed to ensure that rural areas would be considerably more heavily represented than urban. All rural districts were to be as nearly equal in population as possible, and so were all urban districts, but, "for every four persons of the population included in each rural electoral division there shall be seven persons in the population included in each urban electoral division."[49]

The first redistribution by Commission in 1957 resulted in there being 36 rural divisions with an average population of 11,512 (with a very narrow range of from 10,851 in Churchill to 12,133 in Hamiota) and 21 urban divisions with an average population of 20,405. Here, the smallest was St. James (19,248) and the largest was Brandon (24,572). When it is remembered that the *Act* enjoined the Commissioners to take into consideration the usual factors of community or diversity of interest, the means of communication, the physical features of the area, "all other similar and relevant factors" and, as far as possible, to keep the boundaries of municipalities intact, they were remarkably successful, within the constraints of the two distinct quotas, in producing equality of representation. Their success suggests that the criteria are not as inhibiting as is sometimes proclaimed.

In 1968 an amendment to the *Electoral Divisions Act*[50] abolished the formal distinction between urban and rural districts as defined in 1957 and also abolished the two separate quotas.

The amendment substituted a new formula which in principle is very similar to that of the federal *Electoral Boundaries Readjustment Act* of 1964. The relevant section reads:

> In determining the area to be included in, and in fixing the boundaries of, any electoral division, the commission shall consider
>
> (a) special geographic conditions, including the sparsity, density, and relative growth of population of a region of the province, the accessibility of a region of the province, and the size or shape of a region of the province; and

(b) any special diversity or community of interests of the inhabitants of a region of the province; and shall allow a variation in the population requirement of any electoral division where, in its opinion, those considerations, or any of them, render a variation desirable; but in no case shall the population of any electoral division in the province as a result thereof vary from the quotient obtained (by dividing the population of the province by 57) . . . to a greater extent than twenty-five per cent more or twenty-five per cent less.[51]

On this basis the Commission proceeded to a new redistribution in 1968, and although the formal distinction between rural and urban constituencies was no longer to be applied, the Commission still did not choose to ignore the old distinctions altogether. The members reported that in their view

the rule as to the density and sparsity of population indicated that the population of the electoral divisions in the Metropolitan Corporation of Greater Winnipeg should be substantially greater than that of rural divisions in southern Manitoba, and that in the far northern areas of the province the population of electoral divisions should be close to the permissible minimum, with a somewhat larger number where a large town is included within such an electoral division.[52]

The criteria in section 11 of the *Act* meant that using the 1966 census figures, the smallest district would have a population of 12,672 and the largest a population of 21,120. On this basis they recommended that there be 28 constituencies for the rural sections of the province, with populations ranging from 12,715 to 16,461, and 29 for Brandon and Metropolitan Winnipeg, with populations ranging from 16,396 to 20,485. The increase in the number of Winnipeg seats from 20 to 27 and the corresponding reduction in the number of seats from rural Manitoba, on the one hand, and the "surprise" victory of the New Democratic Party in the 1969 elections, on the other, are, of course, not unconnected.

In Ontario an independent boundary commission was appointed in 1962 to inquire into the redistribution of provincial electoral districts.[53] The Commission was not constrained by any particular formula, nor was it specifically enjoined to produce districts of approximately equal populations. All that was required of it was that it should give consideration to:

(1) the concentration of population in various areas of the Province as indicated by the 1961 Federal census;
(2) the varying conditions and requirements regarding representation as between rural and urban electoral districts;
(3) the existing and traditional boundaries of the electoral districts of the Province;
(4) the community or diversity of interests of the population of such districts;

(5) the means of communication between various parts of such districts, together with the physical features thereof;

(6) all other related and relevant factors, and, with particular reference to rural electoral districts shall, as far as practicable, include the whole of any one municipality in one electoral district.[54]

In its preliminary report, which was confined to those parts of Metropolitan Toronto outside the limits of the City of Toronto, in other words, the suburban sprawl, the Commission set out its own criteria. These were not required by the terms of reference, but they were certainly not contrary to the letter or spirit of those terms. The Commission turned directly to the question of the proper relationship between rural constituencies, urban constituencies, and constituencies which were partly rural and partly urban. "We have proceeded on the basis that a reasonable relationship of population for such classes of constituencies would as far as is feasible be as follows: for urban constituencies a population of 60,000-75,000, for rural constituencies a population of 25,000-50,000, and for urban-rural constituencies a population of 50,000-60,000."[55]

The preliminary report was followed early in 1965 by a report for the remaining parts of the province. In this report the commissioners stated the population (according to the 1961 census) of each of their proposed new districts. But, although they based their operation on the pattern described above, they used neither the lower nor the upper limits. The smallest of the new districts, Thunder Bay, had a population of 32,728, and the largest, Brantford, 67,416.[56]

The *Reports* provoked considerable dissension and discussion and in April, 1965 the Ontario Legislative Assembly referred them back to the Commission in order that it might "give consideration to submissions relating to electoral district boundaries made by interested persons or to be made by such persons during such period as the Commission may prescribe." On this basis the Commission proposed a number of fairly substantial changes to its original recommendations, but did not alter the number of seats to be allocated to Metropolitan Toronto, the City of Toronto, or the rest of the province.[57]

Despite the numerous changes, there were a great many individual constituencies, including some of the smallest as well as some of the largest, where the recommendations in the preliminary report were accepted unaltered in the final report. A comparison of the two sets of recommendations did not show up any obvious patterns in the changes and there appears to be nothing to indicate that any party gained anything other than accidental or coincidental advantage from the revised report.

The amended report was accepted by the Legislature and, with only a few minor amendments, was passed into law, becoming effective for the 1967 provincial elections.[58] It seems safe to assume that this pattern of redistribution: initial proposals by an independent body working within a general framework acceptable to the Government, the opportunity for interested parties to examine the initial proposals and to submit briefs for their revision, a final report, and formal action by the legislature closely following the recommendations in the independent reports but allowing some opportunity for amendment of minor details; will continue to be the basic pattern in Ontario for some time. It is a generally successful procedure.

A good deal of attention has already been given to the recommendations of the British Columbia Commission of Inquiry into the Redefinition of Electoral Boundaries. This Commission was set up by Order-in-Council in August, 1965. The terms of reference were quite straightforward. The Commission was charged with the responsibility for making recommendations redefining electoral districts to secure "proper and effective representation of the people of all parts of the Province," and in arriving at their recommendations they were to take into account, "where feasible," historical and regional claims for representation. Certain formal restraints were imposed. The Commission was not to recommend any district which would comprise "fewer than 7,500 registered voters having regard to present population and apparent population trends to the year 1975," and they were to recommend a Legislative Assembly of not fewer than 48 nor more than 52 members.[59]

On this basis the Commission proceeded with its inquiry and submitted its report to the Lieutenant-Governor of the Province in January 1966. Unfortunately the Government which appointed this Commission virtually ignored its recommendations, including those set out in the Commission's Terms of Reference. The 1966 redistribution was, in effect, a Government decision. Thus, although the Commission was instructed to recommend no district with fewer than 7,500 registered voters, the final distribution scheme adopted by the Government included five such districts, two of them with fewer than 5,000 registered voters. Again, the Government's plan produced a Legislative Assembly of fifty-five members, although the Commission was required to recommend no more than fifty-two. One is left with the conclusion that the British Columbia Government would like to have the provincial electoral boundaries defined by an independent commission, because this is a very democratic thing to do, but at the same time it was not prepared to risk the possible political consequences of actually accepting the recommendations of such a commission.

The only other province to consider seriously redistribution by an independent body is Alberta which appointed an Electoral Boundaries Commission in 1969.[60] The Commission submitted its first *Report* in November 1969 but at the time of writing further legislative action had not been taken. The new procedure was initiated in April 1968 when the

Alberta Legislative Assembly appointed a Committee on Redistribution Procedure. Its terms of reference were: "To study various methods in use in Canada for redistributing Legislative seats, whether by Independent Commission, Legislative Committee or a combination of these methods, and to recommend to the next regular session of the Legislature the method considered best suited for adoption in Alberta, together with recommendations for guide rules and draft legislation. . . ."[61]

Predictably the Committee recommended the setting up of an independent commission, although it is one with a rather unusual composition: a Judge of the Supreme Court, the Clerk of the Executive Council, "an independent citizen nominated by the Speaker, with the concurrence of the Premier and the Leader of the Opposition," two further members who would be nominated by the Leader of the Opposition, "one from the largest and one from the next largest opposition parties in the House," and two "Government members".[62]

The Committee further recommended that redistribution, based on voter population figures rather than total population, be carried out after every second General Election (but not more than once every eight years). The Committee took note of the fact that there was increasing urbanization in Alberta and that this therefore required a shift in the base of representation. There were, however, "limitations to the extent to which such a shift can properly be made." It proposed securing these limits by a formula which would ensure that urban constituencies would contain the largest populations. The total voter population of the urban areas, as defined in the committee's *Report*, would be divided by a figure which would be 25 percent above the average voter population for all constituencies in the Province. This would give the number of urban seats, and the remaining seats would then all be divided more or less evenly among the balance of the population to produce the rural constituencies. To achieve fuller representation for the urban areas without unduly enlarging the area to be covered by the more sparsely populated rural areas, the Committee recommended that the membership of the Legislature be increased from 65 to 75.

The principal recommendations of the Committee were accepted in May of 1969 and the Electoral Boundaries Commission was established. Under the terms of the *Act* the Commission submitted a preliminary report to the Speaker of the Assembly in November 1969.[63] The report was then to be published in the *Alberta Gazette* after which the Commission would hold public hearings. The Commission could then, "after considering any further representations made to it, and not later than February 15" submit a further report to the Speaker with such amendments as it considered advisable. The Assembly itself still retains considerable authority over the redistribution, for once the final report of the Commission is received the Assembly, by resolution, "approves or approves with alterations the proposals of the Commission." After this the Government will introduce a Bill to establish the new electoral divisions in accordance with the resolution.[64] As, at the time of writing, these final stages are still in the future, it is not known to what extent the Assembly will exert its authority and override the Commission or to what extent it will consider such authority merely a reserve power for special circumstances and feel itself obliged to accept the Commission's recommendations.

In none of the other provinces is there any form of independent redistribution authority. Redistribution is entirely a matter of Government initiative, sometimes, as in Nova Scotia, by an *ad hoc* select committee of the Legislature. In New Brunswick the electoral district boundaries are contained as a Schedule to the Elections Act.[65] A Royal Commission which was appointed in Prince Edward Island in 1961 to consider all aspects relating to the election of members to the Legislative Assembly included among its other recommendations a proposal for redistribution of seats which would have taken one district from Kings County and added one to Queens.[66] The government did not accept this recommendation, choosing instead to increase the representation of Queens County while leaving Kings County alone. The present district boundaries are described in sections 165 to 169 of the Provincial Election Act.[67]

In the remaining provinces the electoral boundaries are defined in a separate *Act*, introduced by the Government.[68]

## DISTRIBUTION OF FEDERAL SEATS AMONG THE PROVINCES

A separate problem arises when we leave the question of drawing electoral division boundaries within a province and proceed to the broader question of determining exactly how many federal seats each province will have to begin with. While Canada has taken a major step forward with the establishment of independent boundary commissions for the drawing of boundaries within provinces, the present procedure for the allotment of seats to the various provinces is the result of a series of historical compromises and *ad hoc* solutions to pressing political issues.

The original method of allocation, which was adopted in 1867 and which remained in force until 1946, was in its outline fairly simple. The Province of Quebec was given a fixed membership of 65 and a quota was obtained by dividing the total population of Quebec by 65. This quota was then used to determine the number of seats to be allotted to each of the other provinces. The total membership of the House could thus vary with each redistribution.

The number of exceptions which overlaid this basically simple structure gradually became more complex and led finally to the establishment of a new set of rules which, however, were no less complicated than the old.

The first qualification was that the population base for Quebec was to be restricted to that drawn from the old boundaries, before the extension of the province in 1912. Secondly, it was provided that when the quota was divided into the population of any province, any remainder over half a quota would entitle the province to an additional member. The third rule, incorporated into the 1915 Amendment to the *British North America Act*, was designed to protect the declining Maritime provinces. This rule provided that no province could have fewer members of the House of Commons than it had Senators.[69] It now guarantees both Prince Edward Island and New Brunswick more seats than can be justified by strict application of population principles. A further rule was written into the scheme to protect provinces in which the population was declining, or at least growing less rapidly than in the country as a whole. This rule provided that no reduction could be made in the representation of any province unless, after any census, the ratio of its population to the total national population had declined by more than one-twentieth of the same ratio at the previous census. Further complications also arose after 1867 as new provinces entered Confederation and were given, as the price of their entry, a number of seats in excess of their population entitlement.

The present rules, basically as adopted in 1946 but somewhat altered in detail, are as follows:[70]

1. Two seats are set aside for the Yukon and the Northwest Territories.
2. The number of members to which the provinces, exclusive of the territories, are entitled is set at 261, although this number may be altered slightly by the application of other rules.
3. Each province's allocation of seats is calculated by dividing the total population of all the provinces by 261 to obtain a quota, and then by dividing the population of each province by the quota.
4. If this operation produces a total of less than 261 members, the necessary additional seats are awarded to the provinces having the largest remainders after the application of rule 3.
5. No province can have fewer members than it has senators and if the calculations under rules 3 and 4 produce for any province a result less than the senate total, then rules 3 and 4 cease to apply to that province, and the province is given a number of members equal to its senate representation. The procedure then is to deduct from the total population of all the provinces, the population of those provinces protected by this rule, and to deduct from 261 the members assigned to those provinces. The calculations under rules 3 and 4 are then made again for the remaining provinces.

6. No province shall have its representation reduced by more than 15 percent below the representation to which such a province was entitled at the last redistribution. This rule is not cumulative. That is to say, the calculation at any one redistribution is based on the actual entitlement of the province, not on the number of seats held, if this is higher than the entitlement by virtue of a prior application of the 15 percent rule. Thus in 1952, Saskatchewan's representation, which should have been reduced from 20 to 15, was held at 17 by the 15 percent rule. However, in 1966 the basis for the calculation was the 15 seats to which Saskatchewan was actually entitled and representation could drop by 2 below this figure before the 15 percent rule would again come into effect. This, in fact, happened and Saskatchewan's membership is now 13. The 15 percent rule saved Nova Scotia one seat in 1966.

7. No province may have its representation so reduced that it would have fewer members than another province with a smaller population. This rule has not yet been called into effect, although it means that no province with a population larger than either New Brunswick or Nova Scotia can have fewer than 10 members, as these provinces are guaranteed a minimum of 10 by rule 5.

8. Any extra seats which may result from the application of rules 6 and 7 are added to the total of 261 seats and are not included in the divisor used in rules 3, 4, and 5. This has meant that Saskatchewan's extra 2 seats under rule 6 in 1952 raised the House membership to 265, and Nova Scotia's extra seat under the same rule in 1966 has produced a House of 264 members.

Table 3: 5 shows how the present distribution of seats in the House of Commons was calculated.

## Table 3: 5

### DISTRIBUTION OF SEATS IN THE HOUSE OF COMMONS
(1966 Redistribution, based on 1961 Census)

Total members for initial calculation: 263    Population of Canada: 18,238,247

Deduct

|                          |   |        |
|--------------------------|---|--------|
| Yukon                    | 1 | 14,628 |
| Northwest Territories    | 1 | 22,998 |
|                          | 2 | 37,626 |

Remainder for calculation
of 1st quota                  261                    18,200,621

First quotient for 261 seats, =    69,734

| Province | Population | Population 69,734 | Remainder | Arithmetical No. of Seats | Actual No. of Seats | No. of Seats in 1952 |
|---|---|---|---|---|---|---|
| Prince Edward Island | 104,629 | 1 | 34,895 | 1 | 4(i) | 4 |
| New Brunswick | 597,936 | 8 | 40,064 | 8 | 10(ii) | 10 |

Recalculation of quotient deducting population and seats for P.E.I. and N.B.
Number of seats = 247;  Population =  17,498,056;  Quota =  70,842

| Province | Population | Population 70,842 | Remainder | Arithmetical No. of Seats | Actual No. of Seats | No. of Seats in 1952 |
|---|---|---|---|---|---|---|
| Newfoundland | 457,853 | 6 | 32,801(vi) | 7 | 7 | 7 |
| Nova Scotia | 737,007 | 10 | 28,587 | 10 | 11(iii) | 12 |
| Quebec | 5,259,211 | 74 | 16,903 | 74 | 74 | 75 |
| Ontario | 6,236,092 | 88 | 1,996 | 88 | 88 | 85 |
| Manitoba | 921,686 | 13 | 740 | 13 | 13 | 14 |
| Saskatchewan | 925,181 | 13 | 4,235 | 13 | 13 | 17 |
| Alberta | 1,331,944 | 18 | 56,788(v) | 19 | 19 | 17 |
| British Columbia | 1,629,082 | 22 | 70,558(iv) | 23 | 23 | 22 |
| TOTALS | | 244 | | 247 | 248 | 249 |
| Add   Prince Edward Island | | | | | 4 | 4 |
| New Brunswick | | | | | 10 | 10 |
| Yukon | | | | | 1 | 1 |
| Northwest Territories | | | | | 1 | 1 |
| Total Membership of House | | | | | 264 | 265 |

Notes:
(i)   Prince Edward Island is guaranteed a minimum of 4 seats by rule 5.
(ii)  New Brunswick is guaranteed a minimum of 10 seats by rule 5.
(iii) Nova Scotia's loss of 2 seats is reduced to a loss of 1 seat by application of
      the 15% rule (rule 6), increasing the size of the House by 1.
(iv) British Columbia, with the largest remainder, gets the first additional seat.
(v)  Alberta, with the second largest remainder, gets the second additional seat.
(vi) Newfoundland, with third largest remainder, gets third additional seat, bringing
      total for allocation up to 247.

## GERRYMANDERING

The extreme cases of the manipulation of electoral boundaries for partisan
purposes, as in the classic Essex County (Massachusetts) district of 1812

from which the term "gerrymander" originated, are readily recognized and are the usual subject matter of comment. Gerrymandering is not simply a matter of misshapen or distorted districts, but rather a process of gaining the maximum advantage from district boundaries, and especially if it is an "unfair" advantage. The main problem arises from the fact that any pattern of districts will confer some real or apparent extra benefit on some one or another of the parties, and it is therefore difficult to distinguish an impartial districting scheme which by chance favours one particular party, from one which is deliberately manipulated or perverted to ensure that it does grant that favour.

As long as the drawing of constituency boundaries is carried out by the legislature with the majority party in control, the charge of gerrymandering will always be levied against any boundary proposals and the legislature will never be completely successful on refuting those charges. Redistribution by independent commissions is the first major step in removing both the fact and the appearance of the gerrymander — in a democratic system it is as important to remove the appearance of partisan manipulation of boundaries as it is to abolish the fact of such manipulation.

The following simplified model will show that even compact, contiguous boundaries for equal-population districts can be drawn to confer partisan advantage, and that no matter how they are drawn they will appear to confer partisan advantage.

Let us suppose a community of 225,000 voters, to be divided into three compact, contiguous electoral districts of 75,000 each. Let us suppose, further, that a homogenous, working-class, predominantly "left wing" group of voters make up just over one-third of the community's voting population and are concentrated in the southern section. In the northern section live an equally homogenous, middle-class, "right wing" set of voters. Here is a map of the community with the working-class area shaded. The working-class population is thus about 90,000 and the middle-class about 135,000.

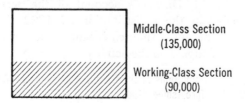

Middle-Class Section
(135,000)

Working-Class Section
(90,000)

The problem is how to draw impartially the boundaries of the three electoral districts. Three apparently straightforward solutions are possible, and as each produces a different result, the drafters will be charged with gerrymandering by whichever party feels that it has not got out of the scheme all that it expects.

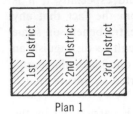 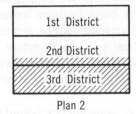 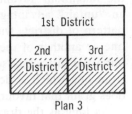

In Plan 1, the "right-wing" party candidates win all three districts with about 45,000 votes to their opponents' 30,000. The "left" vote is dissipated among all three districts. In Plan 2 each party wins one district without any serious opposition, and the "Right" has sufficient strength to win the 2nd District by 60,000 to 15,000. In Plan 3, with the "Right" vote concentrated in the 1st District, the "Left" vote spread over two districts is sufficient to capture these by 45,000 to 30,000 in each case. Straight lines on a map can give one party three, two or one seats, and the other nil, one, or two. Which, if any, of these schemes is a gerrymander?

It is probably a truism to say that if the legislature is responsible for its own districting plans, the majority will use its strength to maximize party advantage. But if the gerrymander is so blatant as to override all other criteria and to ignore any pretence at impartiality, the protest will be loud and the maneuvre may even backfire.

The reliance on gerrymandering for partisan advantage is not solely an American weakness, although perhaps in some of the state legislatures it has been practised with a dedication and enthusiasm not common elsewhere. Certainly it is true that in Canada until very recent times the gerrymander was a normal weapon in the political battle and if it has now disappeared from the federal scene it is still alive and flourishing in most of the provinces. R. M. Dawson's account of the gerrymander of the federal constituencies in the redistribution of 1882 should dispel any lingering doubts that because America invented the term "gerrymander," it has maintained a monopoly on the activity.

The most thorough and ambitious of the Canadian Gerrymander Acts was that of 1882. It merits, therefore, some study in itself as the best example of this particular kind of political manipulation in Canadian history; it surpassed the others in scope, in apparent skill and shrewdness, in lack of scruple, and in the volume of denunciation and disapproval which it aroused. More important, however, is its value as an illustration of the low state into which contemporary political morality had fallen: that a prime minister could introduce, and a Parliament pass, a measure of such a kind, speaks for itself and needs little or no elaboration. Finally, the results of the gerrymander furnish a third motive for its study, for they suggest that the Canadian electorate, accustomed as it was to political corruption in various forms, was at last beginning to revolt at such practices and to give indications of possessing a rudimentary public conscience.[71]

The gerrymander of 1882 was quite shameless and apparently no effort was made to disguise its overt political motives in polite euphemisms or statements of high principles. Perhaps the most interesting aspect of this constituency manipulation, in which all traditional arguments for preserving the integrity of county boundaries were abandoned whenever and wherever it was convenient to do so, is that it failed utterly in its purpose. Professor Ward has noted that the governing party was "all but annihilated in the areas it had most carefully gerrymandered."[72] There were two principal reasons for this failure: in the first place the government had inadequate information about the strength of its support and the intentions of the voters and, in the second, the gerrymander was so blatant, so patently corrupt, that the opposition was able to use it as a campaign plank and so encourage public reaction to this kind of politics. This popular reaction is a constant threat to the over-enthusiastic use of the gerrymander.

One of the commonest arguments for insisting that electoral divisions conform to existing county and city boundaries is that such boundaries will impose limits on the exercise of the gerrymander. This is basically a sound argument and there is no question but that in drawing the electoral district boundaries for a provincial legislature the need to conform to an existing pattern of county boundaries does restrain a partisan map-maker. This is, in fact, undoubtedly the strongest of all arguments for maintaining these traditional boundaries. In another sense, however, reliance on the county can itself be a form of gerrymander.

Whenever some body outside the legislature is charged with responsibility for drawing electoral boundaries it is required to pay due regard to "community of interest," which is almost invariably extended to be a defense of historic county or borough limits as the base of representation. Yet the socio-economic and demographic patterns of population are not static, and today will only occasionally and accidentally conform to the pattern of political subdivisions laid down in the nineteenth century. A system of representation, rationalized as a desirable concession to community interests, but based on historic political subdivisions which no longer encompass genuine communities, may be no more than a gerrymander for the perpetuation of the *status quo*.

## SINGLE AND MULTI-MEMBER CONSTITUENCIES

As will be recalled, the traditional pattern of representation in Britain before the 1832 reform was for each county and each enfranchised borough to return two members. It was not until 1885 that this pattern of dual representation was first seriously challenged and the double-member constituency became the exception rather than the rule. It was, however, an exception which lasted well into the twentieth century so that even in the election of 1945 there were fifteen districts which returned two members. All have now been abolished, and every constituency now returns a single member.

Similarly in Canada all members of the House of Commons are now elected from single-member districts although, as in Britain, historical reasons helped a few two-member districts survive until recently. There were five two-member districts in 1921, four from 1915 to 1930, and two from 1935 until the redistribution of 1966.[73]

The provincial legislatures, however, present a much more complicated picture. During the past fifty years nine of the ten provinces have had some experience with double- or multi-member districts.[74] On a number of occasions districts have returned three, four, or five members and in the case of Winnipeg between 1920 and 1945, even ten members. Some provinces have experimented with systems of proportional representation for their large multi-member metropolitan districts, combined with plurality or preferental voting systems in the remaining single-member districts. Table 3: 6 summarizes the recent history of single- and multi-member districts in the provinces and indicates that while the percentage of members elected from dual- or multi-member districts is declining, the decline is not particularly rapid. Even in the 1960s some 20 percent of the members of the provincial legislatures were elected from districts returning more than one member. The multi-member district might not now be as common as it once was, but it is not yet obsolete.

Most multi-member districts are a result of the application of the principle that the boundaries of electoral districts should conform with the boundaries of other governmental units — counties, cities, etc., a principle which itself may be based on a deep sense of tradition, a desire to maximize administrative efficiency, a concession to the spirit of community interest, or a belief that the multi-member district will confer some partisan advantage. There is also the possibility that the necessity of conforming to existing boundaries may reduce the opportunities for gerrymandering. County and city boundaries are visible and constraining criteria, with their visibility as perhaps their greatest value.

The British Columbia Commission of Inquiry into the Redefinition of Electoral Districts devoted a whole section to the matter of single- versus

## Table 3: 6
### MEMBER ELECTED FROM SINGLE- AND MULTI-MEMBER DISTRICTS IN THE PROVINCIAL LEGISLATURES

| Province | Year | Total Number (100%) | Single-Member | | Dual-Member | | Multi-Member | | |
|---|---|---|---|---|---|---|---|---|---|
| | | | No. of Members | % | No. of Members | % | | No. of Members | % |
| British Columbia | 1920 | 47 | 37 | 78.7 | — | — | 1x4 1x6 | 10 | 21.3 |
| | 1924 | 48 | 38 | 79.2 | — | — | 1x4 1x6 | 10 | 20.8 |
| | 1933 | 47 | 34 | 72.3 | 6 | 12.8 | 1x3 1x4 | 7 | 14.9 |
| | 1937 | 48 | 35 | 72.9 | 6 | 12.5 | 1x3 1x4 | 7 | 14.6 |
| | 1941 | 48 | 36 | 75.0 | 6 | 12.5 | 2x3 | 6 | 12.5 |
| | 1956 | 52 | 34 | 65.4 | 12 | 23.1 | 2x3 | 6 | 11.5 |
| | 1966 | 55 | 41 | 74.5 | 14 | 25.5 | — | — | — |
| Alberta | 1921 | 61 | 49 | 80.3 | 2 | 3.3 | 2x5 | 10 | 16.4 |
| | 1926 | 60 | 50 | 83.3 | — | — | 2x5 | 10 | 16.7 |
| | 1930 | 63 | 51 | 81.0 | — | — | 2x6 | 12 | 19.0 |
| | 1940 | 57 | 47 | 82.5 | — | — | 2x5 | 10 | 17.5* |
| | 1952 | 61 | 48 | 78.7 | — | — | 1x6 1x7 | 13 | 21.3 |
| | 1959 | 65 | 65 | 100.0 | — | — | — | — | — |
| | 1963 | 63 | 63 | 100.0 | — | — | — | — | — |
| | 1967 | 65 | 65 | 100.0 | — | — | — | — | — |
| Saskatchewan | 1921 | 63 | 57 | 90.5 | 6 | 9.5 | — | — | — |
| | 1934 | 55 | 49 | 89.1 | 6 | 10.9 | — | — | — |
| | 1938 | 52 | 46 | 88.5 | 6 | 11.5 | — | — | — |
| | 1944 | 53 | 47 | 88.7 | 6 | 11.3 | — | — | — |
| | 1948 | 52 | 45 | 86.5 | 4 | 7.7 | 1x3 | 3 | 5.8 |
| | 1952 | 53 | 46 | 86.8 | 4 | 7.5 | 1x3 | 3 | 5.7 |
| | 1960 | 55 | 46 | 83.6 | 2 | 3.6 | 1x3 1x4 | 7 | 12.8 |
| | 1964 | 59 | 48 | 81.4 | 6 | 10.2 | 1x5 | 5 | 8.5 |
| | 1967 | 59 | 59 | 100.0 | — | — | — | — | — |
| Manitoba | 1920 | 55 | 45 | 81.8 | — | — | 1x10 | 10 | 28.2 |
| | 1949 | 57 | 43 | 75.4 | 2 | 3.5 | 3x4 | 12 | 21.1 |
| | 1958 | 57 | 57 | 100.0 | — | — | — | — | — |

(Continued)

| Province | Year | Total Number (100%) | Single-Member No. of Members | % | Dual-Member No. of Members | % | Multi-Member No. of Members | | % |
|---|---|---|---|---|---|---|---|---|---|
| Ontario | 1923 | 111 | 103 | 92.8 | 8 | 7.2 | — | — | — |
| | 1926 | 112 | 112 | 100.0 | — | — | — | — | — |
| | 1934 | 90 | 90 | 100.0 | — | — | — | — | — |
| | 1955 | 98 | 98 | 100.0 | — | — | — | — | — |
| | 1963 | 108 | 108 | 100.0 | — | — | — | — | — |
| | 1967 | 117 | 117 | 100.0 | — | — | — | — | — |
| Quebec | 1923 | 85 | 85 | 100.0 | — | — | — | — | — |
| | 1931 | 91 | 91 | 100.0 | — | — | — | — | — |
| | 1939 | 85 | 85 | 100.0 | — | — | — | — | — |
| | 1944 | 91 | 91 | 100.0 | — | — | — | — | — |
| | 1948 | 92 | 92 | 100.0 | — | — | — | — | — |
| | 1956 | 93 | 93 | 100.0 | — | — | — | — | — |
| | 1962 | 95 | 95 | 100.0 | — | — | — | — | — |
| | 1966 | 108 | 108 | 100.0 | — | — | — | — | — |
| New Brunswick | 1920 | 48 | 1 | 2.1 | 14 | 29.2 | 3x3 6x4 | 33 | 68.7 |
| | 1925 | 48 | 3 | 6.3 | 14 | 29.2 | 5x3 4x4 | 31 | 64.5 |
| | 1930 | 48 | 1 | 2.1 | 14 | 29.2 | 3x3 6x4 | 33 | 68.7 |
| | 1948 | 52 | — | — | 12 | 23.1 | 5x3 5x4 1x5 | 40 | 76.9 |
| | 1967 | 58 | 4 | 6.9 | 14 | 24.1 | 6x3 3x4 2x5 | 40 | 68.9 |
| Nova Scotia | 1920 | 43 | — | — | 28 | 65.1 | 2x3 1x4 1x5 | 15 | 34.9 |
| | 1925 | 43 | — | — | 32 | 74.4 | 2x3 1x5 | 11 | 25.6 |
| | 1933 | 30 | 22 | 73.3 | 8 | 26.7 | — | — | — |
| | 1949 | 37 | 27 | 73.0 | 10 | 27.0 | — | — | — |
| | 1956 | 43 | 37 | 86.0 | 6 | 14.0 | — | — | — |
| | 1967 | 46 | 40 | 87.0 | 6 | 13.0 | — | — | — |

**(Continued)**

| Province | Year | Total Number (100%) | Single-Member | | Dual-Member | | Multi-Member | | |
|---|---|---|---|---|---|---|---|---|---|
| | | | No. of Members | % | No. of Members | % | | No. of Members | % |
| Prince Edward Island | 1923 | 30 | — | — | 30 | 100.0 | | — | — |
| | 1966 | 32 | — | — | 32 | 100.0 | | — | — |
| Newfoundland | 1949 | 28 | 22 | 78.6 | 6 | 21.4 | | — | — |
| | 1956 | 35 | 33 | 97.1 | 2 | 2.9 | | — | — |
| | 1962 | 42 | 40 | 95.2 | 2 | 4.8 | | — | — |
| SUMMARY Total No. of Members elected in all elections in all provinces. | 1920-1929 | 1,408 | 1,019 | 72.4 | 208 | 14.7 | 14x3 14x4 7x5 3x6 3x10 | 181 | 12.9 |
| | 1930-1939 | 1,267 | 938 | 74.0 | 172 | 13.6 | 11x3 20x4 4x6 2x10 | 157 | 12.4 |
| | 1940-1949 | 1,325 | 1,021 | 77.0 | 148 | 11.2 | 15x3 14x4 7x5 2x10 | 156 | 11.8 |
| | 1950-1959 | 1,453 | 1,139 | 78.4 | 172 | 11.8 | 18x3 13x4 2x5 2x6 2x7 | 142 | 9.8 |
| | 1960-1969 | 1,649 | 1,323 | 80.2 | 182 | 11.1 | 21x3 14x4 5x5 | 144 | 8.7 |

* Alberta, Aug. 1944: In addition there were 3 "non-partisan" representatives of the armed forces.

multi-member constituencies, concluding that multiple ridings were not to be recommended. The arguments presented in support of multiple ridings, said the commission, were few and mostly weak. Perhaps the strongest argument was that "two or even three members may help to preserve the unity of a riding." Two other arguments demonstrated, in the Commission's view, "an abdication of political responsibility in favour of local caution." These arguments were, first, that by electing members of more than one party, a constituency "could play it safe and maximize its chances of having a representative on the government side." Secondly, the district could increase its chances of being represented by a Minister of the Crown.

The Commission found the whole weight of the argument against multiple districts. It expressed the view that "a multiple riding may completely extinguish an important minority, that could easily win in a portion of the riding, and may be suspected of having been designed to do so: that a weak candidate may get in on the merits of his party colleagues and that the sense of individual responsibility is weakened."[75] Despite this very strong argument against multi-member districts, this was another of the Commission's recommendations which the British Columbia Government chose not to implement.

The weaknesses of the multi-member district are most apparent under a plurality voting system where each voter has as many votes as there are seats to be filled, and where strong party loyalties increase the tendency to bloc voting. It is almost inevitable that wherever there are strong partisan divisions, split-ticket voting will become the anomaly (frequently the consequence of error on the part of the voter) and the one party will win all the seats in the district.[76]

The following results, from the Saskatchewan provincial elections of 1960, in which four parties each put up three candidates for the three-member district of Saskatoon, illustrate the less desirable features of multi-member districts. The figures have been rounded to the nearest hundred.

| 1st C.C.F. Candidate | 16,200 | C.C.F. Vote: |
| 2nd   "        " | 15,900 | 47,900 (43.4%) |
| 3rd   "        " | 15,800 | 3 seats |
| | | |
| 1st Liberal Candidate | 11,600 | Liberal Vote: |
| 2nd   "        " | 11,300 | 34,200 (31.0%) |
| 3rd   "        " | 11,300 | 0 seats |
| | | |
| 1st Conservative Candidate | 7,000 | Conservative Vote: |
| 2nd   "        " | 7,000 | 19,700 (17.8%) |
| 3rd   "        " | 5,700 | 0 seats |

| | | |
|---|---|---|
| 1st  Social Credit Candidate | 3,000 | Social Credit Vote: |
| 2nd   "       "        " | 2,900 | 8,700 (7.8%) |
| 3rd   "       "        " | 2,800 | 0 seats |

There is a great deal of speculation about the impact of multi- or single-member, districts, but hard evidence is extremely hard to come by, especially in Canada where there has been so little research on provincial elections. So many variables enter into an election that trying to isolate the effect of the structure of the constituencies from post-election aggregate data is, at best, only partly successful. Nevertheless, there are certain generalizations that can be stated with reasonable confidence. In the first place, under any system of proportional representation, large multi-member districts will help smaller parties and factions. On the other hand, where there is a plurality system of voting, combined with relatively stable partisan allegiances, then multi-member districts may encourage bloc voting which can permanently exclude representatives of even quite strong parties. There is no doubt whatever that to the extent that minority party strength exhibits any geographic concentration — whether along economic, racial, or ethnic lines — then dividing a multi-member constituency into a number of single-member districts (or, to employ a widely used American term, "districting") will increase the opportunities for minority party representation.

On balance it would appear that the multi-member district returning three or more members, under a plurality voting system, is so susceptible to block voting and the denial of adequate representation to significant minorities, that it is obstructive to the democratic process. On the other hand, in the more densely populated urban concentrations, rigid insistence on single-member districts can result in a pattern of artificial constituencies with no natural or historic boundaries to curb gerrymandering. In these circumstances the two- or three-member riding may be a useful innovation. Certainly the arguments weigh heavily on the side of a dominant pattern of single-member constituencies, but the case for strict adherence to nothing but single-member districts has not been proved. At the federal level the average population of all ridings is large enough to require that all shall return just one member, but in provincial legislatures where the average population per member may number only a few thousands, an exclusive pattern of single-member constituencies may mean the imposition of quite artificial boundaries in already compact urban communities. In such circumstances the two- or three-member district may still have a useful role to play. It is a case that needs much more examination, and a great deal more evidence, before a final verdict is passed.

## CONCLUSION

The constituency is the arena within which the basic electoral battle is fought and it would be strange indeed if the structure of the constituency system and the political values embodied in that structure, together with the voters' perception of both structure and values, did not materially influence the voters' electoral behaviour. The following, therefore, are the principal hypotheses suggested by the preceding pages, hypotheses which, hopefully, will form the basis of the kind of intensive behavioural research which is far beyond the scope of this book.

It is first of all suggested, and this much is already confirmed in many studies, that one of the variables affecting voter participation is the level of political cynicism, the voter perception of the integrity of the system.

It is then further suggested that the level of cynicism, normally proposed as a product of the voter's socio-economic-educational background, is even more directly influenced by the objective integrity of the system. That is to say, we find many instances where the political elites regard the election machinery as a device to be manipulated for the advantage of the majority party, where such attitudes are overt and only thinly disguised by polite democratic euphemisms, and then we find other examples where all parties seem united in the desire to remove from the election system as much partisan bias as possible. It is hypothesized that the voter reacts directly to such attitudes and that levels of political cynicism and voter participation are directly related to the levels of institutional impartiality built into the system. The hypothesis requires much further testing, but we may note the high levels of voter participation, and the general high level of political integrity in New Zealand, where there is a long tradition of entrusting the task of creating constituencies to impartial commissions working to criteria which leave little opportunity for partisan bias, and contrast this with the general low participation and high cynicism in the southern United States where an even longer tradition has held that the drawing of constituency boundaries is an acceptable political instrument for preserving the power of established elites.

A further hypothesis, directly related to the constituency, is that the criteria most likely to produce not only a non-partisan constituency structure, but also some public evidence that the structure is as free from bias as possible, would include:

(1) The dominating role of equal-population factors in all but a few rare, very special circumstances;

(2) regular redistributions according to specific, known rules; and

(3) redistribution by an independent, largely *ex officio,* Commission.

Other criteria may emerge from these, but these three remain as the core, all essential to an unbiased arena for electoral contests.

# FOOTNOTES

[1] The cube relationship will be examined more closely in Chapter Four.

[2] W. J. D. Boyd, "Suburbia Takes Over," *National Civic Review*, 54 (6), 1965, 294.

[3] See, for example. L. S. Amery, *Thoughts on the Constitution*, Oxford University Press, London, 1953 and C. Hollis, *Can Parliament Survive?* London, Hollis and Carter, 1949.

[4] John Locke, *Second Treatise on Civil Government*, London, J. M. Dent & Sons Ltd., Everyman's Library edition, par. 157.

[5] Reform Bill of 1832, 2 Will. IV, London, Her Majesty's Stationery Office, chap. 45.

[6] Canada, *House of Commons Debates*, 1872, 926.

[7] Canada, *House of Commons Debates*, 1899, 3442. Reproduced with the permission of the Queen's Printer for Canada. For further material on the historical debates on numbers versus communities in Canada, see N. Ward, *The Canadian House of Commons: Representation*, University of Toronto Press, Toronto, 1963, 19-58.

[8] Canada, *House of Commons Debates*, 1952, 1430. Reproduced with the permission of the Queen's Printer for Canada. See also N. Ward, "The Redistribution of 1952," *Canadian Journal of Economics and Political Science*, 19 (3), 1953, 343.

[9] S.C., 1964, chap. 31.

[10] The figures, based on the 1961 census, are from Canada, Chief Electoral Officer, *Report of the 26th General Election, 1963*, Table 5, XII-XVIII.

[11] The debate is examined at some length in T. H. Qualter, "Representation by Population: A Comparative Study," *Canadian Journal of Economics and Political Science*, 33 (2), 1967, 246-268, and more will be said about it later.

[12] S.C. 1964, chap 31, sec. 13 (c). Reproduced with the permission of the Queen's Printer for Canada.

[13] Australia, *Commonwealth Electoral Act*, 1918-1965, sec. 19.

[14] Reproduced from T. H. Qualter, "Representation by Population: A Comparative Study," *op. cit.*, 261.

[15] See, for example, the "Index of the Relative Value of the Right to Vote," devised by P. T. David and R. Eisenberg in *Devaluation of the Urban and Suburban Vote*, Charlottesville, University of Virginia, two volumes, 1961 & 1962; G. Tyler's index in "Court Versus Legislature; the Socio-Politics of Malapportionment," *Law and Contemporary Problems* 27 (3), 1962, 390-407; and A. L. Clem, "Measuring Legislative Malapportionment: In Search of a Better Yardstick," *Midwest Journal of Political Science*, 7 (2), 1963, 125-144.

[16] Developed by M. J. Dauer & R. G. Kelsay in "Unrepresentative States," *National Municipal Review* 44 (11), 1955, 571-575, and 587, as corrected in *National Municipal Review*, 45 (4), 1956, 198.

[17] G. Schubert and C. Press, "Measuring Malapportionment," *American Political Science Review*, 58 (2), 1964, 305.

[18] David and Eisenberg, *op. cit.*, 3.

[19] Yukon, the Northwest Territories and the four Prince Edward Island seats.

[20] In Canada as a whole registered voters for the 1968 elections represented 54.3% of the total population in 1966. In Spadina the figure was only

34.3% and in Vancouver Centre it was 74.7%. These were, however, very special cases and the vast majority of constituencies closely approached the norm.

21 Alberta, Legislative Committee on Redistribution Procedure, *Report*, April 2, 1969, 7 and 10.

22 R. M. Dawson, *The Government of Canada*, 4th edition revised by Norman Ward, Toronto, University of Toronto Press, 1963, 341.

23 T. H. Qualter, "Representation by Population: A Comparative Study," *op. cit.*, 250-251. There is more on the same theme in this paper.

24 Qualter, *ibid.*, 252.

25 Canada, House of Commons, *Objections Filed with Mr. Speaker Pursuant to the Electoral Boundaries Readjustment Act*, Jan. 19, 1966 to Feb. 18, 1966.

26 Manitoba, Electoral Divisions Boundaries Commission, *Report*, Winnipeg, 1968, par. 5.

27 Mr. G. H. Aiken (PC, Parry Sound-Muskoka) Canada, *House of Commons Debates*, 1964, 772.

28 Qualter, *op. cit.*, 254.

29 British Columbia, Commission of Inquiry into Redefinition of Electoral Districts, *Report*, Jan. 1966, 15-16.

30 *The Works of Thomas Jefferson*, Volume IV, collected and edited by Paul Leicester Ford, New York and London, G. P. Putnam's Sons, 1904, 85-86.

31 British Columbia, *op. cit.*, 16.

32 *Loc cit.*

33 *Ibid.*, 19.

34 *Ibid.*, 21.

35 *Ibid.*, 22.

36 United States Commission on Inter-Governmental Relations, *Report to the President*, 1955, 39.

37 N. Ward, "A Century of Constituencies," *Canadian Public Administration*, 10 (1), 1967, 107.

38 Like the *Canada Elections Act*, none of the provincial acts requires that the candidate shall reside in the constituency he wishes to contest.

39 See, for example, R. Hanson, *The Political Thicket*, Englewood Cliffs, Prentice-Hall, 1966, 35-36.

40 N. Ward, "The Redistribution of 1952," *Canadian Journal of Economics and Political Science*, 19 (3), 1953, 353.

41 In *The Canadian House of Commons: Representation*, Toronto, University of Toronto Press, 2nd edition 1963, N. Ward describes each redistribution from 1869 to 1947, and in "The Redistribution of 1952," in *The Canadian Journal of Economics and Political Science*, 19 (3), 1953, 341-360, and "A Century of Constituencies," in *Canadian Public Administration*, 10 (1), 1967, 105-122, he brings the account up to the redistribution of 1966.

42 *B.N.A. Act*, sec. 51 (1).

43 J. Pope, *Confederation Documents*, Toronto, 1895, sec. 25 of "First Draft of the British North America Bill."

44 S.C., 1964, chap. 31, secs. 5 and 6.

45 A large number of objections were filed with Mr. Speaker between Jan. 19, and Feb. 18, 1966 and were debated at great length on several days between April 27 and May 6, 1966. See the *Debates* for this period for details. Objections ranged over the fields of the philosophy of representation, of

numbers versus communities, and the unique claims of rural interests for special representation.

46 S.M., 1957, chap. 18.

47 *Ibid.*, sec. 8 (2). It was further provided, in sec. 8 (6) that if the president of the University was unable to act then his place would be taken by the Dean of the Faculty of Arts and Sciences.

48 *Ibid.*, sec. 13.

49 *Ibid.*, sec. 11 (6) (c).

50 S.M., 1968, chap. 21.

51 *Ibid.*, sec. 11 (2).

52 Manitoba, Electoral Divisions Boundaries Commission, *Report*, Winnipeg, 1968, par. 5.

53 Ontario, *Journal of the Legislative Assembly*, Vol. 96, April 18, 1962, 171.

54 *Ibid.*

55 Ontario, Special Commission on Redistribution of Electoral Districts in Ontario, *First Report*, Dec. 14, 1962, 3.

56 Ontario, Special Commission on Redistribution of Electoral Districts in Ontario, *Report*, 1965. The Dauer-Kelsay index for these proposed districts was 41·2.

57 Ontario, Special Commission on the Redistribution of Electoral Districts in Ontario, *Final Report*, Dec. 1965.

58 S.O., 1966, chap. 137.

59 British Columbia Commission of Inquiry into the Redefinition of Electoral Districts, *Report*, Jan. 1966, 5.

60 S.A., 1969, chap. 27.

61 Alberta, Legislative Committee on Redistribution Procedure, *Report*, April 2, 1969, 1.

62 *Ibid.*, 8.

63 Alberta, Electoral Boundaries Commission, *Report*, Nov. 21, 1969.

64 S.A., 1969, chap. 27, secs. 7-11.

65 S.N.B., 1967, chap. 9, Schedule C.

66 Prince Edward Island, Royal Commission on Electoral Reform, *Report*, March, 1962, 10-12.

67 S.P.E.I., 1963, chap. 11, secs. 165-169.

68 Quebec, *Territorial Divisions Act*, S.Q., 1965, chap. 10. Newfoundland, *House of Assembly (Amendment) Act*, S.N., 1962, chap. 81.

Saskatchewan, *Legislative Assembly Act*, R.S.S., 1965, chap. 3, Nova Scotia, *House of Assembly Act*, R.S.N.S., 1954, chap. 117.

In the case of Quebec one should note, in addition, the provisions of section 80 of the *British North America Act* which were intended to protect the then English majority in the eastern townships. The section reads, in part:

> Provided that it shall not be lawful to present to the Lieutenant Governor of Quebec for Assent any Bill for altering the Limits of any of the Electoral Divisions or Districts mentioned in the Second Schedule of this Act, unless the Second and Third Readings of such Bill have been passed in the Legislative Assembly with the Concurrence of the Majority of the Members representing all those Electoral Divisions or Districts, and the Assent shall not be given to such Bill unless an Address has been presented by the Legislative Assembly to the Lieutenant Governor stating that it has been so passed.

Quebec is the only province in which the authority of the provincial legislature over the drawing of provincial legislative district boundaries is constrained by the provisions of the *British North America Act*.

[69] *B.N.A. Act*, 1915, 5-6 Geo. V, chap. 45 (U.K.).

[70] See *B.N.A. Act*, sec. 51. Also see N. Ward, "The Redistribution of 1952", *Canadian Journal of Economics and Political Science*, 29 (3), 1953, 350, for a very much clearer exposition.

[71] R. M. Dawson, "The Gerrymander of 1882," *Canadian Journal of Economics and Political Science*, 1 (2), 1935, 197.

[72] N. Ward, "A Century of Constituencies," *Canadian Public Administration*, 10 (1), 1967, 110.

[73] The five were: Queen's (P.E.I.), Cape Breton South and Richmond (N.S.), Halifax (N.S.), Saint John City and Counties St. John and Albert (N.B.), and Ottawa (Ont.). The four from 1925 to 1930 were: Queen's, Halifax, Ottawa, and St. John-Albert. From 1935 there were only two: Queen's and Halifax, and these were abolished as two-member seats in 1966.

[74] The exception is Quebec.

[75] British Columbia, Commission of Inquiry into the Redefinition of Electoral Districts, *Report*, 1966, 47.

[76] For an examination of bloc voting and split-ticket voting in federal two-member constituencies, see: N. Ward, "Voting in Canadian Two-Member Constituencies," *Public Affairs*, 1946 (reprinted in J. C. Courtney, *Voting in Canada: A Selection of Papers*, Prentice-Hall of Canada, Toronto, 1967, 125-129), and the three papers by Morris Davis: "Did They Vote for Party or Candidate in Halifax?" in John Meisel, *Papers on the 1962 Election*, University of Toronto Press, Toronto, 1964, 19-32; "Ballot Behaviour in Halifax Revisited," *Canadian Journal of Economics and Political Science*, 30 (4), 1964, 538-558; and "A Last Look at Ballot Behaviour in the Dual Constituency of Halifax," *Canadian Journal of Economics and Political Science*, 32 (3), 1966, 366-371.

# FOUR

## HOW AND UNDER WHAT CONDITIONS?

A Parliamentary election is a process whereby voters, organized into constituencies, elect representatives from among a slate of candidates. But the process itself is complicated and involves decisions about the method of recording and counting the votes, about the functions and responsibilities of election officials and the method of their appointment, about the number and location of polling places, about the design of ballot papers, about security measures to safeguard the ballot boxes and to protect the voters from violence or intimidation, about measures to reduce the opportunities for bribery, corruption, and fraud and to preserve the secrecy of the ballot, and about adjudicating disputed elections. Questions of this type are raised in this chapter.

### THE ELECTORAL SYSTEM

Throughout this book reference has been made to the "election system" by which is meant that whole complex of all the elements of voter, candidate, constituency, and procedure. One of those elements is the "electoral system," a term here confined to the manner in which votes are recorded and counted.[1] Thus one can refer to a plurality electoral system, or a preferential electoral system, as one of the variables in a total national election system.

There exists a great deal of general discussion about the relative merits of different electoral systems[2] and there is little to be gained from reopening this general discussion here, except insofar as it relates to specifically Canadian problems.

The first point to note is that at present there is one electoral system common to all eleven election systems in Canada, and that is the plurality or "first-past-the-post" system under which the voter may mark his ballot with as many X's as there are seats to be filled, and those candidates who have the greatest number of X's are declared elected. Any lengthy consideration of the more esoteric alternatives is therefore irrelevant to the Canadian scene.

The second point is that not only do all eleven systems now vote under a plurality scheme, but also in all but three provinces the plurality system has been the only one in use in this century. The three provinces which have experimented with, and finally abandoned, other voting systems are all in the west: British Columbia, Alberta, and Manitoba.

British Columbia's experience with preferential voting has been the briefest, having been adopted for two elections only, those of 1952 and 1953. In those elections a preferential, or alternative, ballot was adopted by which the voter marked the names on his ballot in order of preference. In the thirty-six single-member districts the voter received a single ballot to be marked 1, 2, 3, etc. and in the two- and three-member ridings he was given two or three separate ballots. The system was apparently introduced by the government in order to prevent gains by the C.C.F. in three-cornered contests. It was the expectation of the government, a foundering coalition of Liberals and Conservatives, that electors who gave their first choice to a Liberal would give their second choice to a Conservative and *vice versa*. Under this notion the C.C.F. could win only in those constituencies in which it gained an absolute majority.[3]

This strategy revealed a fundamental misunderstanding of the mechanics of preferential voting. The most important second-choice votes are not those of the leading contenders, for these will not be taken into account, but those of the candidates on the bottom of the ballot, the ones that are to be eliminated. If, after the first count, no candidate has a clear majority, attention should be directed away from the leading candidates for there is nothing they can do now to affect the outcome, and focussed on the trailing candidates for it is the second preferences of these losers which will determine the results. Preferential balloting enormously increases the power and significance of defeated candidates.

The Government in British Columbia in 1952 had also seriously misinterpreted the mood of the electorate and would have been defeated whatever system had been used. At the end of the first count the results showed the C.C.F. leading in 21 seats, Social Credit leading in 14, Liberals in 9, Conservatives in 3, and the Independent Labour candidate in 1. These, of course, would have been the final results in a plurality system. The Government then further miscalculated the distribution of second preferences of defeated candidates and actually lost seats on the second count. The final results were: Social Credit 19, C.C.F. 18, Liberal 6, Conservative

4, and Independent Labour 1.[4] On this basis the Social Credit party proceeded to form a minority government and at the next elections, held just a year later, converted its minority position into that of a clear majority, which it has maintained ever since.

The province returned to a simple plurality electoral system for the 1956 elections, but with no significant change in the relative standing of the parties. Thus it seems that while the introduction of a preferential ballot was a major contributing factor in the initial victory of the Social Credit party, there is no confirming evidence that the continuation of that system beyond 1953 would have further strengthened or inhibited the continued success of Mr. Bennett's Government.

From 1926 to 1959 Alberta operated under two different electoral systems, using the alternative, or preferential, ballot in the rural single-member districts, and the single transferable vote in the two multi-member districts of Edmonton and Calgary. Since 1959, however, the province has been divided into single-member districts, and all candidates have been elected on a straight plurality system. The detailed results published after each Alberta provincial election, which give figures for both the first and the final count in each constituency, make it possible to assess the consequences of the preferential or single transferable vote, although, as Table 4:1 demonstrates, they are surprisingly minor consequences.[5]

## Table 4: 1 (A)
### EFFECTS OF PREFERENTIAL VOTING IN RURAL CONSTITUENCIES OF ALBERTA, 1940-1955

| Election Year | No. of Candidates Elected by an Absolute Majority on the First Count | No. of Candidates Leading on the 1st Count and Elected on the 2nd Count | No. of Candidates Trailing on the 1st Count and Elected on the 2nd Count | Total Candidates Elected |
|---|---|---|---|---|
| 1940 | 20 | 25 | 2 (a) | 47 |
| 1944 | 39 | 7 | 1 (b) | 47 |
| 1948 | 39 | 8 | — | 47 |
| 1952 | 38 | 10 | — | 48 |
| 1955 | 32 | 12 | 4 (c) | 48 |
| Total | 168 | 62 | 7 | 237 |

| | Leading on first count | Elected on 2nd count |
|---|---|---|
| (a) | One Independent Social Credit | One Social Credit |
| | One Social Credit | One Independent |
| (b) | One Independent | One Social Credit |
| (c) | Four Social Credit | Four Liberal |

## Table 4: 1 (B)
## EFFECTS OF THE SINGLE TRANSFERABLE VOTE IN CALGARY AND EDMONTON 1940-1955

| Election Year | No. of Candidates Leading on First Count and Elected on Second Count | No. of Candidates Trailing on First Count and Elected on Second Count | Total No. of Candidates Elected |
|---|---|---|---|
| 1940 | 8 | 2 (a) | 10 |
| 1944 | 9 | 1 (b) | 10 |
| 1948 | 7 | 3 (c) | 10 |
| 1952 | 9 | 4 (d) | 13 |
| 1955 | 9 | 4 (e) | 13 |
| Total | 42 | 14 | 56 |

| Elected | Position on 1st Count | Defeated |
|---|---|---|
| (a) One Social Credit | 7th (Calgary) | One C.C.F. |
| One Social Credit | 13th (Edmonton) | One Independent |
| (b) One Social Credit | 9th (Edmonton) | One Independent |
| (c) One Liberal | 7th (Calgary) | One Labour |
| Two Social Credit | 7th & 9th (Edmonton) | One Independent & One Liberal |
| (d) One Independent, & One Liberal | 7th & 8th (Calgary) | One Ind. Labour & One Soc. Cr. |
| One Liberal & One Social Credit | 12th & 16th (Edmonton) | One Social Credit & One Liberal |
| (e) One Liberal | 7th (Calgary) | One Conservative |
| One Liberal and Two Social Credit | 10th, 11th & 12th (Edmonton) | Two Liberal and One C.C.F. |

## Table 4: 1 (C)
## SUMMARY OF TABLES 4: 1 (A) & 4: 1 (B)

| Total Seats Unchanged on Second Count | Total Seats Changing Hands on Second Count | Total number of Seats |
|---|---|---|
| 272 | 21 | 293 |

### Table 4: 1 (D)
### NET PARTY GAINS AND LOSSES OVER FIVE ELECTIONS

| Party | Seats Gained on Second Count | Seats Lost on Second Count | Net Gain or Loss |
|---|---|---|---|
| Social Credit | 9 | 8 | + 1 |
| Liberal | 9 | 4 | + 5 |
| C.C.F. | — | 2 | − 2 |
| Independents | 3 | 3 | — |
| Others | — | 4 | − 4 |

Manitoba, too, has used a combination of preferential and single transferable ballots. From 1920 until 1945 Winnipeg was a single electoral district returning 10 members under a scheme of proportional representation, by a single transferable vote. In the elections of 1949 and 1953 the representation of Winnipeg was increased to twelve and the city was divided into three electoral districts, each returning four members. In the same period St. Boniface was established as a two-member district. Proportional representation was continued in all four multi-member districts.

The pressure for the introduction of the single transferable vote came mainly from those who apparently believed that formal political parties were inherently evil and that proportional representation was the most effective tool for breaking the hold of party organization.[6] One cannot put all the responsibility on the electoral system, but it is a fact that for many years in Manitoba there was a virtual cessation of party activity in the normal sense of this term. Indeed it seems much more likely that the general political culture which made a virtue of non-partisanship helped perpetuate proportional representation and to rationalize its operation than that coalition government was a product of the electoral system. If the latter had been the case one would have expected non-partisanship to have developed in Alberta.

In rural Manitoba the alterative (preferential) ballot was used in the single-member districts, but only for a much briefer time, in the three elections of 1927, 1932, and 1936. Beginning with the election of 1958 all balloting in Manitoba provincial elections, rural and urban, has been based on the traditional Canadian system of plurality vote in single-member districts.

Unfortunately the only official returns available from Manitoba do not give details of the first or subsequent counts, but only of the final results and it is not possible to calculate the actual effects of the single transferable vote in Metropolitan Winnipeg, to find which candidates, trailing on the first count, were brought to victory by transferred votes.

Whatever may have been the advantage of preferential ballots or single transferable votes, all provinces have now abandoned these systems and the simple majority or plurality is the standard procedure across the country. Yet for a time great hopes were held out for the various alternatives to the standard electoral system. Writing in the *Canadian Forum* in 1935, for example, Professor Frank Underhill concluded that the "establishment of P.R. in our main metropolitan urban centres and some form of alternative vote in the rural areas is urgently needed if our democratic system of government is not to become a meaningless gamble."[7] More recently Professor Paul Fox restated the argument that plurality systems produce "absurd results," and that it is only through proportional representation that a truly representative legislature can be elected.[8] Later in the same article Fox accepted as an obstacle to P.R. that it might produce a legislature which was too representative of minority interests and therefore one in which majority government would be impossible. He therefore proposed that P.R. be introduced only in the major metropolitan areas. Seymour Lipset concluded that if "Alberta or Saskatchewan were to adopt a system of proportional representation, we would soon see the end of one-party rule."[9]

In part the enthusiasm for proportional representation stems from excessive hopes as to its effects. Admittedly experience with proportional representation in Canada has been limited and has been confined to four western metropolitan areas. As there is no evidence, one can only speculate about the consequences of applying proportional representation to large multi-member rural areas or to eastern suburbia. Yet such knowledge as exists should lead to a revision of opinions as to the radical nature of proportional representation through the single transferable vote. All the evidence suggests that it has not really made all that much difference and most results achieved under the single transferable vote are very much what would have occurred under plurality voting.

Canadian experience with proportional representation, limited as it is, has been confined to that system known technically as the single transferable vote under which each voter is presented with a list of all candidates for a multi-member district normally returning between five and a dozen members. With fewer than five to be elected the advantages of the transferable vote are very much reduced, and with more than twelve the ballot paper becomes too long, too confusing to the voter. The voter himself marks one, two, three, or more names with numbers to signify the order in which he prefers them. Votes are then transferred from those candidates with more votes than are needed for election and from those who have the fewest first preferences and given to second or third preferences until the exact number of members are elected.[10]

Most Canadian critics of the prevailing plurality system have such a scheme in mind. Professor Fox, for example, writes that the only sure way of giving all the voters representation is "to enlarge the constituency so that it has a number of seats and to fill these seats in proportion to the way the electorate votes. This, in a nutshell, is the system of voting known as proportional representation. It had quite a vogue in Canada about 30 years ago when cities like Winnipeg, Calgary, Edmonton, and Vancouver adopted it."[11] Of course, the single transferable vote does not necessarily produce a legislature which mirrors the party divisions in the electorate. The transfer of votes may indeed strengthen the position of the dominant party. The proportionality element refers more to the procedure for allocating second preferences than to the representation of parties.

Table 4: 2 summarizes the results of the application of the single transferable vote in Calgary and Edmonton in 1952 and 1955, the last two elections in which such a system was used. It shows, first of all, the actual number of seats won by each party in the two multi-member districts. It then shows the number of seats that might have been won had seats been

**Table 4: 2**

**COMPARISON OF POSSIBLE EFFECTS OF DIFFERENT ELECTORAL SYSTEMS IN CALGARY AND EDMONTON, 1952 and 1955**

|  | S.C. | Cons. | Lib. | C.C.F. | Other |
|---|---|---|---|---|---|
| **1952** | | | | | |
| Actual number of seats won | 7 | 2 | 3 | 1 | — |
| Number of seats allocated in strict proportion to share of first-preference votes | 7 | 2 | 2 | 2 | — |
| Number of seats allocated if first-preference votes are considered to be single votes under a plurality system | 7 | 2 | 2 | 1 | 1 |
| **1955** | | | | | |
| Actual number of seats won | 6 | 2 | 5 | — | — |
| Number of seats allocated in strict proportion to share of first-preference votes | 5 | 2 | 5 | 1 | — |
| Number of seats allocated if first-preference votes are considered to be single votes under a plurality system | 4 | 3 | 5 | 1 | — |

allocated to each party strictly in proportion to their share of the total of the first preference votes. Finally it shows the results that might have been achieved if a plurality system had been applied, and if those candidates leading on the first ballot had been declared elected.

As can be seen the single transferable vote offers few advantages over the plurality system as far as the balance of party strength is concerned. In 1952 the single transferable vote gave the Liberals one more and the C.C.F. one less seat than strict proportionality would have allocated. A plurality vote would have taken one C.C.F. seat and given it to an Independent. Again in 1952 the single transferable vote did no more than give the Social Credit one additional seat at the expense of the C.C.F. A plurality count would have taken one from Social Credit and given it to the Conservatives.

Part of the difficulty seems to stem from a tendency to ascribe to the single transferable vote system consequences which can follow only from the party list system common in several European countries. Under this kind of voting pattern the entire territory is divided into large multi-member districts and the elector casts his vote, not for the individual candidate as such, but for the party list.[12] Seats are then allocated among the parties on a proportional basis. This kind of party-oriented proportional representation has never been adopted in Canada and as it requires the almost total formal subordination of the individuality of the candidate to the dominance of the party hierarchy it would be alien to the Canadian political tradition. But a party list electoral system is the only system which will automatically produce a legislature which will reflect more or less accurately all the major divisions of organized political opinion in the country.

Another reason for the support for proportional representation is the evidence of the weaknesses of plurality voting which have led some to conclude that any change must be an improvement. The system as we know it has two major defects: (a) it produces individual constituency results in which a candidate may be elected although rejected by a substantial percentage of the voters, and (b) the representation of the parties in the legislature is frequently quite disproportionate to their support in the country. The party with the largest number of votes tends to win considerably more than a proportionate number of seats and losing parties usually get far fewer seats than their popular support would warrant.

The first proposition is easy enough to demonstrate. In the 1968 federal elections, for example, 145 out of 264 members were elected with less than half the total vote in their constituencies. Some individual constituencies have produced quite extreme distortions of the popular will. In the federal district of Springfield (Manitoba) in 1935 the Liberal candidate was elected with only 24.7 percent of the vote, and in the 1957 federal election in Burnaby-Richmond (British Columbia) the Social Credit member won his seat with only 26.0 percent of the total vote. But these extreme cases are noted and remembered because they are not the norm and if the experience with the alternative vote in Manitoba and Alberta is any guide then the great majority of those who are leading on the first count (and are thus elected under a plurality system) would also be elected if a second count were taken under a preferential system. An alternative ballot would ensure that the winning candidate did have a clear majority of votes in the single constituency, but that is all it would do.

The second proposition is also easily substantiated. The relationship between the percentage of votes cast for a party and its percentage of seats in the legislature appears at first to be totally haphazard, and irrational. Thus, for example, the Liberals in 1930, with 45.5 percent of the popular vote, received 37.1 percent of the seats in the House of Commons, yet in 1935, with only 44.9 percent of the vote, they obtained 70.6 percent of the seats. Then, in 1963, the Progressive Conservatives won 35.8 percent of the seats with only 32.8 percent of the total vote while five years earlier the Liberals, with a slightly higher share of the vote (33.6 percent) won only 18.5 percent of the seats. The same apparent disparity between the share of the vote and the share of seats is evident at the provincial level. In Alberta, for example, in the 1967 elections, the Social Credit party won over 80 percent of the seats with less than 45 percent of the vote, and in 1955 in Ontario the Progressive Conservatives won 84 out of the 98 seats with only 48.5 percent of the popular vote. Similar illustrations can be found in every province.

Yet the electoral system is not as irrational as these results might indicate. It has been shown that the relationship between any party's share of the popular vote in federal elections and its share of seats in the House of Commons is surprisingly consistent. There is obviously not a direct one-to-one relationship, but the plurality electoral system does distribute representatives as a mathematical function of the votes received in a manner perhaps even more precise and consistent than one might reasonably have expected in a country as large and as diversified as Canada.[13]

The relationship has been expressed as the "cube law" which predicts that the ratio of seats won by each party in any given election will be close to the cube of the ratio of the share of the popular vote. It will not, of course, be an exact relationship and a certain margin of error is expected and tolerated.

> The problem is one of relating certain empirical data to a set of theoretical equations. In the case under consideration the data are a series of election results which will be dependent to some uncertain degree on such irregular and unpredictable variables as candidate's personality, the emergence in some constituencies of purely local issues running contrary to national trends, situa-

tions where the contest in constituencies is so close that mere chance must determine which candidate receives the few score vital extra votes, and the appearance of additional candidates who might take votes from the front runners. Given this measure of unpredictability it is unlikely that any simple mathematical formula which would match up all the data exactly could be devised.[14]

Nevertheless it can be shown that even within the context of Canadian federal politics in which during the past fifty years new parties have appeared on the political scene, and others have disappeared altogether, in which there have been major shifts in the regional bases of party support, and in which there have been several redistributions of seats, the cube formula will produce predicted results surprisingly close to those which have actually occurred. Table 4: 3 compares the predicted results under the "cube law" and the actual results, first, for the winning party in each federal election since 1921, and secondly for the trailing parties.[15]

The most important recent study of the impact of the electoral system on other aspects of the Canadian political process is the article by Professor Alan Cairns which appeared in the first issue of the new *Canadian Journal*

### Table 4: 3 (A)
### COMPARISON OF PREDICTED AND ACTUAL RESULTS FOR THE LEADING PARTY IN EACH FEDERAL ELECTION FROM 1921 to 1968

| Election | Leading party | Predicted no. of seats | Actual no. of seats | Difference | Difference as percentage of total no. of seats | Difference as percentage of leading party's total |
|---|---|---|---|---|---|---|
| 1921 | Liberal | 120 | 116 | −4 | 1.7 | 3.4 |
| 1925 | Conservative | 125 | 116 | −9 | 3.7 | 7.8 |
| 1926 | Liberal | 119 | 128 | +9 | 3.7 | 7.0 |
| 1930 | Conservative | 127 | 137 | +10 | 4.1 | 7.3 |
| 1935 | Liberal | 161 | 173 | +12 | 4.9 | 6.9 |
| 1940 | Liberal | 172 | 181 | +9 | 3.7 | 5.0 |
| 1945 | Liberal | 130 | 125 | −5 | 2.0 | 4.0 |
| 1949 | Liberal | 187 | 193 | +6 | 2.3 | 3.1 |
| 1953 | Liberal | 172 | 171 | −1 | 0.4 | 0.6 |
| 1957 | Prog. Cons. | 108 | 112 | +4 | 1.5 | 3.7 |
| 1958 | Prog. Cons. | 201 | 208 | +7 | 2.6 | 3.4 |
| 1962 | Prog. Cons. | 113 | 116 | +3 | 1.1 | 2.6 |
| 1963 | Liberal | 149 | 129 | −20 | 7.5 | 15.5 |
| 1965 | Liberal | 139 | 131 | −8 | 3.0 | 6.1 |
| 1968 | Liberal | 168 | 155 | −13 | 4.9 | 8.4 |

## Table 4: 3 (B)
## COMPARISON OF PREDICTED AND ACTUAL RESULTS FOR THE LOSING PARTIES (EXCLUDING "OTHERS") IN EACH FEDERAL ELECTION FROM 1921 to 1968

| Election | Party | Predicted no. of seats | Actual no. of seats | Difference | Difference as percentage of total seats |
|---|---|---|---|---|---|
| 1921 | Conservative | 50 | 50 | 0 | 0 |
| | Progressive | 60 | 65 | +5 | 2.1 |
| 1925 | Liberal | 91 | 99 | +8 | 3.3 |
| | Progressive | 25 | 24 | −1 | 0.4 |
| 1926 | Conservative | 102 | 91 | −11 | 4.5 |
| | Progressive | 17 | 20 | +3 | 1.2 |
| 1930 | Liberal | 104 | 91 | −13 | 5.3 |
| | Prog. & UFA | 10 | 12 | +2 | 0.8 |
| 1935 | Conservative | 56 | 40 | −16 | 6.5 |
| | CCF | 11 | 7 | −4 | 1.6 |
| | Social Credit | 11 | 17 | +6 | 2.4 |
| | Reconstruction | 2 | 1 | 1 | 0.4 |
| 1940 | Conservative | 48 | 40 | −8 | 3.3 |
| | CCF | 10 | 8 | −2 | 0.3 |
| | Social Credit | 7 | 10 | +3 | 1.2 |
| 1945 | Prog. Cons. | 70 | 67 | −3 | 1.2 |
| | CCF | 21 | 28 | +7 | 2.9 |
| | Social Credit | 10 | 13 | +3 | 1.2 |
| 1949 | Prog. Cons. | 48 | 41 | −7 | 2.7 |
| | CCF | 15 | 13 | −2 | 0.8 |
| | Social Credit | 7 | 10 | +3 | 1.1 |
| 1953 | Prog. Cons. | 55 | 51 | −4 | 1.5 |
| | CCF | 19 | 23 | +4 | 1.5 |
| | Social Credit | 15 | 15 | 0 | 0 |
| 1957 | Liberal | 120 | 105 | −15 | 5.7 |
| | CCF | 17 | 25 | +8 | 3.0 |
| | Social Credit | 15 | 19 | +4 | 1.5 |
| 1958 | Liberal | 54 | 49 | −5 | 1.9 |
| | CCF | 7 | 8 | +1 | 0.4 |
| | Social Credit | 2 | 0 | −2 | 0.8 |
| 1962 | Liberal | 108 | 100 | −8 | 3.0 |
| | NDP | 15 | 19 | +4 | 1.5 |
| | Social Credit | 29 | 30 | +1 | 0.4 |
| 1963 | Prog. Cons. | 81 | 95 | +14 | 5.2 |
| | NDP | 12 | 17 | +5 | 1.9 |
| | Social Credit | 23 | 24 | +1 | 0.4 |
| 1965 | Prog. Cons. | 87 | 97 | +10 | 3.8 |
| | NDP | 23 | 21 | −2 | 0.8 |
| | Social Credit (RC) | 14 | 14 | 0 | 0 |
| 1968 | Prog. Cons. | 66 | 72 | +6 | 2.3 |
| | NDP | 19 | 22 | +3 | 1.1 |
| | Social Credit (RC) | 10 | 14 | +4 | 1.5 |

*of Political Science.*[16] Professor Cairns developed two separate themes: (a) the Canadian party system "exacerbates sectional cleavages, sectional identities, and sectionally oriented parties"[17] and, (b) the electoral system is a major determinant of the party system. The two themes are, of course, intimately related, although it is the first point, the effect of the party system on the "politics of sectionalism" that is most convincingly demonstrated. Professor Cairns, in his critique of the traditional view of Canadian party politics as "politics of moderation, or brokerage politics, which minimize differences, restrain fissiparous tendencies, and thus over time help knit together the diverse interests of a polity weak in integration,"[18] effectively shows that the traditional view is "at best questionable, and possibly invalid" in that it attributes to the party system what "is simply inherent in a representative democracy." By this argument Cairns has compelled Canadian political scientists to reassess the role of Canadian parties and his paper must become a landmark in our understanding of the operation of the political process in this country.

But it is the other side of his case that is of the greatest concern here and it is the hardest part of the argument to make, largely because so little attention has been paid to the causal impact of the electoral system on the party system in Canadian politics. The general conclusion reached by Cairns is summed up in a single paragraph:

> The following basic effects of the electoral system have been noted. The electoral system has not been impartial in its translation of votes into seats. Its benefits have been disproportionately given to the strongest major party and a weak sectional party. The electoral system has made a major contribution to the identification of particular sections/provinces with particular parties. It has undervalued the partisan diversity within each section/province. By so doing it has rendered the parliamentary composition of each party less representative of the sectional interests in the political system than is the party electorate from which that representation is derived. The electoral system favours minor parties with concentrated sectional support, and discourages those with diffuse national support. The electoral system has consistently exaggerated the significance of cleavages demarcated by sectional/provincial boundaries and has thus tended to transform contests between parties into contests between sections/provinces.[19]

There can, of course, be no dispute with this general proposition. The electoral system has produced the effects which Professor Cairns has claimed of it and the electoral system is much more of a determinant factor in Canadian party politics than most commentators have so far allowed. There is still one objection. While Professor Cairns has shown that a structure of single-member constituencies with a plurality vote will produce the results he describes, he does not show that it will be the only electoral system to produce such results.

The two most frequently proposed alternatives to the single-member plurality system are the preferential ballot in the single-member district and the single transferable vote in districts electing from five to a dozen members, and these are the only two alternatives which have been applied at all in Canada. There is neither empirical evidence from Canada, or elsewhere, nor theoretical necessity, which suggests that either of these two most favoured alternatives will have any very different overall impact on the party system. The preferential ballot in the single-member district may mean that in constituency X, candidate A will be elected rather than candidate B, but it has not, and there is no reason why it should have, any systematic or long-term effect on the representation of parties, sections, or interests. As has been noted the single transferable vote in the typical metropolitan constituency electing fewer than twelve members produces a balance of party representation not inherently different from that to be expected under a simple plurality vote.

Either system will continue to give disproportionate weight to the leading party or to any party with concentrated sectional support and either system will discourage, with minimal rewards, minor parties with diffuse national support. By bestowing its rewards unevenly either system will present a distorted image of the sectional bases of party support.

The only alternative electoral systems which are likely to produce any radical restructuring of the party system or of party representation in the legislature are various varieties of the party list system of voting in constituencies returning twenty or more members. Only a division of Ontario into perhaps no more than four constituencies in which the number of members allocated to each party is proportional to the share of the total vote would have enabled, for example, the C.C.F. in 1945 to translate its 14.4 percent of the popular vote into 12 seats (instead of winning none at all) and only a single constituency for the whole of Saskatchewan would have reduced the C.C.F.'s representation there from 18 seats to 9. Hence Professor Cairns is correct; for the C.C.F. to have won 12 seats in Ontario and 9 in Saskatchewan in 1945 would have given a truer picture of the real basis of support of the party, and thus prevented many later misconceptions, than the 18 from Saskatchewan and none from Ontario which resulted from the application of the single-member constituency system.

But this kind of proportional representation in which the legislative strength of the parties is a fairly close mirror image of their total national support, and in which the diffuse national support of some parties, if it is not too diffuse, will be reflected in some kind of legislative support, will not be achieved except through the adoption of some radically different electoral system on a multi-member district, party list basis. And there are overwhelming cultural and political traditions which make the introduction of any such radical innovation a most unlikely proposition in Canada at the present. Voting by a party list system is not now a viable option in Canadian politics, federally or provincially.

## THE ELECTION OFFICIALS

Essential to the operation of any election is a body of officials, persons responsible for the announcement of candidates, the preparation and distribution of ballot papers, the conduct of the poll, the counting and recording of votes, and the official declaration of results. Obviously these are all sensitive areas wherein there are maximum opportunities for fraud and corruption and great care ought to be taken to ensure that, however appointed, the election officials act in a genuinely non-partisan manner. This is important not only in the sense that a corrupt or biased election system is incompatible with the spirit of democracy, but also in that the voters' perception of election corruption will tend to determine the level of political cynicism and alienation. Few today are surprised or disturbed to discover that election administrators in past generations did not even begin to approach the necessary high standards of non-partisanship, but it is a matter of concern that even now shortcomings and occasional unfortunate lapses are still accepted as part of the normal order of things.

Until comparatively recently in most areas, and as is still the case in others, the operation of an election was almost entirely a matter for the individual constituency itself, subject only to the general law. The wording of the Writ made it clear that it was not the Government or the central administration which conducted the election, but the returning officer in the constituency. The Writ, addressed to the returning officer, says, in the name of Her Majesty the Queen, that "We command *you* that . . . *you* do cause an election to be made according to law . . . that *you* do cause the nomination of candidates at such election to be held . . . and if a poll become necessary that the same be held . . ."[20] and so on. A general election is, in effect, no more than the sum of a series of particular elections administered by local officials.

This is still fundamentally the position, with the prime responsibility for the conduct of the election remaining with the returning officer, but since 1920 there has been, at the federal level, an overall supervision and co-ordination through a Chief Electoral Officer who ensures that there are recognized and uniform practices and procedures.[21] The new Chief Electoral Officer, who was made directly responsible to Parliament and not the Government of the day, was given the status of a deputy minister and the same degree of tenure as a Supreme Court judge. He was to be paid directly out of the consolidated fund as a further guarantee of his independence.

While the returning officers were the direct administrators of an election, the Chief Electoral Officer was given authority to "properly direct" them and, "in the case of incompetency or neglect of duty on the part of any of them, recommend his removal and the appointment of another in his stead."[22] This authority in itself did much to correct the partisan bias which seemed so much a feature of earlier elections. The authority of the Chief Electoral Officer was further emphasized by granting him the right to "exercise general direction and supervision over the administrative conduct of elections with a view to ensuring the fairness and impartiality of all election officers and compliance with the provisions of this Act."[23]

Although it is probably true that the introduction into the system of a Chief Electoral Officer has been one of the most important single steps in establishing both the fact and the appearance of non-partisanship, the change did not, and could not, solve all problems immediately. The Chief Electoral Officer could recommend the removal of a returning officer but he could not himself directly intervene in the administration of an election in any constituency, and as long as returning officers were themselves appointed by the government of the day, the Chief Electoral Officer's authority over them was severely circumscribed. Nevertheless the establishment of the office was a major step forward and made easier the subsequent steps.

All the provinces except Alberta now also provide for a Chief Electoral Officer, but although there appears to be little or no published material on how well or badly these officers have performed their tasks, it is clear that there are considerable variations in their responsibilities and independence. The most detailed provisions are in the *Quebec Election Act,*[24] which defines the office of the Chief Returning Officer. The *Act* specifies his salary ($25,500), requires that he be appointed by a resolution of the Legislative Assembly and gives him the same tenure and pension rights as a district judge. He may not have been a candidate in any federal, provincial, or municipal election during the ten years preceding his appointment and he must take an oath "well and faithfully to perform" the duties of his office without partiality or favour. He is given authority, subject to certain specified rules, to suspend or dismiss other election officers.

The Manitoba Act is less specific in defining the general functions of the Chief Electoral Officer, saying no more than that he is "to have supervision and charge of the conduct of every election held under this Act." His qualifications are also left, probably deliberately, vague. He is to be "a suitable person" appointed by the Lieutenant-Governor-in-Council. The most distinctive features of the Manitoba provisions for a Chief Electoral Officer relate to questions of tenure. The Chief Electoral Officer can be removed "by the Lieutenant-Governor-in-Council only by order-in-council made on an address of the assembly carried by a vote of two-thirds of the members voting thereon." He can be suspended upon "the written advice of the majority of a committee consisting of the President of the Council and the recognized leaders of the members belonging to the several political parties in opposition." These requirements would mean that except in circumstances where one party held almost all the seats in the legislature, the Chief Electoral Officer would be virtually irremovable and his independence of action is in fact guaranteed.[25]

Three provinces, Ontario, Nova Scotia, and Prince Edward Island, specify that the Chief Electoral Officer shall be a provincial civil servant, with Ontario and Nova Scotia requiring also that he be a barrister.[26] The two maritime provinces have identically worded sections on the responsibilities of the Chief Electoral Officer. He is to "exercise general direction and supervision over the administrative conduct of elections;" and "(b) enforce on the part of election officers, fairness, impartiality and compliance with this Act."[27]

The principal duties of the Chief Electoral Officer in New Brunswick and Newfoundland are worded in terms exactly following those of Nova Scotia and Prince Edward Island, but the appointment is less detailed, there is no specification of qualifications, and tenure and independence are less certain.[28]

The other two provinces have much less detailed provisions and the words of the acts leave a great many more questions unanswered. Saskatchewan, for example, provides that the Lieutenant-Governor-in-Council shall appoint: "an elector residing within the province to be the Chief Electoral Officer during pleasure;" and that the Chief Electoral Officer is to be paid such salary "as may be fixed by the Lieutenant Governor in Council."[29] The law in British Columbia is even more general, it being required merely that "The Lieutenant-Governor in Council shall appoint a Chief Electoral Officer who shall have general supervision of the administration of this Act."[30] While Alberta has no one with the official title of Chief Electoral Officer, the Clerk of the Executive Council acts in this capacity.

Despite the creation of the office of Chief Electoral Officer the single most important post in an election is still that of the returning officer in each constituency. Both the fact and the appearance of integrity in the election system follow from the procedure for the appointment of the returning officer and the manner in which he carries out his duties.

At the federal level there have been several changes in the procedure for appointing returning officers, although none of them has so far guaranteed the highest possible level of non-partisanship (in fact some of the changes would seem to have been designed to ensure that non-partisanship would not be too serious a threat to the government).

Section 42 of the *British North America Act* empowered the Governor General to issue Writs for the election of members to the House of Com-

mons "to such Returning Officers as he thinks fit," and the person so appointed was to conduct the election in accordance with the electoral law in
the province in which his constituency was situated. This arrangement
appeared to maximize the opportunities for partisan conduct and it is clear
from numerous accounts that a great many returning officers took
advantage of the opportunity.

An attempt to remedy the situation was made with the passing of the
*Dominion Election Act* of 1874 which abolished the Governor General's
discretion and required that the Writ be addressed to "the Sheriff or to
the Registrar of Deeds, or to one of the Sheriffs or of the Registrars for the
Electoral District or a portion of the Electoral District for which the
election is to take place."[31] The Sheriff or Registrar was to be *ex
officio* returning officer. In constituencies where there was neither a
Sheriff nor a Registrar of Deeds, then the returning officer would be "such
other person" as the Governor General appointed. This practice of appointing *ex officio* returning officers from either the local government
administrators or regional offices of the national government is, and has
long been, the standard practice in Great Britain, New Zealand, and
elsewhere.

If partisanship in election administration is to be minimized by the use
of *ex officio* election officials then, of course, it is essential that the officials
themselves be non-partisans. There is no conclusive evidence about the
extent of partisan behaviour on the part of the returning officers appointed
after 1874 although there were clearly a number of Conservatives who
were convinced that many of the returning officers, largely appointed under
Liberal provincial administrations, were unfairly partisan. This, whatever
the actual facts of the case, was the argument used by the Conservatives
to restore the appointment of returning officers to federal government
control in 1882.[32]

From 1882 until 1925 returning officers were appointed only for the
election to which the Writ referred, "and it was accordingly inevitable, . . .
that appointments should, as a general rule, be made from among the
political supporters of the Government of the day; in practice each returning officer no doubt was chosen usually on the recommendation of the
person or persons by whom the local party patronage was controlled."[33]

A further consequence of the partisan appointment of returning officers
was that the subordinate election officials, the deputy returning officers
and poll clerks whose appointment was made by the returning officer, were
also chosen largely on the basis of political friendship. All this meant that
the political party in power had full administrative control over the election
machinery. This does not mean that all, or even the majority, of election
officials abused their authority, but there was always the suspicion that
they might. As the Chief Electoral Officer noted in 1926:

Most of the complaints made relate to matters in which the election officer concerned has been quite right or, although mistaken, has acted in good faith, but his conduct has aroused an unfounded suspicion of partisanship in the minds of persons opposed in political interest: the fact that appointments are generally made from among supporters of the party in power naturally inclines supporters of the opposite party to think that unfair administrative tactics are intended to be or are in fact resorted to. In some cases, however, the present mode of the selection of election officers does induce on the part of appointees a mistaken idea that they owe a duty to the party to which they belong rather than to the state by which they are employed and paid.[34]

Here, in these words, is the whole substance of the case against the partisan appointment of election officials. It is not enough to establish that, even though appointed by the party in power, the majority of election officers have behaved with scrupulous impartiality. As long as they receive their appointments as political favours they will always be suspected of returning the favour. When, therefore, in the course of their duties they make decisions which, although proper, are to the advantage of the party which appointed them, their actions will be seen as biased and will thus reflect adversely on the voters' perception of the integrity of the system. And in its ability to mould or preserve a genuine democratic political system any sub-system such as the election process will be severely constrained by the voters' perception of it.

What should have been a major change took place in 1925 when an amendment to the *Dominion Elections Act* provided that henceforth returning officers, instead of being appointed for one election only, should hold office "during pleasure" like other servants of the Crown.[35] This permanence, however, proved illusory for, with the change of government in 1926, the appointments of most existing returning officers were cancelled and new appointments made in their place.

A further, and apparently the final, attempt at reform was made in 1929 when an amendment to the *Dominion Elections Act* imposed the burden of appointing returning officers directly on the Chief Electoral Officer.[36] In one sense this was a successful experiment and following the 1930 elections the Chief Electoral Officer reported that "the number of administrative difficulties and complaints against returning officers showed a notable decrease."[37] On the other hand, as Professor Ward has noted, the Chief Electoral Officer had, of necessity, to rely on the advice of local people familiar with each constituency and such local people, interested enough to advise the Chief Electoral Officer, were almost always partisans.[38] The experiment, therefore was not continued and in 1934 the Government re-established its authority to appoint all returning officers, on a "permanent" basis.[39] There have been no further changes in the formal rules and returning officers are still appointed by the Government, presumably on the advice of the chief spokesman in each constituency of the party in power in Ottawa. But the practice seems to be slowly improving.

There is still, however, some element of partisan preference in the selection of returning officers. All the returning officers responsible for the conduct of the 1957 elections had, of course, been appointed by Liberal governments. The Progressive Conservatives, elected in 1957, replaced 53 of these in time for the 1958 elections but were content to leave most as they were. More substantial changes took place before the 1962 elections when the Conservative government replaced a further 171 Liberal appointees, as well as 12 of their own 1958 appointments. Between 1962 and 1963, 2 more Liberal and 22 Conservative appointments changed hands. Thus, when the Liberals returned to office in 1963 they were confronted with the fact that only 37 of the returning officers appointed before 1957 still held their posts, and 226 were Conservative nominees. Surprisingly, perhaps, between 1963 and 1965 the new Liberal government appointed only 52 new returning officers, 3 of whom were for constituencies where the original Liberal appointments had not been changed by the Conservatives. Confronted with an overwhelming number of Conservative appointments after their election in 1963 the Liberals made fewer changes than between 1953 and 1957 when 74 Liberal appointees had been replaced. The redistribution of 1966, by abolishing numerous old constituencies and creating many new ones, demanded extensive replacement and reappointment of returning officers and a genuine comparison between the elections of 1965 and 1968 is not, therefore, possible.

At the provincial level there is surprisingly little that can be said about returning officers. All are appointed by the provincial governments and in certain cases there are provisions for the removal of a returning officer who engages in "politically partisan conduct." But those in each province who will know how close the statutory provisions are to the political reality, who could describe the varying levels of impartiality or partisanship, have not made their knowledge public. The statutory provisions pertaining to returning officers in the provinces are summarized in Appendix Two.

The comparisons in these Appendices in themselves make interesting reading. It would be intriguing to know exactly why from Alberta through to Ontario it was deemed to be necessary to legislate against the possibility of ministers of religion acting as returning officers, or why some provinces, but not all, have been prepared to give a returning officer near permanent status. One would also like to know why it is only in the Maritimes that the election law specifically prohibits partisan activity on the part of the returning officer when it is assumed that partisan activity is also frowned on in the other provinces. But in our present stage of knowledge of comparative provincial politics the contrasts remain simply as "interesting."

Apart from a few experts in each province who, as has already been suggested, have kept their knowledge to themselves, there is no real information about the operation of these provisions. In Alberta, Ontario, and Newfoundland, for example, returning officers are technically appointed for only one election. It is not known how many of these returning officers are reappointed at subsequent elections, nor is it known whether the turnover of such "temporary" returning officers is, in fact, any greater than that in those provinces where returning officers appear to be appointed on a more permanent basis. There are, in various sources, numerous anecdotal accounts of partisan bias by returning officers in individual constituencies, but no substantial, documented accounts comparing one province with another, or comparing changes in the practices within any one province over a period of several elections. One cannot say, with any authority, how accurate or how typical are the allegations of partisanship; and as long as our knowledge of the integrity of the election system at the basic level of the constituency remains as vague as this, our perception of the effective operation of democracy in Canada will remain incomplete.

The voters' principal contact with the election administration is with the deputy returning officers and the poll clerks who man the individual polling stations. With one deputy returning officer and one poll clerk to each polling station, there were more than 100,000 of these temporary election officials engaged for the 1968 federal elections. The number needed to staff all the polling booths for a complete set of provincial elections is at least as great, and probably considerably higher than this.[41]

Because of the large number of temporary officials, appointed directly or indirectly by the returning officers,[42] for the most part on the recommendation of the dispensers of party patronage in each constituency, it is inevitable that some will be easily corrupted, some will turn a blind eye to the shady practices of party enthusiasts, and a larger number will simply, through incompetence or lack of training, make many mistakes. It is easy to find the examples of the malpractices and the mistakes, and some of these will be commented on shortly, but there is no reliable information on how widespread these deficiencies are and so one cannot really say what kinds of measures are needed to correct them.

In all provinces there are some attempts to reduce the range of genuine error by providing the deputy returning officers with more or less explicit instructions. The most precisely detailed are those issued to deputy returning officers for federal elections.[43] As well as the general verbal instructions, there is a detailed "Diary of Duties," a step-by-step guide which, if followed exactly, should make administrative error virtually impossible.

The best protection against deliberate malpractice is the presence in the polling station of agents or representatives of the candidates. Such agents, or scrutineers, are entitled, by all the Acts being considered, to be present in the polling place before the poll is opened to examine the ballot box and ensure that it is empty, to come and go through the day to observe the actual conduct of the poll and to ensure that all is done properly, and to attend and witness the counting of the votes. On the theory that the best safeguard against fraud by the friends of one candidate is the presence of friends of another who would suffer by the success of such fraud, this is probably the most efficient arrangement possible.

The point at which it breaks down is where one of the parties has too few resources, or is too poorly organized, to provide the manpower to staff all polling stations — this, unfortunately, is very often the case. Most parties, in most constituencies, can staff most polling stations in the final hours of election day when the drive to ensure maximum turnout of supporters is at its peak, and to witness the counting of the vote, but it is usually only the strongest parties which can maintain observers in every polling place throughout all the hours of voting.

As long as a structure of a large number of polling places, serving at most 300 or so electors is maintained, and there are certain substantial advantages in doing this, one must expect that some of the very large number of people required to staff these places will be unsuited for the work, that there will be temptations to cheat a little on the rules, and that some will not resist this temptation.

## BRIBERY, CORRUPTION, INTIMIDATION, AND OTHER UNSAVOURY PRACTICES

Bribery, corruption, and intimidation were, until very recently, part of the normal procedure of elections in all parts of the world where elections were becoming a meaningful part of the political process. As one Canadian justice asked, "Is not bribery the cornerstone of Party Government?"[44] Writing of conditions in England in the mid-nineteenth century, Cornelius O'Leary commented that "Violence or physical intimidation at elections, although common law offences, tended to be accepted as part of the normal behaviour of a rude and inhumane age," and that "bribery and treating were never more prevalent than in the decades immediately after the passing of the Great Reform Act."[45]

Conditions were obviously no better in Canada in the years after Confederation. Professor Dawson wrote of:

> The low condition of Canadian political morality which was most conspicuous during the first fifty years of responsible government . . . its rise and continuance were due in no small measure to the proximity of the United States; and the temptation for the Canadian politician to emulate in a modest way the methods of a Tweed, a Croker, or a Philadelphia Gas Ring, proved in a de-

plorable number of instances to be irresistible . . . these were evidences of
native sins which had received American inspiration and encouragement and
which corrupted extensively Canadian political life.[46]

In view of the low state of English political morality in the same period
it seems a little unfair of Professor Dawson to put so much of the
responsibility for Canadian corruption on the Americans. It seems that
Canadian politicians were perfectly capable of becoming corrupt on their
own initiative, without anyone's example or help.

The history of electoral corruption in these early days of Canadian
confederation has been outlined by Professor Ward.[47] Today it is still
possible to discover ugly incidents and corrupt practices, but they are increasingly rare and, what is more important, the electors appear to be
increasingly hostile to them. The last point suggests that there are three
separate elements in the reform of the morality of election systems:
positive actions by the legislature to refine the definitions of corrupt practices and to close-off loopholes in their application; improvements in the
machinery for handling allegations of corrupt practices and for discriminat-
ing the genuine from the purely mischievous allegation; and changing
standards of public morality and concern for political morality which
provide some of the impetus and pressure for the first two elements.

All the federal and provincial election acts now devote considerable
care to the defining of corrupt practices and other offences. *The Canada
Elections Act* for example, has comprehensive definitions of bribery,
treating, undue influence, and personation. The description of the "corrupt
practice of treating," which is surely a model of legal draftsmanship, must
cover every possible course of action:

(1) Every person is guilty of the corrupt practice of treating and of an indictable
offence against this Act punishable as provided in this Act, who, corruptly, by
himself or by any other person, either before, during or after an election,
directly or indirectly gives or provides, or causes to be given or provided, or is
accessory to the giving or providing, or pays or engages to pay wholly or in
part the expense of giving or providing any meat, drink, refreshment or provision, or any money or ticket or other means or device to enable the procuring
of any meat, drink, refreshment or provision, to or for any person for the
purpose of corruptly influencing that person or any other person to give or
refrain from giving his vote at such election or on account of such person or
any other person having voted or refrained from voting or being about to vote
or refrain from voting at such election, and every elector who corruptly
accepts or takes any such meat, drink, refreshment or provision or any such
money or ticket, or who adopts such other means or device to enable the procuring of such meat, drink, refreshment or provision is guilty likewise.
(2) Subsection (1) does not apply to
(a) an official agent who, as an election expense, provides food such as sand-

wiches, cakes, cookies, and drink such as tea, coffee, milk or soft drinks at a meeting of electors assembled for the purpose of promoting the election of a candidate during an election; or

(b) any person other than an official agent who at his own expense provides food such as sandwiches, cakes, cookies, and drink such as tea, coffee, milk or soft drinks at a meeting of electors assembled for the purpose of promoting the election of a candidate during an election.[48]

Undue influence is the use, or the threatened use of "force, violence or restraint," and includes any "temporal or spiritual injury, damage, harm or loss," and also any "abduction, duress, or any false or fraudulent pretence, device or contrivance," which "impedes, prevents or otherwise interferes with the free exercise of the franchise."[49]

A person is guilty of the indictable offence of "personation" if he applies for a ballot paper in the name of some other person, whether that name is of a person "living or dead, or of a fictious person," or if, having voted, he applies at the same election for another ballot paper, or if he "aids, abets, counsels, procures or endeavours to procure" the act of personation by anyone else.[50]

All the provincial acts contain provisions similar in intent to the above, although the wording and arrangement is often very different. All define, and prohibit, in some form bribery, treating, undue influence, and personation. All also place some kinds of restrictions on campaign activities on election day, limiting the wearing of ribbons and badges, the displaying of flags, banners, or posters, or the use of loudspeaker systems. Saskatchewan and Nova Scotia[51] specifically prohibit the holding of any parades or demonstrations on election day until after the close of the polls. Only four provinces: Alberta, Manitoba, Quebec, and Newfoundland, follow the federal practice of having their electoral law prohibit the sale of liquor on election day or at least while the polls are open, but in fact abstinence is provided for in many provinces by virtue of other legislation or regulation.[52]

All the acts are similar in making extensive provision for the security of ballot boxes and ballot papers, and all contain clauses which make it an offence for any election official or voter to violate the secrecy of the ballot.

In the matter of peace and good order it is universal practice to give returning officers and deputy returning officers full powers to make arrests and to swear-in special constables. Most also make it illegal to be in the possession of any kind of offensive weapon[53] in a polling station or within a certain specified distance of one, and deputy returning officers are generally given the authority to demand the surrender of such weapons.

Five provinces: Alberta, Saskatchewan, Manitoba, Ontario, and Nova Scotia, further ensure the purity of elections by forbidding any candidate to place any bet or wager on the outcome of the election in his own constituency.

British Columbia specifies one election offence which is unique to that province. From the date of the issue of the Writ until after polling day it is illegal to take any "straw vote" which will "distinguish the political opinions of the voters in any electoral district."[54] This, if strictly enforced, would preclude any pre-election survey research whether or not the results were to be published before the election. There is some case to be made for restricting the publication of "public opinion polls" which are often based on the most dubious techniques and which are published only because it is assumed that they will create some kind of bandwagon effect among the voters. Such polls are simply another kind of election propaganda and one would suspect that most voters are intelligent enough to perceive them as such. But it seems to be a little extreme to attempt to curb a spuriously scientific, and therefore dishonest, kind of propaganda by prohibiting genuine academic research which, if properly carried out, would not be available to the voter until the election was long over.

All these prohibitions, offences, and consequent penalties for their violation seem to be reasonably effective and there does not seem to be any reason to suppose that elections anywhere in Canada today are won or lost by anything other than the choice of the voters.

This does not mean that all is completely pure. The reports which the Chief Electoral Officer submits to the Speaker of the House of Commons after each federal election include the results of any investigations he has made following allegations made to him of improper election conduct. We do not need to review all of these, but some examples are useful. In his report of May 1958 the Chief Electoral Officer reported on the results of an inquiry he had ordered following allegations of offences during the 1957 election in the electoral district of St. Paul's. As a result of these investigations it was established that at the revision of the voters' lists the agents of one of the candidates had added 474 fictitious names to the list. All the agents involved were found guilty and were given short terms of imprisonment.[55] Similar irregularities in the Montreal district of Cartier in the 1958 elections also resulted in prosecutions and sentences. In 1962 charges were laid and convictions obtained in the Trinity and Parkdale constituencies in Toronto. Both cases concerned the deliberate falsification of voters' lists.

On the other hand not all allegations were substantiated. In his *Report* following the 1962 elections, the Chief Electoral Officer noted that allegations of violations of various sections of the *Canada Elections Act* had been made in the constituencies of Bellechasse, Carleton, York West, Chambly-Rouville, and Sainte-Anne, but in each case investigation showed no substantial evidence on which to proceed. One other charge, concerning Rosedale, was dismissed by the Magistrate.[56]

It also appears that during the elections of 1930 Communist party candidates in Toronto and Montreal were subjected to considerable harassment and intimidation by the police, although episodes of this kind now appear to be more rare.[57]

These are only examples and there are others that could have been used; but even in total there are not many, and it should be noted that most of the offences which lead to investigations today concern the deliberate padding of the voters' lists with fictitious names. Personation is probably the major form of election corruption at the present time. But this is a form of activity which is likely to occur only in the anonymous conditions of the big city centres for it is virtually impossible to add any significant number of fictitious names to the lists in rural areas, small towns, or the middle-class suburbs which surround the cities, for in these environments everyone makes it his business to know everyone else.

Direct bribery, treating, and undue influence have declined principally because there is no profit in them any more. Before the extension of the franchise the bribing of a dozen or so voters could secure the election, but the modern constituency, with its thousands of voters, is simply too large to influence through individual bribes and threats.

## ELECTION FINANCE

This is not the place to engage in a detailed commentary on election finance[58] but a few general remarks ought to be made about the implications of the financial structure on the total election process. The problem is summed up in a single phrase in the *Report* of the Committee on Election Expenses which refers to "the possible distortion of the democratic process by the uneven distribution of funds among candidates and parties."[59]

In an era when the direct bribery of individual voters was a normal part of campaign strategy the candidate with the greatest resources obviously had a substantial advantage. The substitution of more subtle campaign techniques and the expansion of the mass media changed the character of the advantage, but did not do away with it all together. It is not true that the candidate who spends the most money will always win. If he is a candidate for a party which is discredited, or which has no traditional basis of support in his constituency, or if he wastes his resources on ill-planned campaigns, the rich candidate will very likely finish up behind a much poorer one. However since elections are costly operations, it is to be expected that over any period of time those candidates with the greatest financial resources will have a genuine advantage, and will be more likely to be elected.

It is therefore argued that the democratic process is threatened or obstructed unless there exists some form of control over election expenses.

> Let us be clear what the problem really is. The legal control of the election expenses of candidates for parliament, including the fixing of maximum figures beyond which they may not go, serves two purposes. One is the elimination of expenditure and practices of a corrupt, unfair, or otherwise undesirable kind. The other is the prevention of overlavish expenditure by exceptionally wealthy candidates. Legal control can do no more. It cannot alter the fact that to contest a modern election is necessarily an expensive affair.[60]

Controls over election expenses can be of three basic kinds, any or all of which could be put into practice at any one time. There can, first of all, be limits on the amounts that candidates can legally spend on their campaigns thus reducing the total cost of the election. Secondly, there may be requirements that candidates report in detail the source of all their campaign funds and account for the manner in which these funds are spent. Finally, there may be provision for the reimbursement of actual campaign expenses out of the public treasury.

At the federal level there is no limit on the amount that candidates and parties may legally spend on election campaigns. The candidate himself is limited to an expenditure of no more than $2,000 paid out of his own money for personal expenses. But this is not in any sense a limit on the amount that may be spent, for the candidate may furnish his official agent with as much money as he wishes. All the restriction means is that sums in excess of $2,000 paid by the candidate must be received and disbursed by the official agent.[61] It is also made clear to potential candidates that there "is no limitation upon the amount which a candidate may lawfully disburse in good faith, or any restriction . . . (except in sections dealing with bribery and treating) . . . upon the objects of such expenditures."[62]

The only two provinces which impose any limit on the amount that may be spent on individual campaigns are Quebec and Nova Scotia. As described in Chapter Two,[63] the 1964 *Quebec Election Act* sets limits on the election expenses that may be incurred by either a recognized party or by individual candidates and then provides for the reimbursement of a portion of the election expenses actually incurred. A Nova Scotia Royal Commission, set up in 1968, made recommendations for Nova Scotia basically similar to those already enacted in Quebec. Legislation to give effect to these proposals was passed in April, 1969.[64]

The *Manitoba Election Act* imposes limits, not on individual candidates, but on the provincial organizations of the parties. The *Act*, in a clause at present unique in Canada, requires that: "The total electoral expenses incurred by the central or general committee of any politcial party, or by or through any officer or member thereof, in connection with a general election for the Legislative Assembly, shall in no case exceed the sum of twenty-five thousand dollars;" and then the parties are still further limited in the kinds of things on which they can legally expend funds. The clause continues: "and no such expenses shall be incurred or authorized except for a central office, the holding of public meetings, radio broadcasting, the presentation of election literature, and the publication, issue, and distribution, thereof."[65] In commenting on this provision one cannot do better than follow Professor Angell:

> It is not known how effective these Manitoba regulations are. This writer has never come across a commentary upon them. If they were really enforced and effective however, there is no doubt whatever that every writer on the subject in Canada would hold Manitoba up as a shining example to be followed. . . . It is feared that this regulation is probably a copy of the federal provision, in effect until 1930, and similarly ignored.[66]

All provinces contain clauses requiring official agents to make complete detailed returns of receipts and expenditures, but, as noted in Chapter Two when questions of the costs of candidature were discussed, there appears to be nowhere, except possibly Quebec, where there is even a pretence at enforcing these regulations. An unsystematic sampling of election expense returns suggests that only candidates who have been defeated are likely to make accurate returns, and then only if they wish to make a virtue out of how little they spent. For the rest, at both the federal and provincial levels, election expense returns are simply not taken seriously. It appears that although the letter of the law is reasonably clear and capable of being enforced, it has in fact been regularly and consistently disobeyed. "The tale is one of quiet but thorough law-breaking in practice, and of genteel but persistent hypocrisy in utterance."[67]

There are two major reasons why the expenses-reporting provisions of the various election acts are unenforced. In the first place no party gains, or thinks that it gains, any clear advantage by initiating any formal complaints about any other party's failure to make accurate returns of expenses, and each apparently considers that there are substantial advantages in leaving things as they are. As long as election campaigns are financed principally from donations by individuals, corporations, associations, trade unions, and so on, there will always be the fear, probably justified, that too much publicity might dry up some of these sources. In the second place it is assumed within the political parties that public apathy would weaken the effectiveness of publicity as a control on the unfair distribution of resources. There is nothing to indicate that there yet exists any widespread public concern over election finance and until such concern is aroused it is hard to see any real effect that the publication of expenses would have on the total election process. Even the problem of donors wishing to remain anonymous could be solved by seeing that donations were made through third parties, or by establishing "Funds for Mr. X" committees. Donations could be made to such a committee and all that the party would be required to report would be the total sum received from the committee. Publicity thus will be an effective control only when there emerges a public interest in, and concern over, the amounts of money spent on election campaigns.

The details of the Quebec scheme for the reimbursement of election expenses have already been described. All the indications are that it is a reasonably successful plan and it is possible that it may eventually be copied elsewhere.

## THE OFFICIAL AGENT

Writing on the elimination of corrupt practices from British elections, Professor W. J. M. MacKenzie concluded that the most important contribution to the subject had been the invention of the post of the official agent who would be legally responsible for the receipt, disbursement, and accounting of all expenses. The device of accounting through an agent, he wrote, was "the neatest technical method of control."[68]

The key ideas behind the principle of an official agent, who serves the same role in Canada as in Great Britain, are simple and precise. Every candidate must appoint an official agent whose major responsibility is to act as the candidate's campaign treasurer. Apart from a few limited and specified exceptions, all money spent by or on behalf of a candidate, if in any way related to his campaign, must pass through the official agent's hands. It is an offense for anyone other than the official agent to pay any election campaign expense, or meet any other election campaign liability (again excluding specified minor items). All campaign contributions must be paid directly to the official agent. After the election the official agent is obliged to make a declaration attesting to the correctness of the itemized statement he makes of all the receipts and expenditures made by him or on his behalf in relation to the conduct of the election. These principles are embodied in the *Canada Elections Act* in a lengthy set of clear and precise regulations regarding the appointment and responsibilities of official agents.[69]

There are only two provinces, New Brunswick and Prince Edward Island, which do not adopt the common practice of requiring every candidate to appoint an official agent with duties and responsibilities very similar to those outlined above.[70] In some cases the candidate can himself act as his own agent, in which case he assumes all the legal responsibilities of agent.

The great advantage claimed of the principle of agency is that it sets up a series of formal rules, and applies penalties for breaking them. It is not necessary under the laws governing official agents to prove that payments were corruptly made, only that they were not made and accounted for by the official agent. It is much easier to prove an act than to prove an intention. If it becomes an offence for anyone other than the official agent to spend any money in support of a candidate, and if it is an offence on the part of the agent not to give a detailed accounting of how he has spent money, then all that should be required for a prosecution ought to be that someone else spent money on behalf of a candidate, or that the agent did not keep proper accounts. This principle could be the most effective machinery possible for the controlling of corrupt, dishonest, or excessive expenditures.

The machinery at present available in Canada, and in most of the provinces, is thus reasonably suited to the job that is required of it. Unfortunately it is a machinery that is never used. "The continual violation of the law thus remains one of the most striking aspects of the whole electoral machinery."[71]

The law regarding the official agent is almost universally ignored because the enforcement provisions are virtually unworkable. At the federal level, for example, the returning officer, to whom agents are supposed to make their expense returns, are under no obligation to obtain one if it is not submitted, and the Chief Electoral Officer has no jurisdiction in the matter. As the matter now stands it appears that the only way in which a full set of election expense returns could be obtained would be for legal action to be instituted in each constituency against each candidate and each agent who failed to observe the regulations. It seems quite clear that such large-scale legal action is unlikely.

Until the law is enforced and automatic and adequate penalties imposed either for failing to submit a return by a specified date, or for making an inaccurate return, the present attempt to control improper or excessive expenditure through a system of reporting will remain a farce.[72]

This is one aspect of the election process in which there do not appear to be any regional or provincial differences.[73] None of the provinces (except Quebec) has any adequate enforcement provisions for the control or reporting of election expenses. The controls themselves exist and could be effective, but in no province is there any willingness on the part of election administrators, candidates, party officials, or members of the public to see that the law is observed and that penalties are imposed for its violation. Given what has already been suggested about the relationship between the public concern for political morality and the actual behaviour of the political actors it is unlikely that any serious effort will be made to restrain the present easygoing disregard of the undesirable consequences of existing practices. This concern will, in itself, only develop when more effort is given to explaining the nature of election expenses and their unproductive character.

The one variable in the total election process which is most firmly in the control of the most active participants, the candidates and their principal campaign assistants, is the one in which the law is most consistently violated and the integrity of the process most seriously threatened. As long as candidates and members are permitted to continue to place their own short-term interests above the law, so will general public disrespect for, and consequent lack of confidence in, the honesty of the system continue to hamper the development of a fully democratic political system.

## TAKING THE VOTE

It is not appropriate now to review the history of the struggle for a secret ballot. It is a battle that has been fought and won and it is not likely to be reopened. The question, then, is not whether there shall be a secret ballot, but how to ensure that it is indeed secret. In the various election systems which have been examined there are on this point no differences in principle, only in the administrative details of how to accomplish two purposes. The first is to ensure that each voter may record his vote in secrecy and afterwards have it counted without the identity of the voter being revealed. The second is to set up sufficient control and supervision to ensure that the only votes counted are those properly marked by voters in the polling booth concerned and that no voter casts more votes than he is legally entitled to.

Generally secrecy is fairly easy to achieve. All that is required is, first of all, that there be a polling booth in which the voter can mark his ballot unobserved by anyone else. This can easily be done either for the familiar paper ballot or for voting machines. Secondly it is necessary that all ballots be identical in appearance and format, that when the ballot is properly folded no mark is visible, and that before it is deposited in the ballot box all identification marks and numbers be removed.

Security is more difficult and measures to preserve it have to be taken at several levels.

The amount of attention given to the first problem, adequate control over the printing of ballot papers, varies in different parts of Canada. All paper for the printing of ballots for federal elections is supplied by the Chief Electoral Officer to the returning officers, who in turn supply the local printers. The sheets of paper as supplied already have printed on them the heavy black lines which separate the candidates' names, and they are perforated and numbered. All that remains for the printer to do is to enter the names of the candidates, and on the back print his own name and address and an impression of a stereotype block, supplied by the Chief Electoral Officer, naming the constituency.[74] The printer in turn must, under oath, complete an affidavit certifying the number of sheets of paper he received, the number of ballot papers he properly printed and delivered, the number of sheets of paper which were not required and were returned, the number of sheets spoiled in printing and returned, and the number of cut-off portions of all sheets out of which ballot papers were cut, and which must also be accounted for and returned.[75]

At the provincial level, the controls in Saskatchewan and Nova Scotia are virtually the same in their effect as the federal regulations.[76] In Alberta and Manitoba also there are controls and safeguards which are similar in general intent although the specifications are somewhat less rigid and detailed.[77] Three provinces, Prince Edward Island, Newfoundland, and British Columbia, are much more lax in their supervision of the production of ballot papers, British Columbia being content merely to state that ballot paper shall "be supplied to the Returning Officer for each electoral district by the authority of the Chief Electoral Officer."[78]

This leaves three provinces, Ontario, Quebec, and New Brunswick, where there is even tighter security in the production of ballot paper. Ontario and Quebec both require that in the manufacture of the paper there shall be a "secret thread" or some other special mark running through every ballot and require that the manufacturer of the paper guarantee that it will be made exclusively for the Queen's Printer and that none of it will be supplied to any other person.[79] Quebec and New Brunswick add a further check in that they require the printer to furnish to the returning officer "the surnames and Christian names of all the persons who have worked at the printing, counting, putting into booklets, packing and delivering of the ballot papers," and then require that all such named persons shall affirm that "they have not furnished ballot papers of the same description to any person except the returning officer."[80]

There seems to be no information available which would justify one saying either that the provinces of Ontario, Quebec, and New Brunswick have found it necessary to enact extremely tight security controls over the printing of ballots because of their experience with corruption and fraud in this area, or that the existence of such controls has prevented the emergence of fraud which the lack of adequate control encourages in Newfoundland and British Columbia.

At the level of the polling station security over ballots is reasonably effective and fraud is possible only with the connivance of both the deputy returning officer and the poll clerk. All the candidates are entitled to have representatives in each polling station to check that the ballot box is empty before the voting commences, to observe the conduct of the poll throughout the day, and to witness the counting of the votes. As long as all major candidates are able to staff all polling stations, the opportunities for fraud are thus considerably reduced. Unfortunately there will always be some polling stations where deputy returning officers will be left unsupervised. Even in these circumstances, however, there is no evidence to suggest that forged, or stolen, ballot papers are a serious problem.

As one further protection against fraud, and to ensure specifically that the voter marks only one ballot, it is normally stipulated that the elector after recording his vote shall hand the ballot paper, folded, to the deputy returning officer, who will examine it to confirm that it is indeed the one he gave to the voter. The deputy returning officer shall then "in full view of the elector and all others present, remove and destroy the counterfoil and the deputy returning officer shall himself deposit the ballot paper in the ballot box."[81] This is a point on which the party leaders give a very poor example. A standard newspaper photograph on election day shows the prime minister, or the leader of the opposition, smilingly depositing his ballot in the ballot boxes. Such a procedure is a violation of a law which has a very sensible purpose behind it and although we do not suspect the leaders of the parties of being personally involved in such corrupt practices, they owe us a better example than this. An irregular procedure ought not to be permitted merely for the sake of the news media.

The marking of the ballots itself raises some problems. Regulations as to acceptable and unacceptable markings on ballot papers have two distinct aims. First of all there is the need to be sure that the voter's intention is clear and that the vote goes to the proper candidate. If there is any ambiguity or doubt the ballot should be rejected. The second purpose is a further safeguard against fraud. The secret ballot was originally instituted to protect the voter against intimidation and to discourage bribery and corruption, by making it difficult for the bribed voter to prove that he had indeed met his part of the bargain and so collect his bribe. These aims are, of course, frustrated if ballots can be marked in such a way that the identity of the voter can readily be discovered.

The real problem arises in trying to balance these two objectives. Too great a concern with secrecy may cause the loss of too many genuine votes, while too little concern with the formalities may lead to the accepting of votes where the intention of the voter is not absolutely clear. The problem might be made clearer by an examination of the requirements for casting a valid ballot in a federal election. There the voter must use a black lead pencil (although not necessarily the one provided in the polling booth) and may not use either a pen or a coloured pencil. He is to use a cross, but no other form of mark. A circle, or a tick, for example, is not acceptable, but two crosses in the one space are. The cross must be within the space containing the name and particulars of the candidate to be voted for, but it may be anywhere within that space.[82]

The effect of these stipulations may be gauged from the breakdown of rejected ballots for the 1953 federal election in Table 4: 4.[83]

### Table 4: 4
### BREAKDOWN OF REJECTED BALLOTS IN THE 1953 FEDERAL ELECTIONS

| | Reason for Rejection | No. Rejected | Percentage |
|---|---|---|---|
| a. | Rejected in total (paper crossed out or otherwise deliberately spoiled) | 22,119 | 36.5 |
| b. | Left blank, no mark of any kind | 7,883 | 13.0 |
| c. | Vote for more than one candidate | 11,189 | 18.4 |
| d. | Writing of some kind on the paper | 3,525 | 5.8 |
| e. | Numbers rather than crosses against candidates' names | 3,610 | 6.0 |
| f. | Ballot marked with a ∨ instead of an X | 8,824 | 14.5 |
| g. | Marked in ink instead of pencil | 2,558 | 4.2 |
| h. | Could have been passed as acceptable | 983 | 1.6 |
| | | 60,691* | 100.0 |

* These rejected ballots represent only 1.06% of the total vote cast.

Rejected ballots in categories (a) and (b) in Table 4: 4 were probably for the most part deliberately spoiled as some kind of protest against either all the candidates or the whole democratic process. Those ballots rejected under category (c) would include all those in which there was an X against two or more names, or in which there was an X against one name and a ∨ against another, or in which one name was crossed out and another marked in some way. In each of these cases there exists some possibility of doubt as to the voter's intention and the ballots are quite properly rejected. The same doubt might arise from ballots with writing or with numbers instead of X's and the rejection of category (d) and (e) ballots is obviously a wise precaution.[84] Since to permit any kind of writing would open up the opportunities for easy identification of the voter, it is safer to reject any ballot with any special marking on it at all. It is the categories (f) and (g) which are the source of the difficulty and it could be argued that if only one name is marked, and the intention of the elector is established beyond reasonable doubt, then the ballot ought not to be rejected merely because of the use of a pen instead of a pencil, or because of the use of a V instead of an X.

This, certainly, is the attitude in the prairie provinces, all of which accept ballots marked otherwise than with an X, or by use of a pen or other writing instrument, provided always that the intention of the voter is clear and that there is no apparent intention of identification. Ontario permits the use of a pen or a pencil, but insists on an X mark. In all other provinces the election acts are as strict as the federal legislation and only ballots marked with an X, with a black lead pencil will be accepted as valid. Full details from each province and for Canada are set out in Appendix Three.

There is no evidence of any increase in fraud with the less stringent requirements in the prairies and it is suggested that on this point of X's and pens there could well be a relaxation elsewhere which would lead to fewer genuine votes being rejected on what is little more than a technicality without any real increase in the opportunities for fraud. The Alberta legislation seems a model that could be followed in other provinces.

## A DIARY OF A FEDERAL ELECTION

As Professor Ward has noted, the "successful management of a modern general election . . . is an administrative task of huge proportions."[85] Some of the elements have been described in detail in the preceding pages, but there are others, perhaps just as important to the efficient conduct of an election, which have not been mentioned at all. These neglected matters have, for the most part, been purely administrative questions about which there has been little debate, or which do not vary greatly from province to province, or which, most importantly of all, do not seem to involve the basic consideration of this whole book, that is, the impact of the election and the electoral systems on the total political process.

These additional details, however, ought not to be disregarded totally and it is proposed, as a means of tying the whole process together in a coherent whole, to summarize the stages of an election in a chronological or diary form. The model is that of a federal election. In the provinces the same general pattern will be followed, although there will, of course, be numerous variations in detail, and for the most part the time intervals will tend to be shorter.

An election commences with the issue of the Writ, but as a great many things must be prepared it is essential that there be plenty of unofficial advance notice. In the case of a general election called near the end of a government's term of office there is no problem and preliminary matters can be dealt with in an orderly fashion in reasonable expectation of a forth-coming election. A snap election, called without any kind of warning or hint, could, however, throw an intolerable burden on the administration.

Before an election officially gets under way the Chief Electoral Officer must be sure that the returning officer in each electoral district is familiar with his duties and responsibilities and is reasonably capable of dealing with them. He must also make certain that there is ready to be shipped to each of these returning officers a complete set of the supplies, documents, forms, and so on which he will need. The returning officers must themselves have divided their districts into polling divisions. In expanding urban areas this may mean that maps must be constantly revised to include new housing subdivisions and to keep the number of electors on each list to a maximum of about 250. Each returning officer must have available complete descriptions of the boundaries of the polling divisions, and he must also have established revisal districts and advance poll districts.

As the election draws closer the returning officer must select rural enumerators and consult with the leading parties about the selection of urban enumerators. Each of the prospective enumerators must receive instructions on how to complete the enumeration and supplies must be made ready.

The election officially begins with the issue of the Writ. The form of the Writ is worth noting. It is issued in the name of Her Majesty, the Queen, and is addressed to the individual returning officer. It advises the returning officer that, on the advice of the Privy Council, the Queen has ordered a Parliament to be held on a specified date and commands the returning officer to "cause election to be made" to select a Member for that Parliament. He is instructed as to the date on which he will "cause the nomination" of candidates to be held and as to the date on which the poll, if one is necessary, is to be conducted.

Upon the receipt of the Writ many things prepared in advance get done officially, the returning officer opens his office and the enumerators are sworn in and set to work. The Writ is the notice to the returning officer to hold an election. The returning officer must, in his turn, notify officially the electors of his district of the fact of the election and of the essential information which they must have. He does this through the Proclamation. This must be printed locally and be issued to every postmaster in the electoral district within six days of the issue of the Writ. The Proclamation announces that an election is to be held. It describes the place where nominations will be received and time and date for their receipt. It also announces the date of polling day, the date and place of the official counting of votes, specifies which polling divisions are urban and which are rural, and gives the name of the returning officer and the address of his office.

The enumeration and revision procedures have already been described in Chapter One and the details do not need to be repeated here. The only point to note at this stage is the effect on the chronology of the election.

The enumeration must commence on the 49th day before polling day (the time interval is shorter in provincial elections) and must be completed by the 44th day. It is these two dates which effectively set the minimum period for the conduct of a federal election at about 60 days. The enumerators must then prepare their copies of the preliminary lists and from these the printing of the preliminary lists begins. On or before the 23rd day before polling day the distribution of copies of the preliminary list to all entitled to receive them must be completed.

In the meantime the returning officer has been attending to the appointment and instruction of *ex officio* and substitute revising officers and seeing to the publication of the Notices of Revision which inform the electorate of the dates of revision (the 18th, 17th, and 16th days before polling day), the hours of revision, the numbers of the regular polling divisions included in each revisal district, and the address of each revisal office. The notice also includes information about the revision procedures and the kinds of matters dealt with at revision — the addition and deletion of names to or from the preliminary lists of voters.

Also by this time the returning officer should have appointed all deputy returning officers, made arrangement for the establishment of all the necessary polling stations, checked that all ballot boxes are prepared, made the preliminary arrangements for the printing of ballot papers, and made sure that nomination papers have been made available to all potential candidates.

Nomination day also falls between the publication of the preliminary lists and the date of revision. In most constituencies nomination day is the 21st day before polling day, although there are a number of special constituencies listed in the *Election Act*, all territories of vast area and poor communications, where nomination day is the 28th day before polling. As nomination formalities have already been outlined in Chapter Two they do not need to be repeated here.

Once formal nominations have closed, the returning officer can authorize the printing of the ballot papers, which will already have been unofficially prepared, and also see to the printing and distribution of the Notice of Grant of Poll. This latter is another of the major public documents which are the formal notifications to the public of certain essential information. The Notice of Grant of Poll officially announces that a poll will be held on a specified day and announces the hours during which the polls will be open. It gives a full description of every polling division and states the address of the polling station within each. This information is especially valuable to the party campaign organizers who devote so much of their energies to seeing that electors become voters, and who need to be absolutely sure that they get voters to the right polling station.

The Notice of Grant of Poll also contains the name, address, and occupation of each candidate and of his official agent. This information must all be printed and distributed within two days of the close of nominations.

After nomination day, and not later than the 12th day before polling day, the returning officer must give public notice of the holding of an advance poll, with full details of the ordinary polling divisions contained within each advance polling district, and the address of each advance polling station. The advance polls themselves are open between 8 a.m. and 8 p.m. on the Saturday and Monday, the 9th and 7th days before polling day and the *Act* sets out quite elaborate procedures for the security and secrecy of the votes cast during the two days. The deputy returning officer at each advance polling station retains custody of the locked and sealed ballot box until 9 p.m. on the ordinary polling day. He is not permitted to open the box or count the ballots until that time, although after every election there are reports of deputy returning officers who have disobeyed this instruction and as a penalty have had their fees withheld.

Of ordinary polling day we need say little, except to note that the results of the count in each polling division, the announcement of which makes up so much of the excitement of an election, are entirely unofficial results.

After the unofficial election-night count the ballot boxes are delivered to the returning officer who has responsibility for their safekeeping until the official addition of the vote, the actual timing of which may vary. It may not be earlier than the 7th day after polling day, but in more remote rural areas it may be longer. The individual ballots themselves will not be counted at the official addition of the vote, but simply the totals reported on the official statement from each polling division. The armed services vote is also included at this point. After the official addition the returning officer certifies in writing the name of the candidate who has obtained the largest number of votes, and will also certify the total number of votes cast for each candidate and the total number of rejected ballots.

If any candidate desires that there should be a recount of the votes, then he must give notice of this within four days of the official addition of the vote. Again there are elaborate and detailed procedures, which do not need to be described here, for the conduct of a recount.

Immediately after the 6th day after the official addition, or, if there has been a recount, immediately after the recount, the returning officer declares elected the candidate who has obtained the largest number of votes. It is important to note that it is the returning officer in each constituency who declares the candidate elected, and no candidate is elected until he has been so declared. A general election is still legally a series of individual elections which local returning officers "cause to be made."

The returning officer makes this official declaration by completing the return to the Writ, which is printed on the back of the Writ calling for the election.

There are a great many other administrative details to be attended to. There are accounts to be checked and paid, supplies and materials to be accounted for and stored, and innumerable forms to be completed or checked or submitted to the Chief Electoral Officer. These are all internal administrative procedures for the more efficient and orderly operation of the election machinery. As far as the principal actors in the drama, the electors and the candidates, are concerned, with the return of the Writ the election is over.


## FOOTNOTES

[1] This is a distinction made by D. Rae in *The Political Consequences of Electoral Laws,* New Haven, Yale University Press, 1967, 13-14, and while it may be difficult to defend the distinction on etymological grounds it has sufficient practical use to adopt it here.

[2] See, for example, E. Lakeman & J. D. Lambert, *Voting in Democracies,* London, Faber & Faber, 2nd ed., 1959, J. H. Humphreys, *Proportional Representation,* London, Methuen, 1911, G. Horwill, *Proportional Representation; Its Dangers and Defects,* London, Allen & Unwin, 1925, J. F. S. Ross, *Elections and Electors,* London, Eyre & Spottiswoode, 1955, and many others.

[3] H. F. Angus, "The British Columbia Election, June, 1952," *Canadian Journal of Economics and Political Science,* 18 (4), 1952, 518.

[4] Figures from *Ibid.* 520 and 522.

[5] Alberta, *Returns: General Election Province of Alberta,* 1940, 1944, 1948, 1952, 1955.

[6] See M. S. Donnelly, *The Government of Manitoba,* Toronto, University of Toronto Press, 1963, 75-78. See also M. S. Donnelly, "Parliamentary Government in Manitoba," *Canadian Journal of Economics and Political Science,* 23 (1), 1957, 20-32 for a fuller account of Manitoba's "propensity for coalition or non-partisan government."

[7] F. H. Underhill, "Our Fantastic Electoral System," *Canadian Forum,* November 1935, reprinted in J. C. Courtney (ed.) *Voting in Canada,* Toronto, Prentice-Hall of Canada Ltd., 1967, 33.

[8] P. Fox, "The Pros and Cons of PR for Canada," *The Financial Post,* August 8, 1953, revised and reprinted in P. Fox (ed.) *Politics: Canada,* Toronto, McGraw-Hill Company of Canada Limited, 2nd edition, 1966, 321-326.

[9] S. M. Lipset, "Democracy in Alberta," *Canadian Forum,* 34, Nov.-Dec. 1954, reprinted in J. C. Courtney (ed.) *op. cit.* 182.

[10] The precise mechanics of this process do not concern us here. They have been sufficiently detailed in many books. See, for example, E. Lakeman & J. D. Lambert, *op. cit.,* chap. vi.

[11] P. Fox, *op. cit.,* 324.

[12] Variations on the basic system do often allow for some limited expression of preferences for individual candidates within the party lists.

13 See T. H. Qualter, "Seats and Votes: an Application of the Cube Law to the Canadian Electoral System," *Canadian Journal of Political Science,* 1 (3), 1968, 336-344.

14 *Ibid.,* 336.

15 Reproduced from Qualter, *ibid.* 341 & 342 and updated to include 1968 results.

16 A. C. Cairns, "The Electoral System and the Party System in Canada, 1921-1965," *Canadian Journal of Political Science,* 1(1), 1968, 55-80. On the relationship between the electoral system and the party system see also D. V. Smiley, "The Two-Party System and One-Party Dominance in the Liberal Democratic State," *Canadian Journal of Economics and Political Science,* 24 (3), 1958, 312-322.

17 A. C. Cairns, *op. cit.,* 57.

18 *Ibid.,* 63.

19 *Ibid.,* 62.

20 S.C., 1960, chap. 39, Schedule No. 1, Form 1. — Writ of Election. My italics.

21 The Office of the Chief Electoral Officer was established by *The Dominion Elections Act,* 1920. S.C., 1920, chap. 46, sec. 19. Reproduced with the permission of the Queen's Printer for Canada.

22 *Ibid.,* sec. 19 (1) (a). Reproduced with the permission of the Queen's Printer for Canada.

23 *Ibid.,* sec. 19 (1) (b). Reproduced with the permission of the Queen's Printer for Canada. See also Canada, Chief Electoral Officer, *Report to the Speaker of the House of Commons,* Dec. 1, 1926, Appendix 1.

24 R.S.Q., 1964, chap. 7, secs. 8-16.

25 R.S.M., 1954, chap. 68, sec. 3 contains most of the provisions on the appointment, powers, responsibilities, and tenure of the Chief Electoral Officer.

26 R.S.O., 1960, chap. 118, sec. 4 (1); S.N.S., 1962, chap. 4, sec. 3 (1); S.P.E.I., 1963, chap. 11, sec. 3 (1).

27 S.N.S., 1962, chap. 4, sec. 4 (1) (a) & (b), and S.P.E.I., 1963, chap. 11, sec. 4 (1).

28 S.N.B., 1967, chap. 9, sec. 5 (4), and S.N., 1954, chap. 79, sec. 33 (a).

29 R.S.S., 1965, chap. 4, sec. 3 (1).

30 R.S.B.C., 1960, chap. 306, sec. 6 (1).

31 S.C., 1874, chap. 9, sec. 1.

32 S.C., 1882, chap. 3, sec. 6 (1). For an account of this period see N. Ward, *The Canadian House of Commons: Representation,* Toronto, University of Toronto Press, 2nd edition 1963, 173-4.

33 Canada, Chief Electoral Officer, *Report to the Speaker of the House of Commons,* Dec., 1926, Appendix 1. Reproduced with the permission of the Queen's Printer for Canada.

34 *Ibid.,* 4. Reproduced with the permission of the Queen's Printer for Canada.

35 S.C., 1925, chap. 42, sec. 3.

36 S.C., 1929, chap. 40, sec. 6.

37 Canada, Chief Electoral Officer, *Report to the Speaker of the House of Commons,* Sept. 1930, par. 3.

38 N. Ward, *op. cit.,* 185.

39 S.C., 1934, chap. 50, sec. 8.

40 Figures compiled from the Reports issued by the Chief Electoral Officer following each general election.

[41] Full comparative figures are not available, but we might note, for example, that for the 1968 federal elections there were 14,338 polling divisions in the province of Quebec. For the 1966 Quebec provincial elections there were 16,424 polling divisions. We could expect similar ratios in the other provinces.

[42] The usual practice is for the returning officer to appoint the deputy returning officers, and for the latter to select and appoint their own poll clerks.

[43] Canada, Chief Electoral Officer, *Instructions for Deputy Returning Officers at Ordinary Polls*, 1962.

[44] Mr. Justice Armour, Dec. 11, 1884, quoted in N. Ward, *op. cit.*, 245.

[45] C. O'Leary, *The Elimination of Corrupt Practices in British Elections, 1868-1911*, Oxford, Clarendon Press, 1962, 3.

[46] R. M. Dawson, "The Gerrymander of 1882," *Canadian Journal of Economics and Political Science*, 1 (2), 1935, 197.

[47] N. Ward, *op. cit.*, 240-258.

[48] S.C., 1960, chap. 39, sec. 66. Reproduced with the permission of the Queen's Printer for Canada.

[49] *Ibid.*, sec. 67.

[50] *Ibid.*, sec. 68.

[51] R.S.S., 1965, chap. 4, sec. 164 (3); S.N.S., 1962, chap. 4, sec. 178.

[52] This is the situation in Ontario, for example. The sale of liquor on election day is forbidden, not by any clause in the Election Act, but by a regulation issued by the Liquor Control Board of Ontario.

[53] Most provinces are content to refer simply to "offensive weapons" with some making a special reference to firearms. Saskatchewan and Quebec see fit to include swords, but it is Newfoundland that is the most weapon conscious: ". . . offensive weapons of any kind, such as firearms, swords, staves, bludgeons, or the like . . ." S.N., 1954, chap. 79, sec. 73 (1).

[54] R.S.B.C., 1960, chap. 306, sec. 166.

[55] Canada, Chief Electoral Officer, *Report to the Speaker of the House of Commons*, May 16, 1958.

[56] Canada, Chief Electoral Officer, *Report to the Speaker of the House of Commons*, October 5, 1962.

[57] Canada, Chief Electoral Officer, *Report to the Speaker of the House of Commons*, September 15, 1930.

[58] There are already a number of extensive studies of election financing in Canada. There are, first of all, Canada, Committee on Election Expenses, *Report*, 1966, which includes an extensive bibliography relating both to Canada and to other countries, and its companion volume, Canada, Committee on Election Expenses, *Studies in Canadian Party Finance*, 1966. It is the comparatively recent publication of these two studies which makes unnecessary any detailed comments here. At the provincial level there is the *Report* of the Nova Scotia Royal Commission on Election Expenses and Associated Matters, published in 1969, and, although it is less readily available, H. M. Angell's *Report on Electoral Reform of the Province of Quebec*, an unpublished manuscript prepared for the Quebec Liberal Federation in 1961.

[59] Canada, Committee on Election Expenses, *Report*, 13.

[60] H. M. Angell, *op. cit.*, 15.

[61] S.C., 1960, chap. 39, sec. 62 (4). See also, Canada, Chief Electoral Officer, *General Election Instructions for Returning Officers*, 1964, Instruction 353.

[62] Canada, Chief Electoral Officer, *op. cit.*, Instruction 355.

[63] See pp. 73-74.

[64] Nova Scotia, Royal Commission on Election Expenses and Associated Matters, *Report,* Halifax, 1969, and S.N.S., 1969, chap. 40.

[65] R.S.M., 1954, chap. 68, sec. 168 (1).

[66] H. M. Angell, *op. cit.,* 39.

[67] N. Ward, *op. cit.,* 259.

[68] W. J. M. MacKenzie, *Free Elections,* London, George Allen & Unwin Ltd., 1958, 153.

[69] S.C., 1960, chap. 39, secs. 62 and 63.

[70] In Saskatchewan he is called "Business Manager," but his duties and responsibilities are similar to those of an official agent elsewhere. In Quebec candidates have been obliged to appoint official agents only since the new *Election Act* of 1964 — R.S.Q., 1964, chap. 7, sec. 376.

[71] N. Ward, *op. cit.,* 263.

[72] *Ibid.,* 263-4.

[73] Quebec's new election law might be an exception to this, but its effects are too recent for any conclusions to be drawn.

[74] S.C., 1960, chap. 39, sec. 28.

[75] *Ibid.,* sec. 28 (6) and Form 36.

[76] R.S.S., 1965, chap. 4, sec. 20 and S.N.S., 1962, chap. 4, sec. 79.

[77] S.A., 1956, chap. 15, sec. 59, and R.S.M., 1954, chap. 68, sec. 63.

[78] S.P.E.I., 1963, chap. 11, sec. 72, S.N., 1954, chap. 79, sec. 58, and R.S.B.C., 1960, chap. 306, sec. 92 (3).

[79] R.S.O., 1960, chap. 118, sec. 63 (2) & (3), and R.S.Q., 1964, chap. 7, secs. 200 & 201.

[80] R.S.Q., 1964, chap. 7, secs. 206 & 207, and S.N.B., 1967, chap. 9, sec. 68 (1) & (3). The wording is identical in each case.

[81] S.C., 1960, chap. 39, sec. 45 (3). The numbered counterfoil protects against forged ballots, but the number is removed before the ballot is deposited to ensure secrecy.

[82] *Ibid.,* and also Form 102 which illustrates samples of ballot papers which should be accepted and of ballot papers which should be rejected.

[83] The figures are as given to the author by the Chief Electoral Officer.

[84] In his *Report to the Speaker of the House of Commons,* of November 12, 1949, the Chief Electoral Officer noted that in the federal district of Regina City in the 1949 elections 460 ballots were rejected on a recount on the grounds that each contained a number which made possible the identification of the voter.

[85] N. Ward, *op. cit.,* 277.

# CONCLUSION

It is difficult to reach a general conclusion in a book which asks more questions than it answers, that is, if it is to be a conclusion and not merely a recapitulation and summary. But from this brief introductory essay on the way in which the election process operates in Canada a set of particular conclusions can be stated.

The administrative and legal machinery, as it exists now in Canada and in the several provinces, is capable of producing a set of reasonably representative legislatures in a reasonably impartial manner. The machinery both at the federal level and in the provinces has been subject to continual review and amendment generally directed to more efficient and more honest administration. Great credit must be given to the federal and provincial Chief Electoral Officers who have initiated or drafted so many of the needed reforms.

Most of the weaknesses and defects, the dubious activities which cast doubt on the integrity of the whole process, arise less from the weaknesses of the law than from the determination of those most involved to disregard the law altogether, especially in questions relating to the supervision and control of election finance. The vested interests of members, candidates, and the party hierarchies have successfully frustrated an essential overhaul of this, the most unsavoury element in the election process.

It can be seen that there are no legal barriers in most of the systems to the creation of a structure of constituencies which would guarantee to each man, not only one vote, but also an equal vote. A set of constituencies all approximately equal in population could be established within existing legal frameworks. This has not been done because those responsible for the

170

actual distribution of populations into constituencies, whether legislators themselves or commissions, have chosen to preserve a large measure of inequality, and especially an inequality which favours the rural areas. All the systems have a rural bias, which has a significant impact on the character of the legislatures, and, such is the strength of the tradition which defends it, it is likely to continue without serious challenge for some considerable time. Even in 1969 Alberta could take the retrograde step of embodying the urban-rural disparities in representation in formal statutory requirements. Rural interests will almost certainly continue to have a more than proportionate voice in legislatures throughout Canada for a very long time.

On the question of candidate selection the law is generally silent although here again those most involved have introduced into the process practices which, if not completely alien to the spirit of democracy, at least do very little to nourish it. Acceptable procedures could be developed for the increased democratization of candidate selection, without necessarily going to the length of introducing popular primaries, but the party hierarchies have been unsympathetic to such developments.

The voting system itself, both federally and in most provinces, produces a disproportionate, but not irrational, relationship between votes and seats won, a relationship which has been remarkably consistent through a series of elections. Nowhere does the electoral system produce a legislature which mirrors exactly the popular support of the parties. The parties which have the largest share of the popular vote, or which are regionally concentrated, receive a far more than proportionate share of the seats, a fact which often leads to misconceptions about the character and regional distribution of the support for a particular party. But a truly representative assembly could be achieved only at a price which few Canadians would be prepared to pay: the introduction of a party list system of voting which would enormously increase the power and authority of the leadership of the parties and a consequent reduction in the influence and independence of the individual member. It would still further undermine the already declining role of the member as a voice for his constituency and make him still more merely a vote to sustain a government in office.

On a more fundamental, comparative level, it can be noted that all the provinces have adopted basically similar election processes. There is little evidence that those drafting election acts, or considering amendments to them, have looked far outside Canada for inspiration. Even in format the eleven election acts are similar, with topics generally dealt with in more or less the same order. In terminology the similarities, especially in the maritimes, are often striking. None of the provinces has apparently even considered such American innovations as the primary, a device which, if properly understood, could be considered America's major contribution to electoral democracy. None has experimented with compulsory registration of electors or with compulsory voting, or with the employment of permanent, *ex officio* returning officers. Apart from British Columbia none has considered alternatives to enumeration and revision for preparing voters' lists, and all still provide that the vote shall be counted in individual polling stations catering to no more than 300 or so voters.

Yet despite these, and many other similarities, which demonstrate a common source and tradition behind the several systems, there exist some equally striking and significant differences. In matters such as the attitude towards the redistribution of constituencies and the measures to be taken to perpetuate or diminish the partisan influence of the government in the drawing of electoral district boundaries; in the concern over the elimination of bribery, intimidation, personation, and other corrupt practices; in the perception of the role of the parties in the election machinery; in the willingness, or otherwise, to reduce administrative barriers to voting; in the willingness to make special provision for those whose special circumstances might otherwise mean they might lose their vote; in the general concern to eliminate partisan bias from the election system, or to manipulate the system to the advantage of the party in power, there are clear and significant differences in the various areas of Canada.

Further, it can be seen that these differences are not inconsistent with what is already known of the political and social traditions of each region. The variations in the election process do not of themselves establish or prove, but they lend considerable support to, the hypothesis that the separate provinces constitute distinct political systems with identifiable political cultures. Of course there are great similarities, greater between some provinces than between others, but the differences are also great. Each province has its own distinctive provincial political "style," a set of values and attitudes, and a way of dealing with things political; and the election process as it has been examined here seems in each case a fair representation of that characteristic political style of each province.

Finally it can be concluded that nowhere does there appear to be a case for a fundamental overhaul of the election law or the administrative machinery set up to operate it. Certainly every election act could be improved, but basic changes are not called for. One would suspect, indeed, that radical changes in the law or administrative procedures, designed to eliminate this or that weakness, would create new, and perhaps even more serious, problems. Such faults and weaknesses as there are in the total Canadian election process do not generally lie in the machinery of elections. Most lie in the minds and attitudes of those who live by the existing machinery. The failure of campaign workers, candidates, and voters to observe the spirit, and often the letter, of the election law are the principal source of whatever dissatisfaction one may have with the process.

The election process is not, in any sense, a failure. We do not need to condemn it, nor to launch a crusade for its reform. It could, of course, be better, but it will only be better when voters, candidates, and party workers are sufficiently concerned over the consequences of its present genuine weaknesses to want to make it better.

# APPENDIX ONE

## CLASSIFICATION OF VOTERS' LISTS

| Class of List | Province | Regulations in Provincial Election Act |
|---|---|---|
| A. Rural and Urban lists closed | Quebec | "No person applying to vote shall be entitled to vote if his name is not entered on the duplicate or copy of or extract from the electoral list in use for voting in the polling station. . . ." sec. 236 (Exception made for electors on revised list, but accidentally omitted from copy at polling station) — sec. 237 |
| | Prince Edward Island | A person may vote if he is otherwise qualified and, "if his name appears on the official list of electors for the polling division in which he intends to vote." sec. 91 (1) |
| B. Rural lists open, Urban lists closed | New Brunswick | For a rural polling division, an otherwise qualified voter may vote, "notwithstanding that his name does not appear on the official list of electors . . ." if, "(a) he is vouched for by an elector whose name appears on the official list of electors for such polling division" and both the elector and the voucher, "subscribes an oath." sec. 76 (3) For an urban polling division, "a person shall not |

174

| Class of List | Province | Regulations in Provincial Election Act |
|---|---|---|
| | | be allowed to vote if his name does not appear on the official list of electors for such polling division." — with some very minor exceptions. sec. 76 (1) |
| | Ontario | For rural polling divisions, regulations are virtually the same as for New Brunswick. sec. 84 (1) For urban polling divisions, ". . . a person whose name has been omitted in error from the polling list but whose name appears on the municipal list of voters for the polling subdivision in which he resides and who is vouched for by a voter whose name is on the polling list and who is resident in the polling division . . ." may vote after taking an oath. sec. 84 (2) |
| | Alberta | For rural polling divisions the regulations are virtually the same as for New Brunswick. sec. 72 (1) There is an added qualification that, "No resident elector shall vouch for more than one applicant voter." sec. 72 (4) In a city constituency, a qualified voter whose name is not on the list of electors, "but whose name is on the Registry of Electors," as already described, may, "make application to the returning officer and he may cast his vote in a special ballot box kept by the returning officer for the purpose. . . ." sec. 72 (5) |
| C. Rural and Urban lists open | Nova Scotia | Generally the provisions are similar to those for rural areas of Alberta, i.e. the elector must take an oath and be vouched for by another qualified elector on the list in the appropriate polling division, provided that such other person, "has not previously vouched during the pending election for a person other than a member of his household." sec. 114 (1) A person in an, "incorporated city, or a town having a population in excess of five thousand persons," may also vote if his name is not on the list provided he first attends the headquarters of the returning officer during certain specified hours and obtains there a certificate entitling him to vote at a polling station under the same conditions as laid down for rural polls. sec. 114 (2) |

| Class of List | Province | Regulations in Provincial Election Act |
|---|---|---|
| | Manitoba | No distinction is made between rural and urban voters. Electors not on the list may apply and be vouched for by a fully registered elector in terms similar to those for rural voters in class B above, sec. 77 (1-3)<br>"No person shall vouch for more than four applicants under this section unless they all reside in one household." sec. 77 (5) |
| | Newfoundland | No distinction is made between rural and urban voters, and vouching is not required. A qualified voter omitted from the list may, "vote at the appropriate polling station established in that polling division, if he takes and subscribes before the deputy returning officer" the appropriate oath. sec. 65 (2)<br>". . . the oaths so taken and filed shall constitute the supplementary list of electors for the polling station concerned." sec. 65 (3) |
| | Saskatchewan | The provisions are very simple. "Every person whose name does not appear on the voters' list and who claims he is entitled to vote at the polling place in which he presents himself to vote shall before voting make the declaration." sec. 87<br>The declaration referred to is similar in wording to the oath required in other provinces, but it is not sworn. |

# APPENDIX TWO

## (A) PROVINCIAL RETURNING OFFICERS: TERMS OF OFFICE

| | |
|---|---|
| British Columbia | ". . . during good behaviour and for such period as may be determined by the Lieutenant Governor in Council." sec. 34 (3) |
| Alberta | For the one forthcoming election only. sec. 3 (1) (a) |
| Saskatchewan | ". . . a returning officer, unless he ceases to be a resident of the constituency or resigns, shall continue in office during pleasure until he reaches the age of sixty-five years at which time he shall cease to hold office but he may, by order of the Lieutenant-Governor in Council, be continued in office beyond the age of sixty-five years for a period to be specified in the order." sec. 6 (2) |
| Manitoba | "(The returning officer's) appointment shall continue as long as he remains a resident of the division and for three months thereafter unless it is sooner rescinded or he dies or resigns." sec. 4 (1) |
| Ontario | Appointed for each election and holds office "until he has completed the work of the general election next following his appointment." sec. 24 (1) |
| Quebec | Term not specified, but apparently permanent only "for cause." See sec. 18 |

New Brunswick    "The office of a returning officer . . . shall not be deemed to be vacant unless he dies, resigns, or is removed from office for cause." sec. 9 (5)

Nova Scotia    "The office of a returning officer . . . is not vacant until he (a) dies; (b) resigns; or (c) is removed from office under subsection (4). sec. 11 (3)
(The details of subsection (4) are set out in Appendix Two (C))

Prince Edward Island    The office of a returning officer is not vacant until he (a) dies; or (b) resigns; or (c) is removed from office under subsection (3). sec. 10 (2)
(The details of subsection (3) are set out in Appendix Two (C))

Newfoundland    Term not specified, but returning officer is apparently appointed for the one election only. See sec. 36

## (B)  PROVINCIAL RETURNING OFFICERS: CLASSES OF PERSONS DISQUALIFIED FROM SERVING AS RETURNING OFFICERS

British Columbia    Members of the Privy Council of Canada; members of the Senate or the House of Commons; members of the British Columbia legislature; members of the British Columbia Executive Council; certain categories of judges; The Registrar, District or Deputy Registrars of the Supreme Court; police magistrates; members of the B.C. legislature for the session immediately preceding the election; candidates for the election; persons found guilty of offences or dereliction of duty at any election within the seven years preceding the election. sec. 35 (1)

Alberta    Members of the Executive Council of Alberta; members of the Parliament of Canada; members of the Alberta legislature; ministers of religion; various categories of judges; persons found guilty at any time of corrupt practices at any election, or of any offence or dereliction of duty under the Election Act; persons convicted of any indictable offence within the ten years preceding nomination day; non-electors. sec. 6 (1)

Saskatchewan    Members of the Saskatchewan Executive Council; members of the Parliament of Canada; members of the Saskatchewan legislature; ministers of religion; various categories of judges and magistrates; the provincial Chief Electoral Officer and the Assistant Chief Electoral Officer; a candidate, or his business manager or representative; persons found guilty of corrupt practices or other offences or derelictions of duty under the Election Act; persons found guilty of any indictable offence within the past eight years; persons disqualified from voting under the Act. sec. 9 (1)

**Manitoba**

Members of the Manitoba Executive Council; members of the Parliament of Canada; members of the Manitoba legislature; ministers of religion; certain categories of judges and magistrates; persons found guilty of corrupt practices or other offences or derelictions of duty under the Election Act; persons found guilty of any indictable offence within five years of the date of the Writ. sec. 5 (1)

**Ontario**

Members of the Ontario Executive Council; members of the Parliament of Canada; members of the Ontario legislature; ministers of religion; judges of federal or provincial courts; members of the Ontario legislature for the session immediately preceding the election; persons found guilty at any time of corrupt practices under the Election Act. sec. 25 (1)

**Quebec**

Minors; persons not domiciled during the past year in the electoral district where they are to act; persons not qualified as electors; persons found guilty of any infraction or crime punishable by imprisonment for two years or more; persons found guilty of practices declared corrupt by the electoral laws of Canada, of the Province or of any municipality; candidates. secs. 21 and 22

**New Brunswick**

Minors; persons who have not been resident for twelve months in the electoral district where they are to act; persons not qualified as electors; persons who have been found guilty of a corrupt practice under the electoral laws of Canada, of any province or of any municipality. sec. 10

**Nova Scotia**          Persons not qualified as electors. sec. 165

**Prince Edward Island**  Persons not qualified as electors. sec. 139

**Newfoundland**

Members of the Executive Council of Newfoundland; members of the Parliament of Canada; members of the Newfoundland legislature; ministers of religion, judges of the Supreme Court; persons who have served in the Parliament of Canada or the Newfoundland legislature in the session immediately preceding the election; persons who have been found guilty of any offence under the provincial Election Act; persons who are intending candidates. sec. 56 (1)

Persons in the employ of any department of the provincial government, or employed upon any public works directly or by contract under any department of government. sec. 111 (a)

## (C)  PROVINCIAL RETURNING OFFICERS: GROUNDS FOR REMOVAL

| | |
|---|---|
| British Columbia | None specified. |
| Alberta | None specified. |
| Saskatchewan | Reaching 65 years of age. See Appendix 2(A). sec. 6 (2) |
| Manitoba | See specifications in Appendix 2(A). |
| Ontario | None specified. |
| Quebec | None specified. |
| New Brunswick | Any returning officer who acts as a canvasser for any candidate; or who is guilty of partisan conduct **after his appointment** may be suspended or dismissed. sec. 11 (1) (bold face added) |
| Nova Scotia | A returning officer who has: attained the age of 65; has ceased to reside in his electoral district; is unable to act; has failed to perform satisfactorily the duties of his office; or is engaging in partisan political activity, may be removed. sec. 11 (4) |
| Prince Edward Island | The returning officer may be removed for causes virtually identical with those specified for Nova Scotia. sec. 10 (3) |
| Newfoundland | None specified. |

# APPENDIX THREE

| | How the Ballot is to be Marked, and the Grounds for Accepting or Rejecting a Marked Ballot.* |
|---|---|
| Canada | ". . . by making a cross with a black lead pencil within the space on the ballot paper containing the name and particulars of the candidate . . . for whom he intends to vote. . . ." sec. 45 (3)<br>Any ballots not so marked will be rejected. |
| British Columbia | The ballot shall be marked "with a black-lead pencil" and "by making a cross in the white square on the ballot-paper opposite to the division . . . containing the name of the candidate for whom he desires to vote." sec. 101<br>Ballots not so marked are to be rejected. sec. 119 (2) |
| Alberta | ". . . with the black lead pencil provided, mark his ballot paper by placing a cross, thus X, on any part of the space containing the name of the candidate for whom he intends to vote." sec. 89 (1)<br>But, "Where a voter has, with an honest intention in favour of one of the candidates whose name is upon a ballot paper and without any apparent intention of identification, marked his ballot paper with some mark other than a cross mark (X) or marked his ballot paper with a pen or pencil other than the pencil provided, clearly indicating in either case an intent |

181

|  | **How the Ballot is to be Marked, and the Grounds for Accepting or Rejecting a Marked Ballot.*** |
| --- | --- |
|  | to mark in favour of a name . . ." it shall be an acceptable ballot. sec. 94 (7) |
| Saskatchewan | "(b) with: (i) the black lead pencil provided; or (ii) a black or blue ink pen; or (iii) a black or blue ball-point pen; mark the ballot-paper." sec. 92 (1)<br>But, a deputy returning officer shall not reject a ballot "that is marked with some mark other than a cross mark (X) if: (i) there is clearly indicated an intent to mark in favour of a name of a candidate; (ii) there is no apparent intention of identification." sec. 111 |
| Manitoba | ". . . by placing the symbol X with the black lead pencil provided therein within the space on the ballot paper. . . ." sec. 90 (1)<br>But a ballot paper shall not be rejected "merely because the voter, without any apparent intention of identification . . . has marked his ballot with a form of cross other than an X, or the figure 1, or ∨, or —, or 0, or other mark clearly indicating an intent to vote for one only of the candidates. sec. 106 (8)<br>A ballot shall not be rejected if, under the same circumstances, it has been marked with "a writing instrument other than the pencil provided in the compartment." sec. 106 (8A) |
| Ontario | ". . . making a cross with a pen or pencil within the white space. . . ." sec. 91<br>No other markings are acceptable. |
| Quebec | ". . . making a cross with the black lead pencil to be found . . . (in the polling booth) within one of the squares specially and exclusively reserved for voting." sec. 247<br>Any other form of marking is specifically rejected. sec. 264 |
| New Brunswick | ". . . by making a cross with a black lead pencil within the space on the ballot papers. . . ." sec. 82 (3)<br>No other form of ballot marking is acceptable. |
| Nova Scotia | ". . . by making a cross with a black lead pencil within the white space. . . ." sec. 101 (a)<br>No other mark is acceptable. sec. 121 |
| Prince Edward Island | ". . . by making a cross with a black lead pencil within the space on the ballot paper. . . ." sec. 83 (a)<br>No other mark is acceptable. sec. 93 |

| How the Ballot is to be Marked, and the Grounds for Accepting or Rejecting a Marked Ballot.* |
| --- |

| Newfoundland | ". . . by making a cross with a black lead pencil within the space on the ballot paper. . . ." sec. 69 (3) <br> No exceptions to this marking are noted. |
| --- | --- |

* This listing refers only to the criteria for accepting or rejecting ballots that are associated with the type of mark that may be made, or with the use of pens or pencils. In every province there are specified other grounds for rejecting ballots including generally: writing on the ballot, voting for too many candidates, or ambiguous markings of any kind.

# ADDENDUM

In December, 1969, a new Election Act was given first reading in the Ontario legislature.[1] The new legislation, based substantially on the recommendations of the Ontario Select Committee on Election Laws, was introduced by Premier Robarts and will almost certainly be passed without substantial amendment. At the time of writing, however, the Bill was still before the House.

The principal changes introduced by the new Bill are as follows:

1. The old Election Boards are to be abolished and their few remaining functions are to be assigned either to returning officers or to the Chief Election Officer.
2. Returning officers, who are at present appointed for a single election only, will be given permanent tenure. "A returning officer . . . shall continue in office until he dies, or, with prior permission of the Chief Election Officer, he resigns." sec. 4 (7) A returning officer who "(a) has attained the age of sixty-five years; or (b) is incapable, by reason of illness, physical or mental infirmity or otherwise, of satisfactorily performing his duties under this Act" may be removed from office. sec. 4 (8)
3. A Minister of Religion is no longer to be disqualified from acting as a returning officer, but Crown Attorneys and Clerks of the Peace are now to be disqualified. sec. 5 (1)
4. It is proposed that there be a fixed day (Thursday) for nomination day and election day — except where the selected Thursday is a statutory holiday. sec. 7 (1) and (2)
5. There are to be some slight changes in the wording of the qualification of voters, although the minimum voting age is maintained at 21. Citizenship is to be defined as "a Canadian citizen or other British subject" instead of

simply "a British subject." The residence qualification will date from polling day rather than the date of the issue of the Writ. sec. 9 (1) Judges of the Federal and Provincial courts, clerks of the peace, Crown attorneys, and magistrates, are no longer to be disqualified from voting.

6. Two enumerators are to be appointed in every polling division, rural as well as urban. sec. 12 Effectively all distinctions between urban and rural polling divisions are to be abolished.

7. The procedure on the revision of preliminary voters' lists is to be considerably simplified.

8. Proxy voting privileges are to be extended from mariners to members of the Canadian forces, to persons who are unable to vote at either the advance poll or on polling day because they are "engaged for hire or reward in the business of transportation by railway, air, water or motor vehicle," or persons medically certified to be incapable of attending at the poll. sec. 35 (1)

9. Some changes are to be made in the format of the ballot paper which would leave a white circle in which the voter could mark his X. sec. 51 (4-6)

10. It is proposed that the deputy returning officer and the poll clerk represent two different political interests with the deputy returning officer being nominated by the candidate for the government party and the poll clerk by the candidate for the strongest non-government party in the constituency. sec. 56

11. The practice of "vouching" for an elector whose name is omitted in error from a voting list is to be abolished except in "territory without municipal organization." sec. 78 (1) This is compensated for by more elaborate machinery for the preparation of voters' lists, and more simplified revision procedures.

12. There are to be numerous changes, some substantial, in the penalties for several offences under the new Act.

13. Some of the most substantial changes concern the whole area of corrupt practices. Sections of the existing act dealing with such matters as bribery, treating, providing refreshments on nomination day or polling day, exerting undue influence, personation, and related items are simply not re-enacted. This is in accordance with a recommendation of the Select Committee on Election Laws which argued that "the existing legislation provides for the creation of certain offences and the determination of certain corrupt practices which may have been relevant to the days before the secret ballot. The Committee believes that these are no longer pertinent to the electoral process in the Ontario of 1969, which enjoys a well informed electorate of high integrity. Further, some of these sections have been clearly **ultra vires** ever since the Parliament of Canada occupied the field of criminal jurisdiction.[2]

The entire Act of 1960 has been completely redrafted and apart from those major changes outlined here there has been considerable rephrasing and reordering of other sections.

At the federal level, late in 1969 Parliament was presented with a set of *Draft Amendments to the Canada Elections Act* as suggested by the Chief Electoral Officer, but as none of these have yet been incorporated in even the first reading of a Bill it seems premature to discuss these proposals at this time.

## FOOTNOTES

[1] Ontario, *The Election Act,* 1968-69, Bill 217.
[2] Ontario, Select Committee on Election Laws, *Preliminary Report,* 1969, par. 15 (x).

# INDEX TO TABLES

1 : 1    Citizenship Qualifications in Federal and Provincial
Election Acts.     7

1 : 2    Minimum Voting Age in Canada and the Provinces.     8

1 : 3    Progress in Votes for Women.     9

1 : 4    Residence Requirements for Voting in Provincial Elections.     14

1 : 5    A Comparison of the Percentages of the Total Voting-Age
Populations who are Registered on Official Voters' Lists.     29

1 : 6    Votes Cast in Ordinary Polls, Advance Polls, and by
Absentee Ballots in the British Columbia General Elections
of September, 1966.     34

1 : 7    Voters, Non-Voters, and Would-Be Voters in the 1966
Elections in British Columbia.     36

1 : 8    Hours of Voting at Federal and Provincial General Elections.     38

2 : 1    The Law and the Fact of Women Members of
Canadian Legislatures.     52

2 : 2    Nomination Requirements.     53

2 : 3    Indemnity of Members of the House of Commons and of
the Provincial Legislatures (1969).     72

3 : 1    Details of the Extent to Which Constituencies Established
in 1966 Varied from the Official Quota of Their
Own Province.     89

3 : 2    Dauer-Kelsay Index Values, Based on Number of Registered
Voters at Recent Federal or Provincial Elections.     92

3 : 3   An Analysis of the Distribution of Population in the Federal
Constituencies (Excluding the Yukon and the Northwest
Territories) According to the 1961 and 1966 Census Figures.   104

3 : 4   The Rural-Urban Character of the 1966 Constituencies
(According to the 1966 Census Figures) Showing the Extent
to which they are Above or Below Provincial Averages,
or Quotas.   105

3 : 5   Distribution of Seats in the House of Commons (1966
Redistribution, Based on 1961 Census).   113

3 : 6   Members Elected from Single- and Multi-Member Districts
in Provincial Legislatures.   119

4 : 1   (A)  Effects of Preferential Voting in Rural Constituencies
of Alberta, 1940-1955.   131
(B)  Effects of the Single Transferable Vote in Calgary
and Edmonton, 1940-1955.   132
(C)  Summary of Tables 4: 1(A) & 4: 1(B)   132
(D)  Net Party Gains and Losses over Five Elections.   133

4 : 2   Comparison of Possible Effects of Different Electoral Systems
in Calgary and Edmonton, 1952-1955.   135

4 : 3   (A)  Comparison of Predicted and Actual Results for the
Leading Party in each Federal Election from
1921 to 1968.   138
(B)  Comparison of Predicted and Actual Results for the
Losing Parties (Excluding "Others") in each
Federal Election from 1921 to 1968.   139

4 : 4   Breakdown of Rejected Ballots in the 1953
Federal Elections.   161

# ABBREVIATIONS

In the citing of laws, statutes, etc., the following abbreviations are used.

R.S.A., 1955, chap. 174   Alberta, *Legislative Assembly Act*, 1955, consolidated with amendments to 1968.

R.S.B.C., 1960, chap. 306 British Columbia, *Provincial Elections Act*, 1960, consolidated with amendments to 1968.

R.S.C., 1927, chap. 147   Canada, *Senate and House of Commons Act*, 1927, including amendment, S.C. 1931, chap. 52.

R.S.C., 1952, chap. 23   Canada, *Canada Elections Act*, 1951, consolidated.

R.S.C., 1952, chap. 33   Canada, *Canadian Citizenship Act*, consolidated.

R.S.C., 1952, chap. 87   Canada, *Dominion Controverted Elections Act*, consolidated.

R.S.M., 1954, chap. 68   Manitoba, *Election Act*, 1954, consolidated with amendments to 1968.

R.S.N.B., 1952, chap. 70 New Brunswick, *Election Act*, 1952.

R.S.N.S., 1954, chap. 117 Nova Scotia, *House of Assembly Act*, 1954, consolidated with amendments to 1969.

R.S.O., 1960, chap. 118   Ontario, *Election Act*, 1960, consolidated with amendments to 1968.

R.S.O., 1960, chap. 208   Ontario, *Legislative Assembly Act*, 1960.

R.S.O., 1960, chap. 420   Ontario, *Voters' List Act*, 1960.

R.S.Q., 1964, chap. 5   Quebec, *Territorial Division Act*, 1964.

R.S.Q., 1964, chap. 7   Quebec, *Election Act*, 1964, consolidated with amendments to 1967.

| | |
|---|---|
| R.S.S., 1965, chap. 3 | Saskatchewan, *Legislative Assembly Act*, 1965, consolidated with amendments to 1968. |
| R.S.S., 1965, chap. 4 | Saskatchewan, *Election Act*, 1965, consolidated with amendments to 1966. |
| R.S.S., 1965, chap. 9 | Saskatchewan, *Public Service Act*, 1965. |
| S.A., 1956, chap. 15 | Alberta, *Election Act*, 1956, consolidated with amendments to 1967. |
| S.A., 1969, chap. 27 | Alberta, *Electoral Boundaries Commission Act*, 1969. |
| S.C., 1868, chap. 25 | Canada, 31 Vic., *Independence of Parliament Act,* 1868. |
| S.C., 1874, chap. 9 | Canada, 37 Vic., *An Act Respecting the Election of Members to the House of Commons*, 1874. |
| S.C., 1882, chap. 45 | Canada, 45 Vic., *Representation Act*, 1882. |
| S.C., 1885, chap. 40 | Canada, 48-9 Vic., *Electoral Franchise Act*, 1885. |
| S.C., 1898, chap. 14 | Canada, 61 Vic., *Franchise Act*, 1898. |
| S.C., 1917, chap. 34 | Canada, 7-8 Geo. V, *Military Voters Act*, 1917. |
| S.C., 1917, chap. 39 | Canada, 7-8 Geo. V, *War Time Elections Act*, 1917. |
| S.C., 1920, chap. 46 | Canada, 10-11 Geo. V, *Dominion Elections Act,* 1920. |
| S.C., 1925, chap. 42 | Canada, 15-16 Geo. V, *Dominion Elections Act Amendment Act*, 1925. |
| S.C., 1929, chap. 40 | Canada, 19-20 Geo. V, *Dominion Elections Act Amendment Act*, 1929. |
| S.C., 1931, chap. 52 | Canada, 21-2 Geo. V, *Senate and House of Commons Act*, 1931. |
| S.C., 1934, chap. 50 | Canada, 24-5 Geo. V, *Dominion Elections Act Amendment Act*, 1934. |
| S.C., 1934, chap. 51 | Canada, 24-5 Geo. V, *Dominion Franchise Act*, 1934. |
| S.C., 1938, chap. 46 | Canada, 2 Geo. VI, *Dominion Elections Act*, 1938. |
| S.C., 1944, chap. 26 | Canada, 8 Geo. VI, *Canadian Prisoners-of-War Voting Regulations*, 1944. |
| S.C., 1948, chap. 46 | Canada, 11-12 Geo. VI, *Dominion Elections Act*, 1948. |
| S.C., 1950, chap. 35 | Canada, 14 Geo. VI, *Dominion Elections Act Amendment Act*, 1950. |
| S.C., 1955, chap. 44 | Canada, 3-4 Eliz. II, *Canada Elections Act Amendment Act*, 1955. |

| | |
|---|---|
| S.C., 1960, chap. 7 | Canada, 8-9 Eliz. II, *Canada Elections Act Amendment Act*, 1960. |
| S.C., 1960, chap. 39 | Canada, 8-9 Eliz. II, *Canada Elections Act*, 1960, consolidated with amendments to 1968. |
| S.C., 1962, chap. 17 | Canada, 10-11 Eliz. II, *Representation Act Amendment Act*, 1962. |
| S.C., 1964, chap. 31 | Canada, 13 Eliz. II, *Electoral Boundaries Readjustment Act*, 1964. |
| S.M., 1901, chap. 11 | Manitoba, *Manitoba Elections Act*, 1901. |
| S.M., 1957, chap. 18 | Manitoba, *Electoral Divisions Act*, 1957. |
| S.M., 1968, chap. 21 | Manitoba, *Electoral Divisions Act Amendment Act*, 1968. |
| S.M., 1969, chap. 38 | Manitoba, *Election Act Amendment Act*, 1969. |
| S.N., 1954, chap. 79 | Newfoundland, *Election Act*, 1954, consolidated with amendments to 1964. |
| S.N., 1962, chap. 81 | Newfoundland, *House of Assembly (Amendment) Act*, 1962. |
| S.N.B., 1967, chap. 9 | New Brunswick, *Elections Act*, 1967, consolidated with amendments to 1968. |
| S.N.S., 1962, chap. 4 | Nova Scotia, *Elections Act*, 1962, consolidated with amendments to 1966. |
| S.N.S., 1969, chap. 4 | Nova Scotia, *Elections Act Amendment Act*, 1969. |
| S.O., 1885, chap. 2 | Ontario, *Franchise and Representation Act*, 1885. |
| S.O., 1966, chap. 137 | Ontario, *Representation Act*, 1966. |
| S.P.C., 1857, chap. 22 | Province of Canada, 20 Vic., *Independence of Parliament Act*, 1857. |
| S.P.E.I., 1954, chap. 14 | Prince Edward Island, *Election Act*, 1954. |
| S.P.E.I., 1963, chap. 11 | Prince Edward Island, *Election Act*, 1963, consolidated with amendments to 1967. |
| S.O., 1936, chap. 8 | Quebec, *Election Act*, 1936. |
| S.Q., 1965, chap. 10 | Quebec, *Territorial Divisions Act*, 1965. |

# INDEX

Absentee ballots, 16, 30-40
  armed forces, 36
  eligible voters, 36-37
  students, 16, 36
Advance polls, 30-40
  custody of ballots, 165
  disadvantages of, 31-37
  eligible voters, 31-32
  federal procedures, 31-32
  provincial procedures, 32-33
Age:
  candidate qualification, 52, 69
  franchise, 8-9
Agents — official:
  *see* Official agents
Aiken, G. H., 126n
Alberta:
  absentee ballots, 16, 36
  advance polls, 32
  age, candidates, 52
    franchise, 8
  ballot papers:
    format, 56-57, 59
    marking, 181
    party affiliations, 56
    security, 159
  betting on elections, 151-152
  candidates:
    age, 52

    deposits, 53
    government contractors, 47
    nomination, 53
    women, 52
  citizenship, 7
  constituencies:
    criteria, 110-111
    single and multi-member, 119, 131
    urban-rural, 93, 110-111, 131, 171
  Electoral Boundaries Commission, 109-111
  enumeration, 27-28
  government contractors, 47
  legislative assembly:
    indemnity of members, 72
    restrictions on members, 50-51
  Legislative Committee on Redistribution Procedure, 126n
  liquor, sale of on election day, 151
  Notice of Grant of Poll, 56
  plurality voting, 131
  political parties affected by electoral system, 131-132
  polling hours, 38
  preferential voting, 131, 137
  redistribution, 109-111
  Register of Electors, 27
  registration, 20

representation — urban-rural, 93,
    110-111, 131, 171
residence, franchise, 14, 16
returning officers, 147, 148, 177,
    178, 180
seats and votes ratios, 137
seats in House of Commons, 114
single transferable vote, 131-132,
    135-137
students, 16, 36
voting lists, 28, 175
women:
    candidates and members, 52
    franchise, 9
Amery, L. S., 125n
Angell, H. M., 70, 71-72, 80n, 155
Angus, H. F., 166n
Armed forces:
    absentee ballots, 36
    advance polls, 32
    candidates, 49
    franchise, 39
    proxy ballots, 37
Armed Forces Voting Rules, 77n, 165
Armour, Mr. Justice, 168n
Australia:
    constituencies, 88, 103
    registration of voters, 19, 21
Avakumovic, I., 79n

Ballot boxes, 151, 164, 165
Ballot papers:
    format, 56-59
    marking, 160-162, 181-183
    party affiliations on, 56-59
    printing, 158-159, 164
    procedures for handling, 160-161,
        165
    rejected, 161
    security, 158-159
    spoiled, 161
Ballot secrecy, 151, 158, 160-161, 185
Beck, J. M., 41n, 61, 64-65, 78n, 79n
Betting on elections, 151-152
Bloc voting, 122-123
Boyd, W. J. D., 125n
Bribery: see Corrupt practices
British Columbia:
    absentee ballots, 33-36
    advance polls, 33-36
    age:
        candidates, 52

franchise, 8
ballot papers:
    format, 59
    marking, 181
    security, 159
candidates:
    age, 52
    deposits, 53-54
    nomination, 53
    qualifications, 51-52
Chief Electoral Officer, 144
citizenship, 7
Commission of Inquiry into the
    Redefinition of Electoral
    Districts, 96-97, 109, 118, 122
constituencies:
    criteria, 96-97, 109
    single and multi-member, 118,
        119, 122
Doukhobors, 12
language, 11
legislature, indemnity of members,
    72
manhood franchise, 3
plurality voting, 131
political party defined, 59
polling hours, 38
preferential voting, 130-131
property, 6
public opinion polls, 152
race, 10
redistribution, 96-97, 109
Redistribution, 1966, 98, 109
Register of Electors, 35
Registrar of Voters, 28
registration of voters, 22, 26, 28-30,
    35, 36, 51
representation, concepts of, 96
residence, 14
returning officers, 177, 178, 180
seats in House of Commons, 114
unopened ballots, 35
women, candidates and members,
    52
    franchise, 9
British subjects:
    defined, 6
    franchise, 6-7
    residence, 13

Cabinet ministers, 48-49
Cairns, Alan, 138, 140, 141

Canada, Committee on Election
   Expenses, 55, 168n
Canada, House of Commons, Special
   Committee on Elections and
   Franchise Act, 42n, 43n
Canadian Forces Reserves, 31
Candidacy, 45-52
Candidates:
   Armed Forces on active service, 49
   availability, 61
   defeated, 67
   deposits, 53-55
   education, 70
   elected on minority votes, 136-137
   election expenses, 70-75, 154-156
   identified with parties, 55-59, 60-66
   independents, 57, 58, 59, 67
   legal qualifications, 46-52, 69, 99
   listed on Notices of Grants of Poll,
      164-165
   motivations of, 66-67
   nomination, 53, 60-66
   nominators, 54, 55
   potential and actual, 45
   recognized party, 57, 58, 64
   rejected by constituency
      associations, 64
   religion, 69-70
   selection process, 45-46, 65, 75-76,
      171
   socio-economic influences, 66-76
   sources of information on, 67-68
   women, 52, 68
   write-in, 76n
Candidates' Official Agents
   *see* Official **Agents**
Charitable Institutions, 6
Chief Electoral Officer, 17, 163, 170
   action on corrupt practices, 152-153
   appointment of returning officers,
      143, 144-147
   authority over official agents, 157
   control over ballot papers, 158-159
   provincial, 143-144
   responsibilities, 142-143
Chinese, 10
Citizenship:
   franchise, 6-8, 184-185
Civil Servants:
   franchise, 3, 4
   political activity, 49-50
Clerks of the Peace, 184

Cleverdon, Catherine, L., 9, 41n
Commercial Travellers, 31, 32
Communities:
   representation of, 84-86, 93, 96
   sociological criteria, 96
Community of Interest, 86, 96, 117
Constituencies:
   Boundary Commissions: *see*
      Electoral Boundary
      Commissions
   classified, 84
   community, 84-86
   county basis, 86, 94, 117, 118
   criteria, 84-87, 93-98
   distribution: *see* Redistribution
   functional, 84
   gerrymandering, 114-117, 118, 123
   maldistribution, 87-93
   population, 83-87, 89, 94, 97,
      106-108
   redistribution: *see* Redistribution
   religious base, 70
   single and multi-member, 58,
      118-123, 131, 133, 140
   urban-rural: *see* Representation,
      urban-rural
Constituency Structure:
   criteria, 82-83, 110-111
   impact on parties, 82-83
Corrupt Practices, 17, 46, 148-153,
      156, 159-160, 185
   defined, 150-151
   franchise, 17
   prevention, 148-149
   provincial laws, 151-153
Counties as communities, 117
Courtney, J. C., 128n
Criminals, 17
Crown Attorneys, 184
Cube Law, 82, 137-139


Dauer-Kelsay Index, 89-92, 97-98
Davis, Morris, 128n
Dawson, R. M., 79n, 94, 116-117,
      149-150
Denis, Jean-Joseph, 9
Deputy Returning Officers, 148-149,
      164, 165, 185
   appointment, 145-146
   corrupt practices, 159-160
   hiring of interpreters, 11-12

Distribution of Constituencies: *see* Redistribution
Donnelly, Murray, S., 63, 78n, 166n
Double-member Constituencies: *see* Constituencies, single and multi-member
Doukhobors, 12

Election Boards, 184
Election Expenses, 70-75, 154-158
   controls over, 154-156
   limited, 73-75, 154-156
   reimbursed, 73-75
Election Officials, 17, 142-149
Election Process, 170, 171
Election Supplies, 163
Election System:
   compared with electoral system, 129-130
   objective integrity, 124
Elections:
   administration, 162-166
   chronology of, 163-164
   cost factor, 70-75
Electoral Boundary Commissions, 94-95, 101-105, 115
   criteria, 102-105
   membership, 101-102
   procedure, 102-105
   reports, 103-105
Electoral System, 129-142
   alternative ballot: *see* Preferential Voting
   compared with election system, 129-130
   defined, 129
   impact on political process, 138-140
   party list: *see* Party List Voting
   plurality voting: *see* Plurality Voting
   preferential ballot: *see* Preferential Voting
   rationality, 137
   single transferable vote: *see* Single Transferable Vote
Engelmann, F. C., 61, 62, 78n
Enumeration:
   advantages, 22-23, 24-25, 29
   chronology, 163-164
   federal, 14, 15, 23-26
   historical development, 22-23
   provincial, 13, 23, 26-28, 185
   students, 15-16
   urban-rural, 23-26, 163
Enumerators:
   appointment of, 23-24, 55, 185
Ermatinger, C. O., 40n
Eskimos, 10-11
Express Company Employees, 32

Fishermen:
   absentee ballots, 37
   advance polls, 31, 32
   proxy ballots, 37
Fox, Paul, 134, 135
Franchise:
   administrative limitations, 1-2
   age, 8-9
   armed forces, 39
   British subjects, 6-7
   charitable institutions, 6
   citizenship, 6-8
   civil servants, 3, 4
   constitutional safeguards U.S.A., 2
   control over, 2-4
   corrupt practices, 17
   criminals, 17
   election officials, 17
   income, 6
   insane persons, 17
   judges, 17
   language, 10-12
   language restraints in wartime, 11
   manhood, 3, 4
   naturalized British subjects born in an enemy country, 11
   property, 3, 4-6, 23, 41n
   race, 10-12
   religion, 10-12
   residence, 12-18, 185
   state control of in U.S.A., 2
   statutory limitations, 1-2
   uniform federal, 3-4
   universal, 5
   veterans, 10
   wartime, 4, 11
   women, 9-10
Franklin Territory, 11

Garner, John, 40n
Gerrymandering, 114-117, 118, 123
Government contractors, 46-47, 50
Graves, W. C., 77n

Great Britain:
civil servants, political activity,
49-50
community representation, 85
corrupt practices, 156
double-member constituencies, 118
*ex officio* returning officers, 145
House of Commons, Select
Committee on Offices or Places
of Profit under the Crown,
76n, 77n
offices of profit under the Crown,
47-48
redistribution, 99
Reform Bill of 1832, 85
registration of voters, 18-19, 20, 22
residence of members of
parliament, 99

Hanson, Royce, 126n
Hindus, 10
Hoffman, J. D., 79n
Hollis, Christopher, 125n
Horwill, G., 166n
House of Commons:
allocation of seats among provinces,
86, 100, 111-114
dual membership with provincial
legislatures prohibited, 51
education of members, 78
indemnity of members, 72-73
representative character, 68-70
residence qualification, 51
seats and votes ratios, 137-140
Humphreys, J. H., 166n
Hydro workers, 16

Income franchise, 5-6
Indians, 10-11
Insane persons, 17
Interpreters hired by deputy returning
officers, 11-12
Intimidation: *see* Corrupt practices
Invalids:
advance polls, 32
proxy ballots, 37
Ireland, citizens of, 6-8

Japanese, 10
Johnson, J. K., 79n
Judges, franchise, 17

Keekatin Territory, 11
Kernaghan, W. D. K., 77n

Lakeman, Enid, 166n
Lambert, J. D., 166n
Language, franchise limitation, 10-12
Laponce, J. A., 40n, 44n
Laurier, Wilfrid, 86
Legislatures, increase in size, 100
Liberal party:
attitude to redistribution, 83
on control of federal franchise, 3, 4
Lipset, S. M., 134
Liquor, sale of on election day, 151,
168n
Locke, John, 85
Loggers:
absentee ballots, 37
residence, 16-17

Macdonald, John A., 86
Mackenzie Territory, 11
MacKenzie, W. J. M., 156
MacKinnon, Frank, 62, 78n
Manitoba:
advance polls, 32
age:
candidates, 53-53
franchise, 8
ballot papers:
marking, 182
party affiliations, 56
security, 159
betting on elections, 151-152
candidates:
age, 52-53
nomination, 63
Chief Electoral Officer, 143-144
citizenship, 7
constituencies:
criteria, 106-107
single and multi-member, 119,
133
urban-rural, 105-107, 133
election expenses, 154-155
Electoral Divisions Boundaries
Commission, 95, 105-107
enumeration, 27-28
language, franchise, 11
legislature:
indemnity of members, 72
liquor, sale of on election day, 151
non-partisanship, 133
plurality voting, 133
polling hours, 38

preferential voting, 133, 137
proportional representation, 133
redistribution, 105-107
registration of voters, 20
representation, urban-rural, 105-107, 133
residence, 14
returning officers, 177,179, 180
seats in House of Commons, 114
single transferable vote, 133
voters' lists, urban-rural, 28, 176
women:
    candidates and members, 52
    franchise, 9

Mariners:
    absentee ballots, 37
    advance polls, 32
    proxy ballots, 37
Meisel, John, 60, 61, 63, 64, 66, 78n
Members of Parliament:
    civil servants, 49-50
    indemnity, 72
    loss of other earning power, 75
    residence in district, 99
Miners, 37
Ministers of Religion:
    residence, 14
    returning officers, 147, 184
Missionary priests, 32
Multi-member constituencies: *see*
    Constituencies, single and multi-member

Naturalized British subjects born in
    an enemy country, 11
Navigators, 32
Neary, Peter, 65
New Brunswick:
    advance polls, 32
    age, franchise, 8
    ballot papers:
        format, 58-59
        marking, 182
        party affiliation, 58-59
        security, 159
    candidates:
        deposits, 53
        nomination, 53, 58
        qualifications, 47, 52
    charitable institutions, 6
    Chief Electoral Officer, 144

citizenship, 7
constituencies:
    single and multi-member, 58, 120
government contractors, 47
income franchise, 5
Indians, 10
language, franchise, 12
legislature, indemnity of members, 72
official agents, 156
polling hours, 38
property franchise, 5
recognized party, 57, 58-59
redistribution, 111
registration of voters, 20
residence, 14-15
returning officers, 178, 179, 180
seats in House of Commons, 112-114
students, 15
voters' lists, 28, 174-175
women:
    candidates and members, 52
    franchise, 9
New Democratic Party:
    attitudes to redistribution, 83
    candidates losing deposits, 55
    election expenses, 71
New Zealand:
    *ex officio* returning officers, 145
    political integrity, 124
    redistribution, 101-102
    registration of voters, 19, 20
Newfoundland:
    advance polls, 32-33
    age:
        candidates, 52
        franchise, 8
    ballot papers:
        marking, 183
        party affiliation, 56
        security, 159
    candidates:
        deposits, 53
        nominations, 53, 65
        qualifications, 52
    Chief Electoral Officer, 144
    citizenship, 7
    constituencies:
        based on religion, 70
        single and multi-member, 121
    democracy, 65

enumeration, 27-28
language, franchise, 12
legislature, indemnity of members,
72
liquor, sale of on election day, 151
logging camps, 16-17
offensive weapons, 168n
polling hours, 38
religion, constituencies, 70
residence, 14
returning officers, 148, 178, 179,
180
seats in House of Commons, 114
students, 14
voters' lists, 28, 176
women:
candidates and members, 52
franchise, 9
Nomination day, 164, 184
Nomination of Candidates: *see*
Candidates, Nomination.
Nomination papers, endorsed by
party leaders, 58-64
Non-voters, classified, 1-2, 18, 38-40
Northwest Territories:
franchise in, 11
seats in House of Commons,
112-114
Notice of Grant of Poll, 56, 164-165
Notices of Revision, 164
Nova Scotia:
advance polls, 32
age, franchise, 8
ballot papers:
marking, 182
party affiliations, 56
security, 159
betting on elections, 151-152
candidates:
availability, 61
deposits, 53, 54
nomination, 53, 58
religion, 69-70
women, 52
charitable institutions, 6
Chief Electoral Officer, 144
citizenship, 7
civil servants, 3
constituencies, single and
multi-member, 120
corrupt practices, 151
election expenses, 73-75, 154-156

language, franchise, 12
legislature, indemnity of members,
72
polling hours, 38
property franchise, 5-6
proxy ballots, 16, 37
recognized party, 57
redistribution, 111
registration of voters, 20
residence, 14
returning officers, 178, 179, 180
school teachers, 14
seats in House of Commons, 100,
113-114
students, 16
voters' lists, 28, 175
women:
candidates and members, 52
franchise, 9
Nova Scotia, Royal Commission on
Election Expenses and Associated
Matters, 168n, 169n

Offensive weapons, 151, 168n
Offices of profit under the Crown,
47-49, 50
Official addition of the vote, 165
Official agents, 73, 155, 156-158,
164-165, 169n
Official lists, 26
O'Leary, Cornelius, 149
Ontario:
advance polls, 32
age, franchise, 8
amendments of *Election Act*,
184-186
ballot papers:
marking, 162, 182, 185
party affiliations, 56
security, 159
betting on elections, 151-152
candidates:
availability, 61
biographical data, 68
deposits, 53, 54
nomination, 53, 62, 65
qualifications, 47, 49
residence, 99
women, 52
charitable institutions, 6
Chief Electoral Officer, 144
citizenship, 7, 184

constituencies:
  criteria, 107-108
  population, 108
  single and multi-member, 120
  urban-rural, 100, 108
corrupt practices, 185
deputy returning officers, 185
election boards, 184
election expenses, 71
enumeration, 23, 185
fixed nomination and election day,
  184
franchise changes, 1969, 184-185
government contractors, 47
language, franchise, 11
legislature:
  increase in size, 100
  indemnity of members, 72
liquor, sale of on election day, 168n
poll clerks, 185
polling divisions, 185
polling hours, 38
property franchise, 3
proxy ballots, 37, 185
race, franchise, 10
redistribution, 107-109
registration of voters, 20
representation, urban-rural, 100, 108
residence, 14, 185
returning officers, 147, 148, 177,
  179, 180, 184
seats and votes ratios, 137
seats in House of Commons, 114
Select Committee on Election Law,
  42n, 185
Special Commission on
  Redistribution of Electoral
  Districts in Ontario, 107-108
voters' lists:
  revision, 185
  urban-rural, 28, 175
vouching, 185
women:
  candidates and members, 52
  franchise, 9

Party List Voting, 136, 141-142, 171
Perlin, George, 65
Person, defined, 10
Personation, 151, 153
Peterson, T., 79n
Plurality Voting System, 122-123,
  130-131, 133, 134-136, 137, 140

Political Culture, 172
Political Parties:
  attitudes to redistribution, 83
  Canadian party system
    characterized, 140
  candidate identification, 55-59,
    60-66
  constituency associations, 62, 82-83
  definitions, 56, 59
  financing, 71-72, 154-156
  impact of electoral system, 130,
    131-132, 140
  importance in election process,
    59-60
  listed on ballot papers, 56-59
  nomination meetings, 60-66
  party leaders, 58, 64
  recognized party, 57-59, 64, 73
  representation, 136
  seats and votes ratios, 137-140
Poll Clerks, 148-149, 185
  appointment, 145-146
  corrupt practices, 159-160
Polling Divisions:
  appointment of enumerators, 23-24
  description of boundaries, 163
  establishment, 164
  hours of voting, 38
  location, 39
  in logging camps, 17
  urban-rural, 20, 23-24, 185
Polling Hours, 38
Polling Stations:
  security, 159-160
  staffing by parties, 149
Population:
  definitions, 88
  representation of, 83-87, 89, 94, 97,
    106-108
Power, C. G., 64
Preferential Voting, 130-134, 137
Preliminary Lists, 164
  distribution, 24-25
  statement of changes and
    additions, 26
Press, Charles, 90
Prince Edward Island:
  advance polls, 32
  age:
    candidates, 52
    franchise, 8
  ballot papers:
    marking, 182

party affiliation, 56
security, 159
candidates:
age, 52
deposits, 53
nomination, 53, 62
women, 52
Chief Electoral Officer, 144
citizenship, 7
constituencies, single and multi-
member, 121
language, franchise, 12
legislative assembly, 41n
indemnity of members, 72
official agents, 156
polling hours, 38
property, franchise, 6, 41n
redistribution, 111
registration of voters, 20
residence, 14, 15-16
returning officers, 178, 179, 180
Royal Commission on Electoral
Reform, 41n
school teachers, 14
seats in House of Commons,
112-114
students, 15-16
voters' lists, urban-rural, 27-28, 174
women:
candidates and members, 52
franchise, 9
Printers, under oath, 159
Prisoners-of-war, proxy ballots, 37
Proclamation, 163
Progressive Conservative Association
of Canada, constitution, 62
Progressive Conservative Party,
attitude to redistribution, 83
Property:
candidates, 51
franchise, 3, 4-6, 23, 41n
franchise, provincial, 41n
land, 5-6
Proportional Representation, 123, 133,
134-135
see also Single Transferable Vote
Provincial Legislatures:
dual membership prohibited, 51
indemnity of members, 72-73
Proxy Ballots, 16, 30-40, 185
prisoners-of-war, 37
provincial regulations, 37, 185
students, 16, 37-38

Public Employees, residence, 16
Public Opinion Polls, 152

Qualter, T. H., 125n, 126n, 167n
Quebec:
advance poll, 32, 33
age:
candidates, 52
franchise, 8
ballot papers:
marking, 182
security, 159
candidates:
age, 52
availability, 61
deposits, 53
independents, 57, 58
nomination, 53, 58, 63-65
recognized party, 57, 58
women, 52
Chief Returning Officer, 143
citizenship, 7
constituencies, single and multi-
member, 120
constituency structure protected by
B.N.A. Act, 127n
democracy in, 65
election expenses, 70-71, 154-156
defined, 74
limited, 73-74
reimbursement, 73-74, 156
reporting of, 157-158
Indians, 10
language, franchise, 12
legislature:
increase in size, 100
indemnity of members, 72
liquor, sale of on election day, 151
offensive weapons, 168n
official agents, 169n
polling divisions, 168n
polling hours, 38
property franchise, 6
recognized party, 57, 58, 64, 73
registration of voters, 20
residence, 14
returning officers, 177, 179, 180
seats in House of Commons,
111-112, 114
students, 15
voters' lists, urban-rural, 27-28, 174

women:
    candidates and members, 52
    franchise, 9


Race, franchise, 10-12
Rae, D. W., 166n
Ralliement Créditiste, attitudes to
    redistribution, 83
Recounts, 165
Redistribution:
    arguments for and against, 82-83,
        93,98
    Australia, 103
    by Boundaries Commissions, 94-95,
        100-105, 115
    criteria, 86, 96-97, 98
    Dauer-Kelsay index, 89-92
    federal-provincial control, 103
    by House of Commons, 98
    by legislatures, 98-99
    machinery, 98-105
    maldistribution: see Constituencies,
        maldistribution by non-
        parliamentary agencies,
        101-105
    party perspectives on, 83
    population quotas, 86-87, 88-89,
        94, 103-105
    provincial allocation of federal
        seats, 86, 111-114
    provincial procedure, 105-111
    responsibility for, 98
    United States, 103
    urban-rural: see Representation,
        urban-rural
Regenstreif, Peter, 71
Registration of voters, 18-30, 35, 36,
    51, 174-176
    based on municipal assessment rolls,
        23
    compulsory, 21, 172
    enumeration: see Enumeration
    falsification of lists, 152-153
    open and closed lists, 27-29
    percentages of population registered,
        29
    permanent lists, 20, 21, 23, 24, 28,
        29, 33
    provincial systems, 20, 22, 26,
        27-28, 29, 30, 35, 36, 51,
        174-176
    systems classified, 18-20, 174-176

urban-rural lists, 28, 175-176
    voluntary, 22, 29
Religion:
    candidates, 69-70
    franchise, 10-12
    represented in legislatures, 70
Representation:
    concepts, 82-85, 93, 96
    functional, 84
    machinery for adjustment: see
        Redistribution
    urban-rural, 28, 83, 91, 93-98, 100,
        103-108, 110-111, 131, 171,
        174-175
Representation Commissioner, 21, 101
Representative system, criteria, 82-83
Residence:
    British subjects, 13
    candidate qualification, 51
    defined, 13
    franchise, 12-18, 185
    loggers, 17
    ministers of religion, 14
    public employees, 16
    school teachers, 14
    students, 15-16
    summer cottagers, 17
    workers temporarily employed, 16
Return to the Writ: see Writ
Returning officers, 142-144, 163, 184
    appointment, 143, 144-147
    appointment of enumerators, 23-24
    authority over official agents,
        157-158
    custody of ballot boxes, 165
    declare candidates elected, 165
    ex officio, 145, 172
    partisan activity, 147
    permanent, 146
    provincial, 147-148, 177-180
    replacement, 147
Returns of receipts and expenditures,
    155-156
Revisal districts, 25, 163, 164
Revisal offices, 25, 26, 164
Revising agents, 25
Revising officers, 25, 164
Revision of lists, 28, 163-164, 185
    deletion of names, 25-26
    fictitious names, 152-153
Ross, J. F. S., 67, 166n
Rothney, G. O., 79n
Royal Canadian Mounted Police, 31

Saskatchewan:
  advance polls, 32
  age:
    candidates, 52
    franchise, 8
  ballot papers:
    marking, 182
    party affiliation, 56
    security, 159
  betting on elections, 151-152
  bloc voting, 122-123
  candidates:
    age, 52
    civil servants, 49
    deposits, 53
    nomination, 53
    women, 52
  Chief Electoral Officer, 144
  citizenship, 7
  civil servants, 49
  constituencies, single and
    multi-member, 119
  corrupt practices, 151
  government contractors, 47
  legislative assembly:
    biographical data, 68
    indemnity of members, 72
  offensive weapons, 168n
  political party, defined, 56
  polling hours, 38
  registration of voters, 20
  religions, represented, 70
  residence, 14
  returning officers, 177, 178, 180
  seats in House of Commons, 86,
    113-114
  students, 15-16
  voters' lists, urban-rural, 28, 176
  women:
    candidates and members, 52
    franchise, 9
Scarrow, H. A., 44n, 60-61, 64, 66,
  78n
School teachers, 14
Schubert, Glendon, 90
Schwartz, M. A., 61, 62, 78n
Scrutineers, 149, 159-160
Seats and votes ratios, 137-140, 171
Secret ballot: *see* Ballot secrecy
Single transferable vote, 131-137
Smiley, D. V., 167n
Smith, David, 68, 78

Smith, Denis, 63, 64, 79n
South Africans, 7
Spafford, Duff, 79n
Special constables, 151
Split-ticket voting, 122
Students:
  absentee ballots, 16, 36
  proxy ballots, 16, 37-38
  residence, 15-16
Suffrage: *see* Franchise
Summer cottagers, residence, 17

Taschereau, L. A., 63, 64
Transportation workers, 31, 32, 33
Treating, 150-151

Ukrainians, 11
Underhill, F. H., 134, 166n
Undue influence, 151
United States:
  franchise laws, 2, 17
  legislators' residence, 98-99
  primaries, 171-172
  redistribution, 99, 103, 124
  registration of voters, 19-20
Unopened Ballots, 35

Voters: *see also* Non-voters
  cynicism, 124, 142
  perception of election system, 124
Voters' Lists: *see* Registration of
  Voters
Voting:
  compulsory, 172
  procedure, 158-162
Vouching, 26, 185

War Veterans, 10
Ward, Norman, 40n, 42n, 67, 76n,
  77n, 98, 100, 117, 125n, 146,
  150, 162
Wilson, J. M., 79n
Women:
  candidates and members, 52, 68
  franchise, 9-10
  members of legislatures, 52
Workers Temporarily Employed, 16
Writ of Election, 15, 142, 162, 163
  return to, 166

Yukon, seats in House of Commons,
  112-114

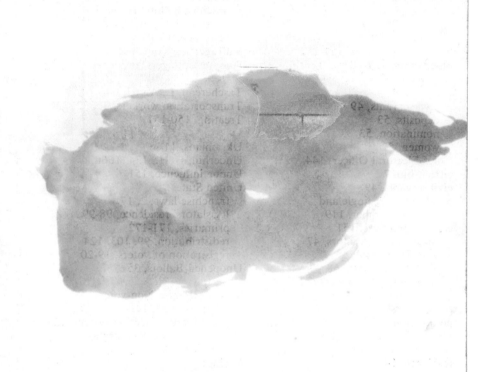